Maritime History as World History

New Perspectives on Maritime History and Nautical Archaeology

UNIVERSITY PRESS OF FLORIDA / STATE UNIVERSITY SYSTEM

Florida A&M University, Tallahassee

Florida Atlantic University, Boca Raton

Florida Gulf Coast University, Ft. Myers

Florida International University, Miami

Florida State University, Tallahassee

University of Central Florida, Orlando

University of Florida, Gainesville

University of North Florida, Jacksonville

University of South Florida, Tampa

University of West Florida, Pensacola

EDITED BY

Daniel Finamore

Foreword by James C. Bradford
and Gene A. Smith, Series Editors

Published jointly by
the Peabody Essex Museum, Salem, Massachusetts,
and the University Press of Florida
Gainesville · Tallahassee · Tampa · Boca Raton
Pensacola · Orlando · Miami · Jacksonville · Ft. Myers

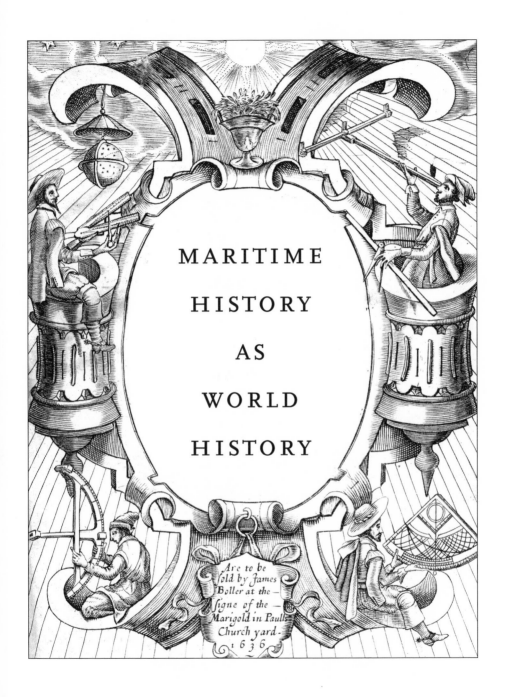

MARITIME

HISTORY

AS

WORLD

HISTORY

Are to be
fold by James
Boller at the —
figne of the —
Marigold in Paull
Church yard.
1636

09 08 07 06 05 04   6 5 4 3 2 1

Library of Congress Cataloging-in-Publication Data
Maritime history as world history / edited by Daniel Finamore.
p. cm. – (New perspectives on maritime history and nautical archaeology)
Includes bibliographical references and index.
ISBN 0-8130-2710-1 (cloth : alk. paper)
1. Naval art and science—History. 2. Navigation—History. 3. Sea-power—
History. 4. Naval history. 5. Underwater archaeology. 6. Excavations
(Archaeology) I. Finamore, Daniel, 1961– II. Series.
V23.M273 2004   909—dc22
2004043733

The University Press of Florida is the scholarly publishing agency
for the State University System of Florida, comprising Florida A & M
University, Florida Atlantic University, Florida Gulf Coast University,
Florida International University, Florida State University, University
of Central Florida, University of Florida, University of North Florida,
University of South Florida, and University of West Florida.

University Press of Florida
15 Northwest 15th Street
Gainesville, FL 32611-2079
http://www.upf.com

Peabody Essex Museum Collections for 2001. Volume 137.
ISSN 1074-0457, ISBN 0-88389-124-7. The Peabody Essex Museum
Collections is an annual monographic series published in Salem, Massa–
chusetts. All correspondence concerning this publication should be addressed
to the Editor, Peabody Essex Museum Collections, East India Square, Salem,
Massachusetts 01970. Previous books are available upon request. This
volume was copyrighted in 2001 by the Peabody Essex Museum.

CONTENTS

FIGURES

Water is unquestionably the most important natural feature on the earth. By volume the world's oceans compose 99 percent of the planet's living space; in fact the surface of the Pacific Ocean alone is larger than that of the total land bodies. Water is as vital to life as air. Indeed, to test whether the moon or other planets can sustain life, NASA looks for signs of water. As such the story of human development is inextricably linked to the oceans, seas, lakes, and rivers that dominate the earth's surface. The University Press of Florida series "New Perspectives on Maritime History and Nautical Archaeology" is devoted to exploring the impact of the earth's water while providing lively and important books that cover the spectrum of maritime history and nautical archaeology broadly defined. The series includes works that focus on the role of canals, rivers, lakes, and oceans in history; on the economic, military, and political use of those waters; and upon the people, communities, and industries that support maritime endeavors. Limited by neither geography nor time, volumes in the series contribute to the overall understanding of maritime history and can be read with profit by both general readers and specialists.

Daniel Finamore's edited collection *Maritime History as World History* exemplifies what this series strives to accomplish. This fine collection of essays by many of the world's foremost authorities presents an updated assessment of maritime history at the beginning of the third millennium; by examining the global impact of maritime exploration, warfare, and commerce on human history, it vividly demonstrates that the story of human development is unquestionably linked to the oceans, seas, lakes, and rivers that dominate the earth's surface. Interaction with the sea is, after all, a fundamental factor of the human experience.

Inspired by a spring 2000 conference held at the Peabody Essex Museum in Salem, Massachusetts, this volume examines the influence of sea power and the sea on human development, beginning with the ancient Japanese, Arabian, and Mediterranean seafarers and continuing through the European worldwide expansion that began in the sixteenth century. Even though the collection covers a broad expanse of time, the authors place their topics into a proper context; maritime affairs have played an integral role throughout human history. But as we enter the third millennium the relative importance of the sea to human society has changed considerably.

Today, television newscasts and newspapers often run stories of sinking oil tankers and the problem of pollution in the world's oceans, cruise ship fires and mysterious shipboard illnesses, multiyear voyages of garbage barges, as well as accounts of naval operations in peacetime and war. These maritime events appear today to be tied more closely to events ashore than ever before. New changes in technology, international law, global commerce, organizational innovation, as well as multinational employment of commercial and naval vessels and the fear of prospective terrorist threats from sea force us to examine the world's oceans from a broader perspective. In the twenty-first century the division between the maritime and terrestrial world has virtually disappeared. Events and issues that previously involved only maritime subjects need to be reexamined today from the perspective of those events and developments occurring simultaneously ashore. It is through this approach, as demonstrated by this fine collection of essays, that maritime history truly becomes a vehicle for understanding global history. As such, the editor and authors' synthetic and substantive assessment of the sea in human history is a welcomed addition to this series.

James C. Bradford
Gene A. Smith
Series Editors

PREFACE

This volume is a collection of essays by many of the world's leading scholars in maritime history, presenting an up-to-date assessment of the field in the early twenty-first century. It offers fresh insights into the impact of seaborne exploration, warfare, and commerce on the course of history and a global perspective on the influence of the sea and seafaring on more than one thousand years of world history, from the independent traditions of ancient Japanese, Arabian, and Mediterranean seafarers to the rapid European expansion around the globe from the sixteenth century onward.

The initial idea for the conference that led to this volume arose during a conversation between Donald Marshall, then Peabody Essex Museum staff publisher for the *American Neptune,* and *Sea History* magazine editor Peter Stanford. Titled the World Marine Millennial Conference, the project was initially conceived of as a way to examine holistically the critical historical events, inventions, and traditions of the last one thousand years of maritime history. As planning began, though, it became obvious that arbitrarily isolating the passing millennium from the greater trajectory of human history would prevent the examination of longer-term trends that began before medieval times and, just as critically, those that are still in force on the seas today. This volume is the fruition of Marshall's and Stanford's bold suggestion that examining large-scale historical developments is of at least as much interest as the individual stories of personal experiences and specific ships. The particularistic and regional studies that make maritime history such engaging reading become the fodder from which greater synoptic histories are synthesized.

With the birth of the idea, an advisory committee was formed to explore the most fruitful strategy. The group proved to be enormously influential in charting the ambitious course we subsequently set for ourselves. The initial committee meeting, hosted by Norman Fiering at the John Carter Brown Library, included J. Revell Carr, Felipe Fernández-Armesto, Daniel Finamore Lewis Fischer, Stuart Frank, John Hattendorf, Roger Knight, Margarette Lincoln, Mary Malloy, Carla Rahn Phillips, Ted Sloan, and William H. White.

Appropriate contributors were then selected using the framework this group laid out.

Of particular significance to the success of this entire endeavor was the enthusiastic and constant support of Mrs. Russell W. Knight. She magnanimously stepped forward and provided the financial backing for the editorial and production efforts on the Massachusetts side of the operations associated with this volume. Staff and volunteers of the Peabody Essex Museum who contributed in a wide range of capacities and at various phases of the project include Jack Bishop, Beatrice Chen, Peg Dorsey, Paul Dustin, Phillippa Eschauzier, Jennifer Evans, Lyles Forbes, Rick Guttenberg, Will La Moy, Don Legere, Marianne McDermott, Eva Ritter-Walker, Laura Roberts, George Schwartz, Samuel Scott, and Louise Sullivan. Essential assistance was also provided by the National Maritime Historical Society staff and volunteers, including Justine Ahlstrom, David Allen, Brig. Gen. Patrick Garvey, Shelley Reid, and Joyce Reiss. The diligence and enthusiasm of this extensive group made every step of the process enjoyable as well as productive.

Dan L. Monroe, executive director and CEO, the Peabody Essex Museum

Introduction

(Maritime) History: Salting the Discourse

DANIEL FINAMORE

Readers discovering the heterogeneous discipline of maritime history for the first time approach it from a wide range of interests, often with substantially divergent expectations. Some, no doubt, begin with an overriding fascination for the watercraft, those indispensable inventions without which, global exploration, transoceanic commerce, seaborne warfare, and innumerable other world-changing events never could have occurred. The chapters in this volume collectively illustrate that the ship has been the primary enabler of much of world history, but aside from those whose concerns lead them directly to the material nexus of all maritime disciplines, many more are motivated by issues less technologically focused.

The term *maritime history*, standing alone, is profoundly uninformative. At its most basic level, it is the history of human interaction with the sea, but most think of it as emerging from a multitude of events in the chronology of seafaring, beginning with the earliest human migrations via boat through the great oceanic voyages and naval battles that have culminated in the modern political map. Maritime history is not a subdiscipline of political history; nor can it be subsumed under any broader rubric of history defined solely by technology, economy, or geography. Human interaction with the sea is a fundamental factor of world history, not a dissociated force of particularistic concern. That point is made unambiguously in the chapters that follow.

The title of this volume, only slightly modified from that of Felipe Fernández-Armesto's lead-off chapter, sets out a framework far broader than what is usually expected of "maritime" histories. Individually and collectively, these chapters emphasize the pervasive impact of maritime activity on interpretations of historical events over several millennia. Admittedly, they form primarily a Western narrative, but looking backward from the world we know today, the events and currents discussed have been as significant for Africans and Melanesians as they have been for Western Europeans. These chapters also lay the groundwork for a broader perspective in the endeavor of conducting a global maritime history, particularly one that incorporates non-Western narratives.

In the introductory chapter, Fernández-Armesto makes no attempt to set maritime history into an explanatory context framed by a larger world history. Instead, he elucidates how the myriad events that entwined humankind with the sea, both those of great renown and those that were never written down but only passed orally through generations, are actually the substance of a world history that reaches beyond regional histories of bounded political entities. The maritime aspects of history are of uniform human consequence to Arabs, Japanese, and Native Americans as well as Western Europeans, eventually intertwining them all.

Environmental factors shape the basics of terrestrial life everywhere, but specialized knowledge of and responses to the environment of the sea have affected more than just the maritime cultures that travel it. Ocean-fronting societies directly influenced other coastal and island cultures by establishing sea routes that resulted in firsthand contact. Impact extended inland as well, where exposure was usually less direct but often no less pervasive. That complex suite of forces included not just exposure to alien disease but often access to new markets and enrichment from ideas and objects of cultural exchange. All of this was a product of the knowledge of winds, currents, tides, and some form of sailing technology that allowed reliable long-distance travel. From this, Fernández-Armesto argues, "global history became a reality. It grew out of maritime history."

Beginning with some of the earliest recorded voyages, Lionel Casson's chapter reads like a series of Iron Age adventures. Laying out the extent of the globe known to the seafaring inhabitants of the ancient Mediterranean—the Greeks, Phoenicians, and Egyptians—Casson tracks the gradual expansion of their world as experimental voyages were taken or information was acquired that allowed more distant travel: across the Mediterranean Sea and out into the Atlantic, south along the coast of Africa, and northward to the British Isles and eventually into the Indian Ocean. Of course, records were made of only a small fraction of the voyages of those times, and incomplete preservation of those that may have been described in writing means that only an arbitrary sample of exploratory voyages taken come down to us today—hence the need for augmenting the historical record with information gleaned from archaeology. Although it is possible that new textual information will contribute to new or revised views of Mediterranean exploration, deepwater shipwrecks as well as coastal terrestrial sites are likely to be the most fruitful future sources for research in this arena.

William D. Phillips examines a period when the most ambitious voyages and the greatest sea distances traveled were not made by southern European mariners but by Polynesians, Chinese, Arabs, and Scandinavians, among others. Sometimes their expansion was a result of extending coastal fishing or trading voyages into deepwater expeditions, motivated by the desire for resources. On certain occasions, this resulted in the permanent migration of the participants. The Crusades, ostensibly of religious inspiration, brought Europeans to the eastern end of the Mediterranean, where they developed their taste for the exotic Asian goods that arrived there by land and sea from as far away as China. Phillips examines explicit and unstated motivations for such expansions in many regions of the globe, arguing that essentially no exploratory voyages were motivated solely by innate curiosity, and that the most successful were those that combined political, economic, and religious motivations. The story of regional histories evolve into truly global history, link by maritime link, as populations trade first through intermediaries and later come face to face via long-distance voyages.

Carla Rahn Phillips offers a novel perspective on Western exploration over the past 500 years that looks comparatively across centuries, nations, and regions of the globe. She treats the odysseys of Malaspina and Verrazano much the same as the modern ventures of Francis Chichester and epic voyage re-enactors, employing "motives, means, and results" as her mode of analysis to identify cultural, national, and personal commonalities that drive initiatives for experimental voyages. The most dramatic and unexpected discoveries were often made by explorers who were fully convinced that they would find something entirely different: Columbus desired a route to the East, Cook sought his Terra Australis, and countless polar explorers hoped for a northwest passage to Asia. Certainly, enterprises were fueled by intellectual curiosity, religion, and commerce, but in Phillips's view, these impulses were more than evenly matched by pure political rivalry. The public support, financial investment, vision, and leadership required to execute most landmark voyages also were driven primarily by unusual people with similar characteristics of personality, no matter what the century.

Justin Manley and Brendan Foley diverge starkly from the preceding discussions of historical motivations for exploration. Their description of twentieth-century advances in undersea technology is a reminder that the exploration of our planet is not yet complete, although sail technology and celestial navigation equipment have given way to far more complex machines. They set the stage for their explication of recent advances in deepocean exploration with a series of startling facts and statistics to illustrate the physical features, chemical composition, and geographic immensity of the world's oceans. Early experiments with dive gear allowed access to gradually deeper waters, but only at great human cost. Breathing equipment for divers gave way to more rugged manned and then remotely operated submersibles and, recently, autonomous vehicles with no tether at all. Initially developed for defense, both vehicles and their acoustic and optical sensors have spun off benefits to the scientific community. Although at least one supposedly scientific project was actually a veiled intelligence operation, information obtained from deepwater survey is the most hopeful prospect for future contributions to the study of early historic and prehistoric seafaring.

Turning from exploration to commerce, Olaf Janzen examines the intercontinental shipping patterns that evolved with the establishment of a maritime world trade network during two centuries of active European colonial expansion. Using the Newfoundland fish trade as an example, he synthesizes characteristics of shipping patterns that utilized the seas as regularly traveled oceanic highways rather than for singular independent voyages. The various transatlantic "triangular trades" took advantage of seasonal oceanic weather patterns and regional demand for foreign goods, while more complex commercial networks kept ships moving in annually repeated patterns along the same sea routes. He emphasizes, however, that viable "oceanic highways" were more than just a pattern of shipping; they were as much the result of a growth in land-based structures of support, namely, the mercantilist economic system.

John Armstrong tackles the critically important coastal trade. Although seemingly of local and regional relevance, coastal, riverine, and canal-based maritime transport formed the backbone of the industrial revolution, moving the majority of raw materials, fuel, and manufactured goods from source to factory to market. He points out just how little academic attention the coastal trade has received, even though it gained much protection by governments and often ran counter to acknowledged shipbuilding and registration trends. The huge volume of cargo moved often meant that carriages and railroads were never positioned to replace coastal shipping but to operate as part of a network that included all of these transport technologies in concert. Urban centers benefited greatly from coastal shipping, carrying food for humans and animals in and waste products out. Although much of it was of low visibility in historical perspective, the vast amount of coasting activity over the centuries has contributed to more distant oceanic voyaging in ways more extensive than the mere redistribution of exotic commodities and the training of sailors. Technologies such as turbines and compound engines were adopted by the higher-risk deepwater operations after introduction and experimentation in the coastal trade.

Addressing the sea as an arena for conflict, John Hattendorf ponders the very definition of "naval history" as a discipline, differentiating between incidents of warfare on the seas and the employment of actual sea power. While many scholars see conflict at sea as the inevitable progression of naval strategy and technical invention, Hattendorf argues that it is usually analogous to critical cultural and political events that occur on land. In harsh contrast to ancient times and even the Napoleonic era, Hattendorf emphasizes the function of modern navies as integral parts of technologically sophisticated fighting forces that are no longer designed merely to defend vulnerable coastlines or trade routes. Modern navies may have fewer vessels than fifty years ago, but their reach is far broader, particularly since they often act in multinational networks of allied nations. Conflict on the seas is rarely the sole result of maritime events. Rather, it is one agent, although a highly mobile and effective one, used to affect a broad array of political and military agendas.

In Richard Unger's view, a necessary precursor to European colonization of landmasses, from Africa to the Americas to the Pacific islands, was the appropriation of the sea itself. He calls the "first era of European colonization" that which established national boundaries across the open ocean. The establishment of boundaries immediately led to conflicts and the subsequent establishment of navies. This process was occurring at least by 870, when Scandinavians started colonizing Iceland, and was fully established by Columbus's first voyage. Evolving hand-in-hand with regular overseas commercial shipping, the act of guarding coasts expanded into protecting strategic waterways, blockading enemy's harbors, and establishing territorial shipping lanes. Naval architecture and armament evolved collaterally to allow longer voyages by heavily armed vessels. By the end of the medieval period, naval battles were waged in distant waters with the assistance of fortified outposts, setting the stage for the organized colonial expansion that was to follow.

The crucial bridge between the early modern state and the empire, Elizabeth Manke argues, required the adoption of an evolved perspective on the oceans as potential political space to be negotiated, claimed, and regulated. The historical trajectories of the Atlantic, Indian, and Pacific Oceans and the European nations who vied for control of commercial shipping through them highlights the competing principles of freedom of the seas versus exclusive governance by individual political entities. Even though the majority of naval engagements have been between European powers, the constant diplomatic negotiations that reapportioned power within maritime states led to advancement of the position of Europeans in particular over others. The resulting overseas commerce acted as a further catalyst to empire.

Compared to preceding centuries, naval activity of the twentieth century was unprecedented in its "magnitude, intensity, and significance." Jon Sumida argues that this necessitates a broader perspective than has traditionally been applied to the analysis of this period. He establishes a conceptual framework that expands upon the traditional interpretive approach, realigning a three-tiered system based on different assumptions: that it is more appropriate to examine the quest for naval supremacy within a transnational system of alliances rather than by an individual nation; that increasingly, the big-gun warships operated within the context of more diversified naval forces that have been underrepresented; and that operations and events, even when influenced by policy and politics, are most profitably examined within economic, financial, or logistical contexts. Such a reinterpretation of twentieth-century naval affairs has broad-reaching relevance for interpretation of modern naval events.

In the closing chapter of the volume, Robert Foulke ventures beyond the literal historical narratives and analyses of the other chapters. Employing literature as his data source, he explores the allure of seafaring within the human psyche, an attraction that is balanced by horror at the dangers and suffering that so commonly accompanies it. He offers an emotional counterbalance to the rational examinations of causality and consequence in maritime history, driving at more universal aspects of the human experience on the sea. And he offers insights into personal interpretations of seafaring experiences of those whose deeds are fleshed out in grander scale in the preceding chapters. The sea voyage is emblematic of more widespread human experience, and in it authors since ancient times have found inspiration allegorically to recount a range of life's voyages, such as initiation into a closed community, a determination to reach utopia, and severe tests of physical or moral potency. Foulke has created a handy ordering of the relevant sea-based literature that reflects on those experiences common to most who ply the ocean waves, both real and imaginary.

Maritime History and World History

FELIPE FERNÁNDEZ-ARMESTO

In 1909, the British government in Malaya commissioned a chaplain from Mergui in British Burma to help conduct a census. Walter Grainge White went to the people he called the Mawken, the northernmost of the *oran laut,* or "sea people," practitioners of the most resolutely maritime culture in the world. A few communities had toeholds on dry land, on unfrequented islands, and coves, where they kept huts to which they could retreat as needed. Most of them, however—and White reckoned their numbers as at least 5,000 at the time—had no homes other than their boats and spent virtually all their time at sea. They came ashore only to trade, build, repair their boats, and, curiously, bury their dead, whom they would not entrust to the waves.

Their material culture was fascinatingly rudimentary and stripped to essentials. Families usually of half a dozen to a dozen people made their homes in dugouts of about twenty-five feet in length with rounded hulls at both ends. This form of construction seemed positively to invite the waves to bounce the occupants up and down and to limit the speed with which they could make headway. Protection against heavy seas was provided by nothing better than long palm stems laid horizontally, one above the other, and caulked with resin to form frail bulwarks a few feet high. Split bamboo stems, lashed with bark thongs, formed a deck that almost covered the boat, except for a hole for bailing with cupped hands or a hollow gourd. On the deck, palm fronds roofed a small hut, high enough to crouch or lie under, to provide the only shelter. Each member of the family had a mat that was spread for sleeping or sitting. When opportune, a mast could be slipped into a hole in a plank amidships, and a palm-leaf sail was hoisted by means of a plaited rope. Otherwise, propulsion was by oar, pivoted on oarlocks of thong. The Mawkens' only implement for fishing was a harpoon, traditionally formed of a bone-tipped stake, for they would not deign to use nets or pots. What could not be speared in passing had to be gathered by hand from the seabed or the rocks. The only fish they ate were, therefore, sluggish catfish, which were vulnerable to the spear, or the crustaceans for which they could dive or clamber. Even in the best of times, this diet could not support life, and they had to trade fish and oyster shells for rice. For cooking, they had a hearth of earth to prevent the deck from igniting. With this truly minimalist technology, they kept afloat throughout the year on a sea racked by storms .[1]

There are many peoples in Southeast Asia who can be said in some sense to be at home on the sea, but most, like the Bugis of Sulawesi, who have a great reputation in the West for their adaptability to an aquatic environment, are essentially peasant landlubbers.[2] The *oran laut*, however, have found ways of making the sea habitable for humans. Only miracles of simplicity or complexity can make this possible. I have recently seen advertisements for apartments in luxury liners that are designed to cruise the world permanently. Their purchasers will be able to claim a place alongside the *oran laut* among the world's few truly seaborne communities.

Apart from permanent ice, the sea is, from a human point of view, the most hostile type of environment in the biosphere. The awe with which, in common with Grainge White, we contemplate the lives of the *oran laut* arises from our conviction that man is not made for the sea, nor the sea for man. Even in a collection of recent work on maritime history, the Mawken seem surprising. Our literature of the sea, for the same reason, is dominated by tales of heroism, madness, and longing for land. This, I suspect, is why marine studies are relatively neglected in the academic world. Of course, from a land-bound perspective, the sea seems literally marginal. Because it is not a normal or "natural" human habitat, it evades the attention of those riveted by the obvious. I feel that I am an inadequate spokesman for the sea. I am the sort of maritime historian who gets seasick in the bath. I am unseduced by the romance of the brine. To me, tar is tacky and the ocean unaesthetic. I never make a sea trip if I can avoid it. In politeness to yachtsmen-hosts, who have assumed that someone who writes so much about the sea must love it, I have spent many hours and days of tedium or discomfort aboard their crafts. I have been drawn to the study of the sea, despite my landward leanings, simply because I recognize its importance.

If one suspends for a moment one's usual way of looking at the world, if one climbs the cosmic rigging and adopts the perspective of those creatures of my imagination, the Galactic Museum-Keepers, it becomes apparent that the sea is not marginal to the land. On our planet, the land is marginal to the sea. The Mawken of Walter Grainge White were modest, retiring folk. They lived on the sea cheerfully but did not pretend to have taken to it willingly. The history they claimed to remember as their own was that of a prosperous farming people driven from their land by invasions of Burmese from the north and Malays from the south. They fled to ever smaller and less viable islands, keeping to their boats when raiders came, and at last abandoned the shore entirely. Their name for themselves meant literally "the sea-drowned." They have, I think, a profound lesson to teach us. Their symbiosis with the sea is a reminder and symbol of the underappreciated role of the sea in human history. I suggest that the sea powerfully conditions the lives of human societies, even in the midmost landmasses, and that it is the supreme arena of the events that constitute global history.

Long-range routes of cultural transmission that have made the modern world what it is have encompassed the world by taking to the sea. The ecological exchanges that accompanied long-range navigation constituted the most astonishing effect of human action on evolution between the rise of species domestication and the development of genetic modification.[3] In this context, maritime history is world history.

Moreover, the sea that hews lands also shapes cultures. The sea is so big, so hugely the greater part of the biosphere, that no region is uninfluenced by its effects. It is the engine of weather systems that help to forge the environment even in lands remote from it. The southern oscillation—the great "swaying" of pressure backward and forward between the Indian and Pacific Oceans—is the biggest weather maker in the world. The Pacific countercurrent we call El Niño is connected with floods and droughts deep in the interiors of Africa and North America. The North Atlantic oscillation determines the severity of winters in the heart of continental Russia.[4] A participant in a National Endowment for the Humanities maritime history summer institute I once taught came from Kansas. When I made the obvious joke about the proximity of Kansas to the ocean, he solemnly told me that he had never been interested in the sea until he found himself living almost as far from it as possible. This is not a case of nostalgia. Absence from the sea made him appreciate the ubiquity of its influence.

The number of maritime cultures in the world, understood as those that are influenced more by the proximity of the sea than by other environmental factors, is far more extensive than commonly supposed. Many great civilizations that are usually described in terms of their landward environments are better understood when reclassified as maritime. Three examples will be enough to illustrate this (though many others could be added). Japan, the first example, is usually regarded as a country with a long, rarely interrupted history of isolation and introspection, and it is true that, for most of their history, the maritime vocation of the Japanese did not take many of them very far from their home islands. The imperial convulsions of the late sixteenth and twentieth centuries, that saw Japan bid for a seaborne empire resembling those of some European powers, are usually seen as freakish and uncharacteristic. Nevertheless, the seaward vocation of Japan has always been strong. Kensai Jochin's bird's-eye view of the country, painted in 1820, brings out the great paradox of Japanese history: a maritime people isolated for many centuries at a time. The landscape is depicted in terms of sailors' landmarks: conspicuous castles, temples, high peaks, and useful harbors. The islands curl around the bay and seem to reach to embrace the sea, emphasizing the shipping that bobs offshore and the intimate relationship of land and water. Even today, most Japanese still live where they have always lived, crammed into narrow shores by the mountains at their backs. The sea around which they huddle is there to be used and feared—a sea without a name, although it has an obvious unity of its own: the system of bays and channels between islands that washes the Pacific shore of Japan from Tokyo Bay to Kyushu. Throughout their history, the Japanese have depended on capricious, unpredictably hostile seas for communications and for a vital part of their diet; rice cultivation in the hinterland was a traditionally laborious business, evoked in an early-tenth-century code of "heavenly offenses": breaking down the ridges, filling in the ditches, overplanting, and wasting the water in the sluices.[5]

In one of Japan's earliest legends, the sea god's daughter gives Prince Fire-fade fishhooks, riches, and victories, but she turns into a dragon in his dreams—a writhing serpent, easily recognizable in the typhoon-coiled ocean Japanese navigators faced.[6] During the medieval shogunate, the political axis of Japan was known as the Seacoast Road, linking the imperial court at Kyoto with the shogun's headquarters in Kamakura.[7] On this shore, in famous verses, the waves wetted the sleeve of the pilgrim Jubutsu while he was asleep.[8] A Chinese satirist of the end of the third century A.D. made fun of the Japanese custom of insuring a voyage by taking a holy man aboard: "If the voyage is concluded with good fortune, everyone lavishes on him slaves and treasures. If someone gets ill or if there is a mishap, they kill him immediately, saying that he was not conscientious in observing the taboos."[9] In the late fourth and early fifth centuries, the proto-Japanese state of Yamato expanded by sea beyond Kansai into neighboring bays and islands. Japanese fleets took part in Korean wars.[10] In the seventh century, Japan is said to have had a navy 400 ships strong.[11] The sea was also the place culture came from: rice cultivation, metallurgy, writing, coinage, Buddhism, and the model of a bureaucratic, self-consciously imperial state—all came from China and Korea. The earth of the rocky woodlands around the shrine of Okinoshima, the sacred "floating mountain" on the sea route to Korea, is full of votive offerings from both shores, forming a fragmentary record of Japan's contact with the world from the fourth to the ninth century.[12] The traditional New Year ship regularly "awakens the world from night."[13] The art of ukiyo-e is full of ships tortured by sea ghosts, surviving storms, or enduring calms. To this day, perhaps the best-known Japanese work of art is Hokusai's *Great Wave of Kanagawa* of about 1805. It depicts a wave, captured in a moment of menace, just before it crashes into dissolving foam.[14]

The needs and perils of the sea were the subject of a diary of an anonymous lady on a homeward voyage more than 1,000 years ago. The writer tells the story of a journey by sea in 936 from Kochi prefecture in southern Shikoku to the Bay of Osaka. On the map, the distance seems short, but in the context of the Japanese empire of the day, it was a crossing from a far frontier, a link between the capital and a remote island outpost. The author is identified as the wife of the returning governor of the province: "Diaries are things written by men, I am told. Nevertheless I am writing one, to see what a woman can do." At the journey's beginning, amid farewells that "lasted all day and into the night," the travelers prayed "for a calm and peaceful crossing" and performed rites of propitiation, tossing charms and rich gifts into the water: jewels, mirrors, and libations of rice wine. The ship pulled out, rowers straining at the oars. "Bad winds kept us, yearning for home, for many days. . . . We cower in a harbor. When the clouds clear we leave before dawn. Our oars pierce the moon." After seven days' sailing, they were delayed by adverse winds at Ominato, where they waited for nine days, composing poems and yearning for the capital. On the next leg, they rowed ominously out of the comforting sight of the shore, "further and further out to sea. At every stroke, the watchers slip into the distance."

As fear mounts and the mountains and sea grow dark, the pilot and boatmen sing to rouse their spirits. At Muroto, bad weather brings another five days' delay. When at last they set out with "oars piercing the moon," a sudden dark cloud alarms the pilot: "It will blow: I'm turning back." A dramatic double-reversal of mood follows: a day dawns brightly, and "the master anxiously scans the seas. 'Pirates? Terror! . . . All of us have grown white-haired.'" Professing terror, the lady manages a literary prayer: "Tell us, Lord of the Islands, which is whiter—the surf on the rocks or the snow on our heads?"

By a variety of techniques, the voyagers elude the pirates. Paper charms are cast overboard in the direction of danger. Prayers are intoned to gods and buddhas "as the offerings drift." Finally, the crew resorts to rowing by night, an expedient so dangerous that only a much greater danger can have driven them to it. They skim the dreaded whirlpool of Awa off Naruto with more prayers. A few days into the third month of the journey, they are prevented from making headway by a persistent wind. "There is something on board the god of Sumiyoshi wants," the pilot murmurs darkly. They try paper charms without success. With increasing desperation, the master announces, "I offer the God my precious mirror!" He flings it into the sea. The wind changes. The vessel glides into Osaka the following day. "There are many things which we cannot forget, and which give us pain," concludes the writer, "but I cannot write them all down."[15]

The journal form makes it possible to be precise about the length of the voyage as described. It began on the twenty-second day of the twelfth moon and ended on the sixth day of the third moon of the new year. For a journey that probably did not exceed 400 miles, the expedition therefore appears to have spent sixty-nine days at sea or in intermediate harbors waiting for a favorable wind. There are all sorts of reasons why this may have been an exceptionally slow journey. The rank of the passengers may have required a stately pace. Reluctance to travel at night may have been greater, in this company, than normal. The presumably large galley may have been compelled to keep inshore, so as to have access to supplies and freshwater, at the sacrifice of open-sea shortcuts. But even if taken as a maximum duration, sixty-nine days seems dauntingly long. Alternatively, the diarist may have stretched the time scale for dramatic reasons to distribute incidents most effectively through the narrative. Even so, the order of magnitude must have been reasonable or the realistic impact of the work would be lost.

The laborious and time-consuming effort of navigating Japanese waters explains, better than any myth of ingrained isolationism, why Japan's imperialism never developed very far until the steamship age. Apart from Japan's home islands and those that most closely neighbored them, Korea and China were objects of sporadic temptations to Japanese imperial visionaries. They could only be approached through zones of terrible typhoons that crush ships against lee shores or cleave them with rocks in the Gulf of Tonkin as navigators approach continental Asia from the east. Occasional Japanese voyagers into the Indian Ocean—like the protagonist of the tenth-century *Tale of the Hollow Tree*, which describes a freak, wind-driven voyage to Persia—were therefore surprised by the amazing rapidity with which communications could be established over vast distances with the aid of the monsoon. The Japanese, by comparison, seemed penned in or pinned down by their winds.

FELIPE FERNÁNDEZ-ARMESTO

The winds were a deterrent to long-range Japanese navigation, an inducement to navigators farther west along Asia's shore. Thanks to the monsoon system that guaranteed a wind at one's back, some seaboard civilizations of the Indian Ocean attained an extraordinary length of outreach in the Middle Ages, when none but the Norse crossed the Atlantic and the Pacific was still an untraversable ocean.

My second example of a maritime civilization commonly misclassified is that of the Arabs. Western travel writers and filmmakers have steeped our image of Arab peoples in the romance and ruthlessness of the desert. Even the Arabs' image of themselves shimmers with the same miragelike effects; they idealize the supposed natural nobility of the desert-dwelling Bedouin and the life of the tent and the camp.

In reality, however, genuine desert dwellers have never been numerous. The heartlands of the civilization that Arabs created and spread across vast areas of the world were in narrow but fertile coastal strips that fringe parts of the Arabian Peninsula, between sand and sea. Especially in Oman, the Hadhramaut, and Yemen, coastal Arabia has all the common geographical conditions for the creation of a seaboard civilization: lands good to sustain life but with no scope to expand to landward and no space, except by sea, to enlarge the base of available resources. There are, nonetheless, serious disincentives to a seafaring way of life. Arabia has never produced much wood with which to build ships. It has no navigable rivers and, relative to the length of the coast, few first-class harbors. Along the Persian Gulf, suitable harbors where freshwater can be taken aboard have always been few and far between. The Red Sea is harder to navigate than the western Arabian desert. According to Ibn Majid, the greatest Arab writer on navigation of the Middle Ages, it "conceals many unknown places and things." Its reputation as late as the sixteenth century A.D. was for "hazards greater than those of the great ocean."[16] It was precisely because it was so hostile to shipping that ancient travelers who did brave it did so with much pride—such as the sailors of the spice-buying expedition sent by Queen Hatshepsut of Egypt and recorded on the walls of her mortuary temple in about 1500 B.C. Therefore, for most of the time—and, indeed, overwhelmingly until the fourth century B.C.— goods arriving in Yemen from farther east would be transferred to camel caravan en route for Egypt or Syria. Even the monsoon system, the regular wind pattern that is nature's great gift to seagoing peoples lucky enough to live on the coasts it serves, was hard for the early Arab navigators to exploit. North of the equator in the Indian Ocean, northeast winds prevail in the winter. For most of the rest of the year, they blow steadily from the south and west. By timing voyages to take advantage of the monsoons, traders and explorers could set out confident of a fair wind out and a fair wind home. As a bonus, the currents follow the wind faithfully. In consequence, the Indian Ocean was the scene of the world's earliest long-range navigation on the open sea, but the Arabian Sea—the arm of the ocean that the Arabs had to cross—is racked by storms throughout the year, and the monsoon is dangerously fierce. Strong shipbuilding techniques were essential to cope with these conditions.

Arabia's early archaeological record is still sketchy, although new work is adding to it all the time. The beginnings of a settled, farming way of life in what is now Oman can be traced back to the fifth millennium B.C. when sorghum was cultivated. Animals were domesticated: dogs, camels, donkeys, and cattle—possibly the hump-backed zebu. In the third millennium, Oman and perhaps Bahrain began to grow in importance as avenues of trade between India and Mesopotamia developed. Early in the third millennium, the name "Dilmun," of disputed location but certainly somewhere in the region, began to become common in cuneiform texts. In the last three centuries of the millennium, the name of the "Kingdom of Magan," generally identified as Oman, was added.[17] Meanwhile, Oman acquired stone buildings, seals decorated in the manner of the Indus Valley, and a reputation for the smelting of copper. In addition to locally mined metal, a persuasive case has been made in favor of the theory that Omani forges also worked with imported metals and ores. By the end of the third millennium, however, the region's role as an entrepôt became concentrated in Bahrain, and the name Dilmun became associated with that island in particular. The results of prosperity are evident in the dressed limestone temples erected in the first half of the second millennium. In the same period, Yemen, the fertile southwest corner of the peninsula, was developing complex irrigation systems and an export trade in the rich aromatics, such as frankincense and myrrh, for which the region was renowned. Goods from Ethiopia, Somalia, and India passed through the hands of Yemeni middlemen on their way to the Middle East or generated tolls that enriched local states or tribes.

The collapse of the Indus Valley civilization, however, had a depressing effect on the Arabian economy. Civilization in Arabia seems to have marked time until late in the last millennium before the Christian era when trade across the Indian Ocean recovered a high level of prosperity. Alexander the Great's desire to launch a campaign of conquest by sea against eastern Arabia was not capricious; at the time, the region contained the impressive walled city of Thaj, with a circuit of dressed stone 2,535 meters in circumference and of an average height of 4.5 meters.[18] The coastal city of Gerrha, probably in the vicinity of the modern al-Jubayl, was an emporium for Arabian aromatics and Indian manufactures. Large numbers of inscriptions in Hasaitic script are still being unearthed. The opportunities for trade in the region are suggested by the apparent wealth of the island staging post of Failaka, occupied successively by Persian and Greek colonists in the third and second centuries B.C.[19] Omani emporia had a glowing reputation among Roman and Greek writers in the two centuries around the birth of Christ. Yemen was regarded as a land where men "burn cassia and cinnamon for their everyday needs." The author of a Greek guide to Indian Ocean trade believed that "no nation seems to be wealthier than the Sabaeans and Gerrhaeans, who are the agents for everything that falls under the name of transport from Asia and Europe. It is they who have made Syria rich in gold and who have provided profitable trade and thousands of other things to Phoenician enterprise."[20]

The history of Arabian seafaring seems, however, to have been interrupted again, or at least almost to have disappeared from surviving sources, during the "dark age" that, according to traditional historiography, preceded the career of the prophet Muhammad in the early seventh century. It resumed with the experience of expansion that followed Muhammad's death. The Sinbad sagas are a few drops in an ocean of stories about the caprice of these seas. My favorite is told by Buzurg ibn Shahriyar, whose father was a sea captain, in the mid-tenth-century text entitled *The Book of the Wonders of India*. It concerns Abhara, a native of Kirman, who, after careers as a shepherd and a mariner, became the most renowned navigator of his day. He made the journey to China and back seven times. To do so once in safety was considered a miracle; to do it twice was incredible. According to the author, no one had ever completed the journey except by accident; it was an exaggeration but representative of the renown Abhara attracted. On the occasion I am thinking of, he was discovered by an Arab crew, captained by the author's father, bound from Siraf for China in the Sea of Tonkin. The famous sailor was alone, afloat in a ship's boat with a skinful of freshwater, in a flat calm. Thinking to rescue him, the crew of the newly arrived ship invited him aboard, but he refused to join, except as captain with full authority and a salary of 1,000 dinars, payable in merchandise at their destination at the market rate. Astounded, they begged him to save himself by joining them, but he replied, "Your situation is worse than mine." His reputation began to tell. "We said, 'The ship has much merchandise and considerable wealth on board and very many people. It will do us no harm to have Abhara's advice for 1,000 dinars,'" and they made the bargain. Declaring, "We have no time to waste," Abhara made them discard all their heavy merchandise, jettison the mainmast, and cut the anchor cables to lighten the ship.

After three days, "a large cloud like a minaret" appeared, the classic sign of a typhoon. They not only survived its onslaught, but Abhara led them profitably to China and, on the way back, was able to steer them to the exact place where some of their lost anchors, cast ashore on barely visible rocks, could be retrieved. There, but for his intervention, the ship itself would surely have come to grief.[21] At one level, the tale reveals how the ocean seemed to those who sailed it: a realm of dramatic changes where only long practical experience, purchased at the risk of one's life, could overcome peril.

At another level, however, the story of Abhara attests to the great advantage of Indian Ocean navigation: if you survived, you could span vast distances in fast times and in both directions. This meant more mutual enrichment, for the merchants and shippers who sent and carried the goods and for the states and civilizations that exchanged them. By almost imperceptible degrees, the spread of conquests and converts along the coasts turned most of the Indian Ocean into an Islamic lake, and Islam came to preponderate in maritime Asia as far east as the Spice Islands. Arab culture was so successful in communicating and catching on that its limits seem more surprising than its reach. The winds dragged eastward. From Yemen, in the age of sail, India and Indonesia were more accessible than Suez, which lay thirty days' voyaging away, beyond the rocks, shoals, and treacherously variable winds of the northern half of the Red Sea. Around parts of the remoter rim of the Indian Ocean world, in Africa and India, Islam has remained a markedly maritime culture, with only patchy penetration inland, where vast, almost untouched hinterlands have stayed hostile or indifferent.

Meanwhile, the limits of Islam were fixed in other directions by the sea and the wind. Although Islam could conquer the eastern and southern shores of the Mediterranean by land-based campaigns, it was extremely hard to get any farther without command of the sea. On the Mediterranean maritime fronts, the winds favored the resisters on the northern and western shores, where the winds blow in the traditional sailing season, giving defenders the weather gauge.[22] Of the great peninsulas of the northern Mediterranean, three were conquered by means of huge investments of manpower and naval effort at different times; but ultimately, Spain, Greece, and the Balkans could not be retained, while Italy was vulnerable only to sporadic attacks. Islamic culture proved almost as hard to spread against the wind as Islamic conquest.

In a collection of essays by maritime scholars, it hardly seems necessary to add the example of the Greeks to that of the Japanese and Arabs. Maritime historians never think of ancient Greece without the sea: the black ships on black-figure vases, the ship catalog of *The Iliad*, the voyages of Jason and Odysseus, and the pursuit of Galatea. To us, who are sea-minded, even the great stage tragedies that take place in the intense, inbred, cramped settings of small courts, city-states, and dysfunctional royal families are linked by offstage sea lanes to the wider world. *The Oresteia* is a tale of homecomings; that of Oedipus ends in exile. Ours is not, however, the common perception. Few of the popular histories and standard textbooks on the Greeks do justice to the maritime dimension. The best way to evoke it, I think, is to recall the earliest known sailing directions in Western history. They were uttered by a poet sweating at a plough, in Boeotia in the middle of the eighth century B.C., where the land was hard and the plough was wearisome. In the annoying manner younger brothers sometimes have, Perses was lounging around, watching Hesiod at work and pestering him with silly questions about how to get rich quickly. The incident really happened, or perhaps Hesiod imagined it, but the poem in which he wrote down the results of the conversation captures a lot of the reality of life on a poor shore, alongside a rich sea. He recast it in the form of a dialogue, and the implied exchange of give and take can be teased out with a fair degree of confidence:[23]

> Greece and poverty are sisters, Perses began, quoting a proverb of which Hesiod was fond. How can I make money easily?

> Work, my brother, that's the way to keep hunger out of the way. You have the better share of our father's land. What more do you want?

> I want to avoid toil, Hesiod. You know me.

> Get a house first, enjoined the elder brother, and a woman and a ploughing ox—a slave woman, not a wife—a woman who can take her turn following the ox.

Hesiod must be imagined continuing his ploughing while he talks, affecting indifference to his brother's next retort:

> I want to buy and sell in distant markets.

In my mind's eye, I see Perses getting up and pacing restlessly at this point. Hesiod begins to sound exasperated:

> Perses, don't be a fool. Our father tried that. He came here in his black ship from Aeolian Kyme, fleeing from the evil penury with which God punished us men. And where did he end up? In this miserable dump of Askra, bad in winter, hard in summer, never good.

But that is why my heart is set on escape—escape from debts and joyless hunger.

Not now, not when the Pleiades plunge into the misty sea, for the blasts of all the winds are blowing. Till the soil, as I tell you, and wait for the sailing season, and then haul your ship to the wine-dark sea and stuff it with cargo. The greater the cargo the greater the gain.

What do you know about sailing? You've only been over the sea once, to Euboia, for the poetry contest. . . .

Where I was victorious with my hymn and carried off the prize, the sacred tripod. But just as God taught me the secrets of composition, so shall he tell me the secrets of navigation for me to confide to you.

Hesiod continues in what I think of as a dreamy, trancelike mode:

For fifty days after the turning of the sun, when harvest, the weary season, is over, you can sail without fear of breaking your ship—unless Poseidon, the shaker of Earth, or Zeus, the king of Gods, makes up his mind to destroy you. For in that spell, the breezes are easy to judge and the sea is unmalicious. You can trust it. But hurry home: never await the new wine or the autumn rains—much less winter's dread onset and the blasts of the south wind. Money may be all you want in life— but it is not worth the risk of death by drowning. And never put all your wealth on board. Be moderate, my brother. Moderation is best in everything.

The visionary's rapture fades. The divine message has been transmitted. Hesiod resumes his ploughing.

Earlier sea-peoples of the Mediterranean disappeared. The megalith builders of the eastern islands were unremembered. The sophisticates of the Cycladic Islands and Crete in the Bronze Age vanished into legend. The Phoenicians were almost expunged from the record. Conquerors destroyed their writings and most of their art and even razed their cities to the ground. The Greeks, by contrast, who took to the sea at almost the same time, nearly 3,000 years ago, for similar reasons, from a homeland with a similar environment, endured against the odds. Their settlements, cities, art, and books survived where the bones of rock poke through the thin skin of the soil. In the fifth century B.C., Plato imagined Greece as a skeleton emerging from desiccated flesh, wasted by sickness.[24] Hesiod complained about the harshness of his own farmland. The very fragility of the environment made the people who lived there want to change it, and, at the same time, they feared the consequences. The gods were always inclined to chastise man's presumption in abusing the gifts of nature. The Scaramander River threatened to drown Achilles for polluting its waters with corpses. Herodotus saw the defeat of Xerxes as punishment for a series of ecologically incorrect excesses: canal building at Athos, bridging the Hellespont, and lashing the waves.[25]

It seems incredible that such a background could nourish the achievements of the civilization founded here, in the southern lands and offshore islands of this hot, dry, rocky salient of eastern Europe, but the deficiencies of the landward environment were countered by the sea. "We live around the sea," said Socrates, "like frogs around a pond," and a glance at the map shows how the Greek world was a network of seaboard communities. Plato reckoned seafaring to be one of mankind's greatest achievements, and even the wood, pitch, and sailcloth to make ships had to be imported, as well as metal for the shipwrights' tools. Building up the wealth necessary to be able to exploit the sea was a long and laborious business. In an environment hostile to agriculture, industry was the only means to acquire wealth. At Athens, Corinth, and a few other centers in the tenth century B.C., finely decorated pots were made for export. Olives, the only surplus farm product, were pressed for their oil. These were the beginnings of a trade that first lined the Aegean and Ionian Seas with cities, and then, from the middle of the eighth century onward, spread over the Mediterranean and Black Seas. Stories of early explorers were collected by the historian Herodotus nearly 2,500 years ago. He told, for example, the story of Coleos of Samos, who crossed the length of the Mediterranean with a freak wind and burst through into the Atlantic between the pillars of Hercules, where the racing current stoppers the sea. He was aiming for Egypt and ended up in southwestern Spain. Here he discovered the El Dorado of the Greeks, the real-life fantasy land they called Tartessos, where Hercules tamed the flocks of Geryon and a king could be said to live for 120 years. "This market," Herodotus reported, "was at that time still unexploited," despite its rich mines: the copper that has stained the banks of the Río Tinto, and the gold, silver, and iron that are concentrated in the pyrite belt. "Therefore when they returned to their own country the men of Samos made more profit from their wares than any Greeks we know of, save Sostratos of Aegina—and there is none to compare with him. They sailed in round freight-ships, but the men of Phocaea, who discovered the Adriatic Sea, made the same journey in fifty-oared vessels."[26]

In the eighth century, increased use of iron tools made agriculture more efficient, but the consequent increase of population made ever more strenuous demands on food and land.[27] As well as a trading people, the Greeks became colonizers, extending the range of their settlements to rich, wheat-growing areas in Sicily, southern Italy, and the north shore of the Black Sea, and then to cash-rich markets in what are now France and Spain. During the seventh century, many of these colonies became impressive cities in their own right. The progress of trade meanwhile is shown by the introduction of coinage in most Greek cities and the building of new and larger ship types. Although Greek writers tended to idealize the hardy farming past, they realized that commerce was the life-blood of their society. Many of them included merchants and sea explorers among their heroes—something unthinkable, for example, in the China of the time, where only farmers, warriors, and scholars were valued.

The call of the sea was not universally felt; Spartans, for example, often preferred to stay in Greece and build up an empire in contiguous territory. This, however, was one of many Lacedaemonian eccentricities of which the gods disapproved: a pair of Spartan imperialists who planned a settlement near Corinth in about 706 were directed by the oracle "to Satyrion, the water of Taras, a harbor on the left, and the place where a goat loves salt water, wetting the tip of his grey beard. There build Tarentum."[28] From other centers, the usual direction of imperialism was outward. Colonies were founded abroad with the blessing of oracles uttered by the gods, especially through the mouths of priestesses at Delphi. In this shrine, the divine pronouncements were relayed from a theatrically effective setting—a tripod throne in the form of writhing serpents rose from a smoking chasm in a cave—and recommended colonization in a baffling array of cases: the founder of Kroton went to Delphi in search of a remedy for childlessness, with no prior thought of starting a colony. In about the 720s, Chalcidians were directed to colonize in order to escape famine. In about 640, Rhodians were told to found a colony in Sicily and share it with Cretans. The founder of Eraclea in Sicily was criticized for omitting the routine preliminaries of oracular consultation. Foundation stories of colonies came to include claims of authorization by the oracle almost as a matter of course because Apollo's fiat conferred legitimacy and appeared to guarantee long life.[29] Colony founding ever farther afield became so much a part of the Greek way of life that a playwright speculated on the chances of founding one in the sky. "Not that we hate our city," the would-be colonists protest, "for it is a prosperous mighty city, free for all to spend their wealth in, paying fines and fees." Aristophanes knew how to tweak his audience into laughing at themselves.[30]

Because the Greek world spread seaward rather than by land, the colonies kept the maritime outlook that characterized the world they came from and neighbors of the sort they already knew. Colonies were usually sited on heavily indented coasts.[31] Yet they could have ended up looking very unlike home, for colonists were outcasts, exiles, criminals, and bastards; they were breakaway frontiersmen forging a new society and not imperial paladins recreating Greece overseas.[32] In some cases, they began their new lives by sheltering in pits.[33] Nostalgia, the needs of commerce, and lack of imagination all conspired to keep them clinging to familiar ties and patterns, reproducing the tastes of Greece, replicating its sentiments, and receiving its visitors. Naucratis, the self-designated "polis" on the Nile delta, had temples to Samian Hera and Milesian Apollo—among other shrines dedicated to Greek cults—and Ionic porticoes.[34] The sixth- and fifth-century dedications of votive cups to Aphrodite show a lively traffic of Greek visitors: sex tourists, directed to Naucratis by Herodotus's praise of the prostitutes; Herodotus himself, perhaps, if he can be identified with a pledge-giver of the same name; and sober travelers, including Aristophanes and Solon, bound for Egypt on business or on a sort of grand tour in search of enlightenment by a great civilization.[35]

Thanks in part to an incomparable terrestrial asset, the silver mines of nearby Laurion, by the fifth century B.C., the richest and most powerful city was Athens, with a fleet big enough to force many other cities to pay tribute. Here Poseidon was said to have disputed possession with Athena, lashing the nearby cliffs with waves churned by his trident. Though we think of Athens as a state organized for art, its own citizens' priorities were war and wealth, and their moralists tended to emphasize the priority of the former. Athens will be safe, according to the words Aristophanes put into the mouth of a playwright of revered high seriousness, "when they shall count the enemy's soil their own, and . . . when they know that ships are their true wealth, their so-called wealth delusion."[36]

The three examples could be multiplied. Their range could extend; island cultures tend to have relationships with the sea that are different from those of seaboard cultures but equally dependent on the sea. Even inland trading communities with no direct outlet to the sea are often deeply affected by the transmissions of culture and transfers of goods that reach them by way of the ocean. One has only to think of ancient Aksum, a highland civilization far from the sea, with trade that linked it across the Indian Ocean to places as far away as China; early medieval Rus, where Viking traders brought the river system into touch with the remote sea lanes they frequented; or later medieval Mwene Mutapa that formed part of the Indian Ocean trading world, thanks to coastal and offshore merchant communities in Sofala and Kilwa.

Histories of these kinds illustrate how sea routes became the highways of long-range transmissions of culture and the framework on which genuinely global history—cultural exchange, that is, that encompasses the world—was built. Yet this process began relatively late. The world had to wait until the last half-millennium for the development of interoceanic navigation, without which the globalizing trends of modern history—the "world system" and "world order" that ensued from the opening-up of world-ranging routes—would have been unthinkable. For most of history, long-range exchange relied on slow, precarious, land-bound routes. These led across deserts and steppes or along great rift valleys or highland hogs' backs or, by snaking "silk roads" through zones so inhospitable that they were safe from marauders. For obvious reasons, land-bound communications could never encompass the globe. Until the oceans were crossed by regular navigable routes, some civilizations were virtually out of reach of others. There were few possibilities for the communication of ways of life between comparable environments across the world of "new Europes" being founded, for instance, in Australia and the South American cone or "new Africas" in the Caribbean.[37] The chances of civilizations colonizing unfamiliar environments were relatively few; there could be no Chinatowns in London or San Francisco, no Japanese agricultural colonies in Brazil, no rubber plantations in Malaya, and no grand piano in Bogotá. There could be no prospect at all of that still-unrealized dream or nightmare: global civilization, produced, in triumph or compromise, by the exchange of influences across world-spanning routes.

Nor could the "inner seas" that were the first seaborne arenas of long-range exchange have a global quality. Even the vast system of navigation that linked the seaboards of maritime Asia with those of the western edge of the Indian Ocean remained largely closed and introspective until the last 500 years or so. All seafarers are alert to the dangers and difficulties of their own seas, and the indigenous literature of the ocean is full of scare stories, calculated to inhibit competitors or instill fear of divine wrath. To storytellers, seas are irresistible moral environments where storms are shafts from the quivers of meddlesome deities; most cultures regard freak winds as phenomena peculiarly manipulable by God or the gods. Those used to the Indian Ocean in the age of sail shared, along with these traditions, a heightened perception of its obstacles. To judge from firsthand accounts, you would have to classify every marine environment as hostile to man.[38] To

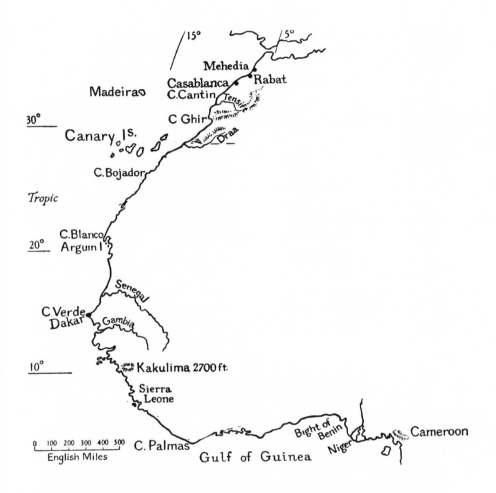

FIGURE I. *Hanno's Voyage* from *History of Ancient Geography* by James O. Thomson (Cambridge, 1948). Reprinted with the permission of Cambridge University Press.

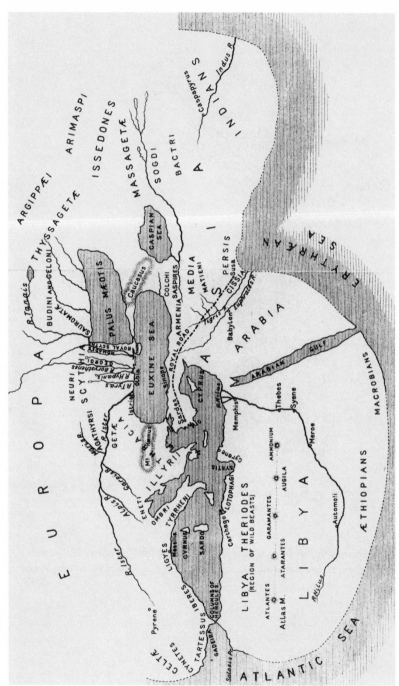

FIGURE 2. *The World According to Herodotus* by Edwin Wilson from *A History of Ancient Geography* by Henry F. Tozer (Cambridge, 1897). Reprinted with the permission of Cambridge University Press.

appreciate the relative benignity of some seas over others, a comparative approach is essential.

There was poetic truth in the old maps that showed the Indian Ocean landlocked because it was difficult to travel beyond it.[39] The lost but much-cited sailing directions known as the Rahnama, which go back at least to the twelfth century, warned of the "circumambient sea, whence all return was impossible." Here Alexander was said to have set up "a magical image, with its hand upraised as a warning: 'This is the *ne plus ultra* of navigation, and of what lies beyond in the sea no man has knowledge.'"[40] Access to the ocean from the east was barely possible in summer, when typhoons tear into lee shores. Until the sixteenth century, the vast, empty expanse of the neighboring Pacific preserved the ocean against approaches from beyond the China Seas. Shipping from the west could enter only by way of an arduous detour through the southern Atlantic and around Africa, while stores wasted and freshwater spoiled. The southern approaches that then had to be crossed were guarded in summer by fierce storms; no one who knew the reputation of these waters would venture between about ten and thirty degrees south or sixty and ninety degrees east without urgent reason in the season of hurricanes. The lee shores toward the tip of Africa were greedy for wreckage at the best of times. From al-Masudi in the tenth century to Duarte Barbosa in the sixteenth, writers of guides to the ocean noted that the practical limit of navigation was to the north of the bone-strewn coasts of Natal and Transkei, where survivors of Portuguese ships wrote *The Tragic History of the Sea*.[41] For most of history, the ocean, therefore, remained chiefly the preserve of peoples whose homes bordered it or who traveled overland, like some European and Armenian traders, to become part of its world. Even within this fairly tight circle of exchange, sailing could be hazardous. Once a ship was afloat on the ocean, the well-frequented routes across two great gulfs—the Bay of Bengal and the Arabian Sea—were racked by storms throughout the year. The ocean system allowed an apparently generous sailing season, from April to June for an eastbound ship, with the southwest monsoon, after which, following an interval during the months of strongest winds, westbound sailing could be taken up with the northeast monsoon. However, to get the greatest benefit from the system, to go farthest and get back fastest with new trade goods or profits, it was necessary to sail in one direction with the tail end of the monsoon in order to reduce the turnaround time, that is, the time a laden ship spent awaiting the new season and the change of wind.

It sounds like an irksome routine of the shipping schedule, but in the age of sail, it was a way of courting death. Particularly on the eastward run, the

late monsoon had the most dreadful reputation among sailors. It was vividly captured by a fifteenth-century ambassador from Persia to the court of
Vijayanagar. He was detained at Hormuz "so that the favorable time for
departing by sea, that is to say the beginning or middle of the monsoon, was
allowed to pass, and we came to the end of the monsoon, which is the season when tempests and attacks from pirates are to be dreaded. . . . As soon
as I caught the smell of the vessel, and all the terrors of the sea presented
themselves before me, I fell into so deep a swoon, that for three days respi-
ration alone indicated that life remained within me. When I came a little to
myself, the merchants, who were my intimate friends, cried with one voice
that the time for navigation was passed, and that everyone who put to sea at
this season was alone responsible for his death."[42]

The choice of this most dangerous sailing time was also imposed on
shipping that began its journey far up the Red Sea. To benefit from the
northerlies that would help them out of that notoriously difficult bottleneck,
sailors had to leave in July, making their open-sea crossing of the Arabian
Sea in August. The ordeal bore one advantage: with the wind at its fiercest,
the journey to India, if not fatal, would be over in as little as eighteen or
twenty days. The alternative was to avoid the season of bad weather by sailing to windward against the northeast monsoon. The dhow, the traditional
vessel of Sinbad, is rigged with triangular sails with this very trick in mind
and can lie close to the wind; that is, it can make headway against the wind
without departing more than a few degrees from its intended course.[43]

As Abhara found, the fabulous rewards of Indian Ocean navigation off-
set its strains and hazards. Under these circumstances, it is not surprising
that trade was internal, and merchants took no interest in venturing far
beyond the monsoon system in search of other markets or supplies.

In comparison with the predictability of monsoons, it was a long time
before trade-wind navigation systems were developed because of the inhib-
iting patterns of winds and currents. Until the trade-wind systems were
explored and decoded, adventurers had no expectation of getting home. The
exceptions to this rule really do seem to prove it. The Waq-Waq navigators
who took Austronesian settlers westward across the southern Indian
Ocean, beyond reach of the monsoon and across the path of the southeast
trades, were evidently unable to sustain communications along the routes
they had pioneered. In about the same period, the Viking enterprise in the
North Atlantic led to Iceland, Greenland, and Vinland by current-assisted
routes, in or just above latitudes where reliable westerlies were known to be
available to take sailors home. The fact that, south of Newfoundland, the
currents along the northeastern coast of America are adverse helps to ex-

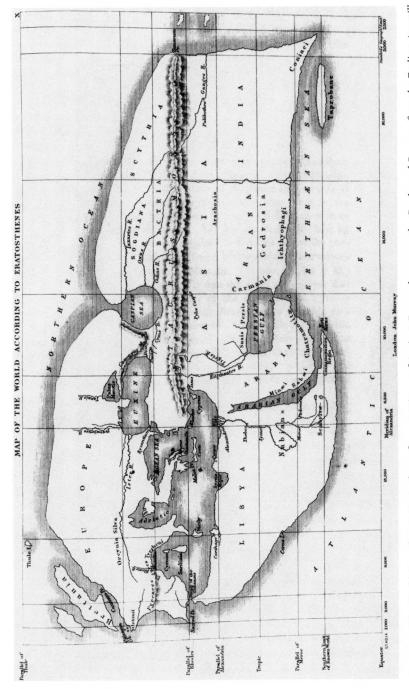

FIGURE 3. *The World According to Eratosthenes from A History of Ancient Geography among the Greeks and Romans from the Earliest Ages till the Fall of the Roman Empire by Edward H. Bunbury (London, 1883).*

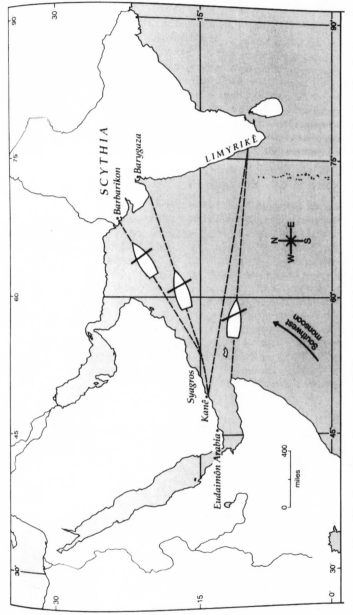

FIGURE 4. *Map of the Open Water Routes to India* from *The Periplus Maris Erythraei: Text with Introduction, Translation, and Commentary* by Lionel Casson (Princeton, c1989). Reprinted by permission of Princeton University Press.

plain the limits of Viking exploration in that area. In the long run, the Viking effort was unsustainable because of the limited economic opportunities to which it led, the constraining effects of climatic change, the grinding ecological problems, and the vulnerability of the western colonies. At about the same time as the Vikings crossed the Atlantic, the Arctic route to Greenland was traversed by Thule Inuit paddling umiaks in summer, from cove to cove, around the northern shore of the New World. This route was discovered in the course of a heroic migration, but it could not be kept open regularly or reliably enough to become an avenue of sustained cultural exchange. The other great navigators of the era, the Polynesian "Vikings of the Sunrise," made their forays deep into the Pacific almost entirely against the wind. By about 1,000 years ago, they had probably reached the limits attainable in those conditions with the technology at their command. Their outposts in Hawaii, Easter Island, and New Zealand could not keep in touch with their islands of origin.

When the trade-wind systems were mastered, the breakthrough was made by mariners from a relatively small range of communities along the Atlantic shores of Europe, from Andalusia in the south to England and Holland in the north. Most known explanations of the worldwide spread of western European influence fail to take account of the apparently essential part played by an Atlantic-side position. The traditional approach is to identify supposed elements of superiority in the society, economy, technology, or, in general terms, the culture of western Europe. Would-be explainers assert, for example, the technical superiority of Western methods of navigation, warfare, and economic exploitation, but the first and one of the greatest of all these far-flung empires, that of Spain, was constructed without any of the industrial technology in which, ultimately and briefly, western Europeans came to be privileged. They appeal to sociocultural explanations in the tradition of Weber, asserting differences in value systems that made some people more prone to commerce and empire than others. There is clearly something wrong, for instance, in an appeal to "Confucian values" when it is used to explain phenomena as diverse and mutually exclusive as the frustration of Chinese maritime imperialism in the fifteenth century, the recovery of Chinese trade in the eighteenth century, and the explosion of business imperialism in the tiger economies of the twentieth century. Nor is it enough to say that the sea was a source of derogation in the East—a Confucian subvalue, a pollutant of caste—whereas it was an ennobling medium for self-consciously chivalric adventurers in the Western tradition because there were many exceptions to this general truth. It is often said that Asian polities were generally hostile to commerce; this is an unconvincing generalization when applied to a vast and diverse world that included states that were, in effect, commercial enterprises. It might be thought that Indian Ocean traders were satiated with the opportunities at hand and that their shipping was fully absorbed by the demands of intraoceanic commerce. While there may be something in this, to ignore genuine opportunities for further self-enrichment seems incompatible with a commercial vocation. Conversely, the progress of western European explorers and conquistadors has been seen as a response to relative poverty, like the desperate efforts of emerging nations today to drill for offshore resources.

I do not mean to dismiss any of these variously useful explanations, or others of similar type, merely to suggest what I believe everyone working in this field suspects: they are not sufficient. We have to acknowledge that the Atlantic is a peculiar ocean and that an Atlantic-side position, especially in western Europe, confers advantages unattained elsewhere. Whereas the Indian Ocean is a sea where navigators look inward, to areas within the monsoonal system and the sea lanes between the storm belts, the trade winds of the Atlantic reach out to the rest of the world. The route discovered by Columbus linked the densely populated middle band of Eurasia that stretches from the eastern edge of the landmass to the shores of the Atlantic, with the environs of the great civilizations of the New World that lay, just beyond his reach, on the other side of the ocean. Along the route pioneered by Vasco da Gama, Atlantic winds drew ships south to the latitudes of the roaring forties that led on to the Indian Ocean and circled the world. Navigators' frustration with the Indian Ocean and the fulfillment of global ambitions in the Atlantic have to be explained in part by one of the inescapable facts of geographical conditioning: the tyranny of the winds. It took a long time for navigators to crack the Atlantic wind code. After an eon of relative inertia, it happened quickly, within the single decade of the 1490s. Once the task was accomplished, the winds drew sailors toward other oceans and other cultures.[44] The Atlantic trade-wind system drew navigators bound for the Pacific or Indian Oceans toward the roaring forties, winds that genuinely girdle the earth. Two-way navigation back and forth across the Pacific became possible after the explorations of Andrés de Urdaneta in 1564 and 1565. The Dutch route across or around the Indian Ocean, using the roaring forties and the West Australian current, was established in the second decade of the seventeenth century. In effect, the fixed-wind systems of the world had been mastered in a spate of frenzied activity lasting little more than 100 years. From then on, worldwide exchanges of biota and culture became possible. Global history became a reality. It grew out of maritime history.

FELIPE FERNÁNDEZ-ARMESTO

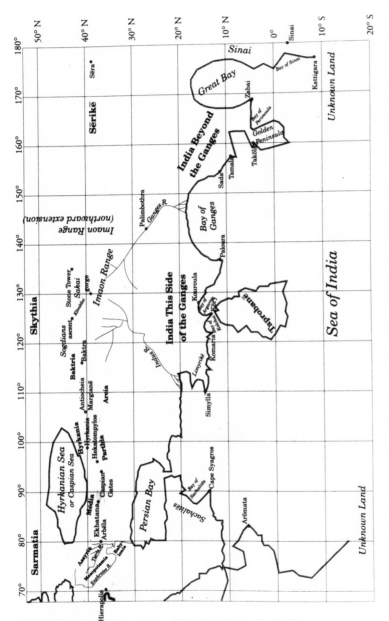

FIGURE 5. *Southern Asia According to Ptolemy* from Ptolemy's *Geography: An Annotated Translation of the Theoretical Chapters* by J. Lennart Berggren and Alexander Jones (Princeton, c2000). Reprinted by permission of Princeton University Press.

Notes

1. Walter Grainge White, *The Sea Gypsies of Malaya* (London, 1922), 40–60.
2. Christian Pelras, *The Bugis* (Oxford, 1996).
3. Alfred W. Crosby, *The Columbian Exchange: Biological and Cultural Consequences of 1492* (Westport, Conn., 1972).
4. Brian M. Fagan, *Floods, Famines, and Emperors: El Niño and the Fate of Civilizations* (New York, 1999), 3–70.
5. David J. Lu, *Japan: A Documentary History* (New York, 1997), 19.
6. Donald Keene, comp., *Anthology of Japanese Literature, from the Earliest Era to the Mid-Nineteenth Century* (New York, 1960), 29.
7. Donald Keene, *Travelers of a Hundred Ages* (New York, 1989), 114.
8. Ibid., 179.
9. Lu, *Japan*, 12.
10. Delmer M. Brown, ed., *The Cambridge History of Japan*, vol. 1, *Ancient Japan* (Cambridge, England, 1993), 124, 131, 140–44.
11. Ibid., 33, 207.
12. Ibid., 312–15.
13. Lawrence Smith, ed., *Ukiyo-e: Images of Unknown Japan* (London, 1985), 39.
14. Muneshige Narazaki, *Hokusai: The Thirty-Six Views of Mount Fuji* (Tokyo, 1968), 36–37; the image should be compared with the great wave the same artist painted later in his career. Henry D. Smith II, ed., *Hokusai: One Hundred Views of Mount Fuji* (New York, 1988), 118–19, 205.
15. Keene, *Anthology*, 82–91; on propitiatory rituals, see Charlotte von Verschuer, *Les relations officielles du Japon avec la Chine aux VIIIe et IXe siècles* (Geneva, 1985), 40–45.
16. Gerald Randall Tibbetts, *Arab Navigation in the Indian Ocean before the Coming of the Portuguese* (London, 1971).
17. Michael Rice, *Search for the Paradise Land: An Introduction to the Archaeology of Bahrain and the Persian Gulf* (London, 1985); and Michael Rice, *The Archaeology of the Arabian Gulf, c. 5000–323 B.C.* (London, 1994).
18. Daniel T. Potts, *The Arabian Gulf in Antiquity* (Oxford, 1990), vol. 2, plates 1 and 2.
19. Ibid., plates 5, 6, and 7.
20. George W. B. Huntingford, ed., *The Periplus of the Erythraean Sea* (London, 1980), 37.
21. Buzurg ibn Shahriyar, *The Book of the Wonders of India: Mainland, Sea and Islands*, ed. G.S.P. Freeman-Grenville (London, 1981), 49ff.
22. John H. Pryor, *Geography, Technology, and War: Studies in the Maritime History of the Mediterranean* (Cambridge, England, 1988), 649–1571.
23. Hesiod, *Works and Days*, ll. 392–420, 450–75, 613–705; Hesiod, *Hesiod, the Poems and Fragments, Done into English Prose*, trans. Alexander W. Mair (Oxford, 1908), ll, 15–17, 23–25.

24. Plato, *Critias*, 1. 111B.

25. Johnson Donald Hughes, *Ecology in Ancient Civilizations* (Albuquerque, 1975), 53–54.

26. Herodotus, *Histories*, 4.152.

27. John Boardman, *The Greeks Overseas: The Archaeology of Their Early Colonies and Trade* (Harmondsworth, England, 1973).

28. Catherine Morgan, *Athletes and Oracles: The Transformation of Olympia and Delphi in the Eighth Century b.c.* (Cambridge, England, 1990), 188.

29. Ibid., 172–78, 186–90.

30. Aristophanes, *The Birds*, in Aristophanes, *Aristophanes' Plays*, trans. B. Bickley Rogers (London, 1924), 133.

31. Anthony M. Snodgrass, "The Nature and Standing of the Early Western Colonies," in *The Archaeology of Greek Colonisation: Essays Presented to Sir John Boardman*, ed. Gocha R. Tsetskhladze and Franco De Angelis (Oxford, 1994), 1–10.

32. Irad Malkin, *Religion and Colonisation in Ancient Greece* (Leiden, 1987); Boardman, *Greeks Overseas*, 163.

33. Gocha R. Tsetskhladze, "Greek Penetration of the Black Sea," in Tsetskhladze and De Angelis, *The Archaeology of Greek Colonisation*, 117.

34. Boardman, *Greeks Overseas*, 119–21.

35. Ibid., 131–32.

36. Aristophanes, *The Frogs*, in Aristophanes, *Aristophanes' Plays*, 1462–4; 431.

37. The phrase "new Europes" is an invention of Alfred W. Crosby, *Ecological Imperialism: The Biological Expansion of Europe, 900–1900* (Cambridge, England, 1986).

38. K. N. Chaudhuri, *Trade and Civilisation in the Indian Ocean: An Economic History from the Rise of Islam to 1750* (Cambridge, England, 1985), 15.

39. See, for example, Kenneth Nebenzahl, *Atlas of Columbus and the Great Discoveries* (Chicago, 1990), 4–5.

40. Hasan, 129–30.

41. Masudi, *Les Prairies d'or*, ed. C. Barbier de Meynard and Pavet de Courteille, 9 vols. (Paris, 1861–1917), 3:6; Mansel Longworth Dames, ed., *The Book of Duarte Barbosa*, 2 vols. (London: Hakluyt Society, 1898), 1:4; and Charles Ralph Boxer, ed., *The Tragic History of the Sea, 1589–1622* (London: Hakluyt Society, 1959).

42. "Narrative of the Journey of Abd-er-Razzak, in *India in the Fifteenth Century*, ed. Richard Henry Major (London: Hakluyt Society, 1857), 7.

43. Alan John Villiers, *Monsoon Seas: The Story of the Indian Ocean* (New York, 1952), 56–57.

44. Felipe Fernández-Armesto, "The Origins of the European Atlantic," *Itinerario* 25 (2000).

2

Seaborne Exploration in the Ancient World

LIONEL CASSON

᛭

Historians of the ancient world lack the abundance and range of evidence available to their colleagues who deal with later ages. This is particularly true in the case of ancient exploration. Most of what we know about it derives from statements in the works of Greek and Roman authors who lived centuries after the journeys or voyages they describe, and so what they report must be subjected to critical judgment. The second major source of information is archaeological finds, and these are limited in what they can offer: an object excavated far from its home merely tells us that it had been brought from there to its find-spot; we can only guess by what route and by whom.

The Mediterranean

The ancient world's first great nations arose at, or not far from, the eastern end of the Mediterranean, and the earliest feats of seaborne exploration came about as sailors pushed westward over its waters. Archaeologists have uncovered on Crete the remains of the highly sophisticated civilization of the Minoans (as historians have named them; what they called themselves is unknown). They were not indigenous but had come to Crete from somewhere on the mainland, possibly Asia Minor, arriving about 3000 B.C. Minoan objects found in other lands show that by at least 2000 B.C., they had established overseas contacts with the Levant, Egypt, the Aegean Islands, and Greece. Ships frequently appear in their art, indicating they were a maritime people, and, indeed, Greeks of classical times held the belief that a mighty sea power existed on Crete in the dim past. It is thus a reasonable guess that it was Minoan mariners who opened up the sea lanes to Crete and from it to overseas destinations.[1]

For the opening of the Mediterranean to its western end, the credit goes to that people celebrated for their maritime skill, the Phoenicians. They accomplished it several centuries before or after 1000 B.C., depending upon whether one follows the traditional dates given by ancient writers or the indications of archaeology. The Phoenicians carried on an extensive seaborne trade from their home ports in the Levant, notably Tyre and Sidon. Seeking to expand their range, they sailed ever farther westward, planting settlements at suitable points along the African and European shores. According to the traditional dates, by 1100 B.C., they had founded the city of Utica some twenty miles north of modern Tunis; by about the same time, they had passed through the Strait of Gibraltar to found Gades, the modern Cadiz; and by 814 B.C., they had founded Carthage, just east of Tunis, which was to become one of the greatest centers of the western Mediterranean. At all three of these sites, the earliest archaeological remains go no further back than the eighth century B.C.; this date still leaves the Phoenicians with the distinction of being the pioneers in the exploration of the western Mediterranean.[2]

The West Coast of Africa

The next advance of the Phoenicians was down the Atlantic coast of Africa. Their first settlement on it was Lixus, situated a modest distance—about forty nautical miles—from the entrance to the Strait of Gibraltar. According to tradition, Lixus was very ancient, and according to the earliest archaeological evidence, it goes back to at least the seventh century B.C. The Phoenicians did not stop at Lixus; some 240 nautical miles farther down the coast, at Mogador (31°34' N), recent excavation has laid bare another Phoenician settlement whose earliest remains also date to the seventh century B.C. Although it was soon abandoned, it revived toward the end of the first century B.C. and became a flourishing town that lasted until the fourth or fifth century A.D.[3]

About 500 B.C., there was a dramatic move forward in the exploration of the Atlantic coast of Africa. It was made by an expedition under the command of a certain Hanno, the ruler of Carthage, whose report of it is the one and only firsthand explorer's account to have survived from ancient times. He had his report inscribed, probably on a bronze tablet, and set up in a temple in Carthage; there a Greek who apparently was interested in such matters saw it and made a translation, a copy of which turned up in a medieval manuscript of the ninth or tenth century.[4]

It is not easy to work out exactly how far Hanno went; almost all the place names he mentions are totally unfamiliar, the descriptions of geographical features rarely offer detail that permits identification with features visible today, and his reckoning of the distances he covered, no doubt based on his estimate of the speed of his ships, is not always trustworthy. The purpose of the expedition was to plant colonies farther along the Atlantic coast; accordingly, Hanno set off with numerous ships loaded with people and provisions. The first leg was in familiar waters, from Carthage through the Strait of Gibraltar and along the part of the Atlantic coast that already had Phoenician settlements on it. He then followed the coast, establishing a number of colonies. He reached a river where nomads and their flocks were camped, and he spent some time with them; most commentators identify the river as the Draa (28° N). Proceeding farther, he planted a colony on a tiny island to which he gave the name Cerne. The location of Cerne is much debated, with a majority favoring an islet north of Cape Blanco (23°50' N). From Cerne, Hanno and his men made an exploratory foray along the sub-Saharan coast, and here the difficulties of following his track increase mightily. They arrived at a "deep and wide river which was infested with crocodiles and hippopotami." This might well have been the mouth of the Senegal (ca. 16° N). Farther on, they came to a promontory with wooded mountains that took them two days to pass; this might have been Cape Verde (14°52' N), the westernmost point of Africa. Still farther along, they came to some islands and, upon landing on one, saw at night "many fires being kindled" and heard the "din of tom-toms." They passed stretches of coast where the land was ablaze; at one point "a leaping flame towered above the others and appeared to reach the stars. This was the highest mountain which we saw." Farther on, at another island on which they landed, they met with "wild people, the greatest number by far being women with hairy bodies; our interpreters called them 'gorillas.'" Hanno's men gave chase, and although the males all scampered out of their reach, they managed to catch up with and subdue three females. They could hardly have taken alive what we call gorillas; the creatures may have been chimpanzees or baboons. By this time, their supplies of food were running low, and the expedition turned about and headed for home.

Hanno is the first to record the sorts of things that later become commonplace in the reports of explorers from Africa: the jungle, the beat of tom-toms, the enormous grass fires that the natives light to burn off stubble and help the following year's crops, and the bands of monkeys. Obviously, he went quite far down the sub-Saharan coast—but how far? Some commentators identify his tall, fire-topped mountain as Mt. Cameroon, which is truly tall (13,370 feet) and a volcano to boot, and bring him under the bulge of Africa all the way to the Cameroons. However, this means squeezing a long voyage—and one beset by the calms his ships would have met in the Gulf of Guinea—into less than two months. Most commentators bring him no farther than Sierra Leone, some eight degrees north of the equator, identifying the mountain as Kakulima in Guinea (ca. 10° N), which, although only some 3,000 feet high, stands out in flat country. There are those who hold that the portion of the narrative dealing with unknown waters is fantasy from the pens of armchair geographers writing centuries later. In any event, whether or not Hanno actually got far down the African coast is an academic question, for his voyage had scant effect on geographical knowledge and none on subsequent history. The shores of Africa below the Canaries (ca. 29° N) were to remain terra incognita until the efforts sparked by Henry the Navigator paid off.[5]

The ancients did know the Canaries. King Juba II of Morocco, who ruled about 25 B.C. to A.D. 25, was a man of great learning and scientific interests, and he sent out an expedition to the islands that returned with a full and accurate report on them. No settlements were ever planted there, to judge from the total absence of archaeological remains. In recent years, divers have discovered in the nearby waters a number of ancient shipping jars, mostly dating from the third century A.D., but these do not prove the existence of settlements of Mediterranean peoples on the Canaries; the vessels that carried the jars could well have been sailing along the Moroccan coast, en route, say, to the town at Mogador, and been blown off course.

What of Madeira and the Azores? There are indications that the ancients may have known of the first. The second probably lay beyond their ken.[6]

The East Coast of Africa

The Greek historian Herodotus tells of a voyage of exploration that, if it actually took place, was a truly remarkable accomplishment. Pharaoh Necho (610–594 B.C.), he states, seeking a water route from the Red Sea to the Mediterranean, decided to investigate the possibility of going around Africa and dispatched a fleet of Phoenician sailors, presumably the best qualified for such an enterprise, to carry it out. They were to leave from a port on the Red Sea, go around the continent from east to west, pass through the Strait of Gibraltar, and land on the north coast of Egypt. The Red Sea was well known to the Egyptians: from as early as 2400 B.C., the pharaohs had been sending ships down it to Ethiopia and Somalia to bring back frankincense and myrrh; the two resins played a vital role in Egyptian religious rites, and these lands were one of the few places where they grew.

FIGURE 6. Woodcut illustration of a fifteenth-century Spanish caravel by Erhard Reuwich (1455–1490) from *Peregrinationes in Terram Sanctam* by Bernard von Breydenbach (Mainz, Germany, 1486), the first illustrated travel book to be printed in the West. Peabody Essex Museum collections. 12 x 8 in.

Necho was totally unaware of how far south Africa extended; he presumably imagined that his Phoenician crews, after going the length of the Red Sea, would very soon be able to turn right and sail westward along the continent's southern coast, thus making the circumnavigation relatively quick and easy. Herodotus reports that it took them three years, including stops each autumn to sow and harvest crops for food. He notes one detail that to him was unbelievable but to us is just the opposite: the sailors said that in going around Africa they had the sun to their right, that is, to their north; indeed, they would have had it consistently so, once south of the Tropic of Capricorn. Herodotus's brief paragraph has engendered pages upon pages of controversy that runs the gamut of opinion, from those who dismiss such a circumnavigation as an impossibility to those who demonstrate how it could have been done just as he describes. The debate is academic: Necho's expedition, like Hanno's, had scant effect. Throughout ancient times, knowledge of the eastern coast of Africa never extended much farther than about 7° S, far short of Africa's tip at approximately 34° S.[7]

The Egyptians had taken the first step in the exploration of the eastern coast of Africa for reasons of trade, procuring frankincense and myrrh as well as other products of Ethiopia and Somalia. The next step was taken by Greek crews acting under the orders of the Ptolemies, the dynasty that grasped the rule of Egypt soon after Alexander the Great died in 323 B.C., and the reason behind this exploration was military. Alexander, in his battles with Indian armies, had to face war elephants; he was impressed by them, and so were the generals who fought at his side. When, after his death, they became rulers of various parts of his conquests and organized military forces of their own, they included an elephant corps—at least those who had access to the source of supply in India. The Ptolemies, off in Egypt, had no such access, so Ptolemy II (282–246 B.C.) launched a program to hunt and train African elephants. This involved setting up bases, first along the eastern coast of the Red Sea and then along the northern coast of Somalia. The bases were by no means simple and rude camps. Capturing wild elephants and then taming them to the point where they could be herded aboard ship for transport back to Egypt required months of training carried on in elaborate facilities by hundreds of people. There had to be corrals, storage sheds for the huge amounts of food the elephants consumed, docks and gangplanks that could handle beasts weighing several tons, and barracks for housing the hunters, keepers, mahouts, guards, and service personnel. When the hunting in a given vicinity was exhausted, the base was given up for a new one farther along. Hence, there was a succession of them right up to Cape Guardafui. In the course of time, traders moved into a good many of the bases after the hunters had left and converted them into trading posts. The final stage in the exploration of the coast came when traders ventured past Guardafui to found posts from scratch south of it; by the middle of the first century A.D., settlements extended to where Dar es Salaam now stands (6°49' S). A few Greek skippers dared to sail, or were blown, into the waters beyond as far as a cape they called Prasum. Prasum marked the southernmost point of the world known to Greek geographers; commentators have suggested identifying it with Cape Delgado (10°30' S), but that is pure guesswork.[8]

Northern Waters

The ancients were only dimly aware of the lands and waters of northern Europe. They knew that amber came from there and, more important, that it was one of the sources of tin, the metal vital for making bronze, and legends persisted that it was a kind of Eden, the happy home of the Hyperboreans, "those beyond the North Wind." The first clear light to be shed on this obscure area was contributed by Pytheas of Marseilles as the result of a voyage to the north he made at about the end of the fourth century B.C. This voyage, unlike Hanno's or that of Necho's Phoenicians, had a signal effect on geographical knowledge: it filled in what had been a blank spot on the map.

Precious little is known about Pytheas himself. We can assume he was a skilled seaman, but he had another unusual qualification for an explorer: he was an accomplished astronomer. He calculated the latitude of his home town, getting it almost exactly right, and it was he who pointed out that the pole star did not mark true north. His own writings have not survived. We know of them only through random citations or paraphrases by later authors who, more often than not, quoted him to express their disbelief or brand him a liar. However, savants best fitted to pass judgment thought otherwise: Eratosthenes, the Greek geographer, and Hipparchus, the Greek astronomer, both accepted Pytheas's findings. We can only guess when and why he embarked on a venture into northern waters. Since Aristotle, who died in 322 B.C., does not mention him but his pupil, Dicaearchus, who died in 286, does, the voyage is usually placed between these two dates, or about 300 B.C. Since Pytheas's account included a detailed description of the mining of tin in Cornwall, commentators have suggested that he may have been sent out by the merchants of Marseilles to investigate access to the source of this vital import.

The first part of his voyage is fairly certain. He passed through the Strait of Gibraltar, sailed around Spain and along the Breton coast, and crossed the English Channel to Cornwall, where he stopped to draw up his report on the operation of the local tin mines. He then circumnavigated Britain, correctly establishing that it was an island, that the island was triangular in shape, and that the shortest side faced the continent. He gives figures for the length of each side, but these, although their proportions are right, are almost double the true figures; presumably he overestimated the sailing speed of his ship.

While in northern Britain, he was told that, six days' sail north of Britain and a one-day sail short of the "frozen" sea, there was an "island of Thule." Here the sun went down at night for only two or three hours and no more. In this region, there was an all-enveloping substance that Pytheas saw himself from a distance but can only describe in an obscure fashion; it was, he notes, "neither sea nor air . . . but a mixture like the sea-lung [a form of shellfish or jellyfish] in which earth and air are suspended." Thule and the "sea-lung" substance have evoked a wealth of conjecture. Thule has been identified as the Shetlands, the Orkneys, Iceland, or northern Norway, but none of these fills all the requirements; the Shetlands and Orkneys are nearer than six days' sail, Iceland is farther, and Norway is to the east and not the north. The mysterious substance has been identified as sea fog or icy slush, phosphorescence, or the play of northern lights, and so on.

Pytheas must have spent some time on land in northern Britain, or other northern places, since he furnishes details about the inhabitants' way of life. He notes that because of the wet climate, they do their threshing in barns (not outdoors, as was the practice in Mediterranean lands), that they brew a drink from honey, and that in the regions near the frozen zone, the only cereal able to be grown is "millet," by which he probably meant oats, a cereal that would have been unknown to him.

For the rest of his voyage, from northern Britain back to Marseilles, our information is hopelessly vague. He mentions an estuary with an island nearby where amber is found. Many commentators take the estuary to be that of the Elbe and the island to be Heligoland and draw the conclusion that he returned home by following the coast of the Continent.

It was an eminently fruitful voyage. It put Britain on the map. It revealed the nature of Arctic day and the existence of frozen seas. It proved that far northern lands were inhabited by real and not mythological people. It even affected the English language: Pytheas's Thule, though we may not know where it is, lives on in our phrase "ultima Thule."[9]

The Indian Ocean

Maritime exploration commonly involves a venture into unknown waters in order to find unknown lands beyond them or known lands conceived to be there. The Greek exploration of the Indian Ocean was not at all like this. The Greeks knew that its waters stretched to the shores of India, and, certainly after the conquests of Alexander the Great, they were very well acquainted with India. In 326 B.C., Alexander had overrun its northwestern part, and several of his successors set up dynasties there that lasted until the second century B.C. Alexander had come to India by land, and direct contact of the Greeks with India continued to be by land. They were aware that the waters from Arabia to India were regularly plied by Arab and Indian traders but had no experience of these waters themselves, for those who plied them wanted no competition and kept them out. Greek shippers brought their goods as far as where Aden now stands; there they exchanged them for goods brought to this point aboard Arab or Indian craft.

About 120 B.C., Greek ships crossed these waters. It came about in a curious way. Toward the end of the reign of Ptolemy VIII of Egypt (146–116 B.C.), guards on duty in the Red Sea brought to the court at Alexandria a half-dead Indian they had found alone on a stranded ship; not understanding his language, they had no idea who he was or where he was from. The king had him turned over to teachers to learn Greek, and, when he could communicate, he explained that, while sailing from India, he had lost his way but managed to stay safely afloat to where he was picked up after all others aboard with him had died of starvation. Thankful for the hospitality he received, he promised he would pilot a group selected by the king to India. At the court at this time was a certain Eudoxus, a leading citizen of the island of Cyzicus and a learned man with a particular interest in geographical exploration; he was chosen to be part of the group and, it is clear, exercised some form of command. Although Eudoxus may have been motivated to some extent by scientific zeal, the king certainly was not; he had in mind the opening of a lucrative trade route, as the aftermath of the voyage makes clear.

What did the Indian offer to do? He was not going to pilot a Greek expedition along the coast of Arabia and Persia to India—any seaman encountered on the docks at Aden could have done that—and, had he done so, ships that regularly plied these waters, or pirates who haunted them, would have kept it from getting very far. What the Indian must have offered was to pilot Ptolemy's group over the open sea to India, where they would avoid interception by either pirates or local traders. This would have involved divulging to them the phenomenon of the monsoon winds, something that Arab and Indian seamen had kept to themselves for centuries. In the waters between Africa and India, from May to September, the wind blows steadily from the southwest; in October it switches direction and until the following May blows steadily from the northeast. Thus, by leaving at the right time, a skipper could ensure himself a fair wind going and coming. Eudoxus's expedition made the voyage without a hitch, bringing back a valuable cargo of perfumes and precious stones. His troubles started when his ship docked in Egypt: the king took over not only the goods to which the crown was entitled but also whatever Eudoxus had loaded on board for his own account. A few years later, the king's successor dispatched Eudoxus on a second voyage to India; this time, he presumably did his own piloting. On the return leg, he failed to set his course exactly right and, as a result, instead of making landfall near Cape Guardafui, he wound up in unknown territory somewhere on the African coast to the south of it. The local tribes were friendly, and he was able to exchange grain, wine, and dried figs—novelties to the natives—for water to replenish his supply. He then followed the shoreline northward to Guardafui, where he was back in familiar waters. Again he was bilked out of his cargo rights, and that led to two attempts to get to Egypt by sailing around Africa from Cadiz, neither of which got very far.[10]

Egypt under the last Ptolemies, from Eudoxus's time to its conquest by Augustus in 30 B.C., was a feeble, poorly run nation. It took scant advantage of the opportunity Eudoxus had opened up: only a handful of ships made the voyage to India. That changed dramatically after Augustus added the country to the Roman Empire. Under efficient Roman rule, its trade with India burgeoned, with more than 100 vessels sailing there annually. Some even ventured into the Bay of Bengal and up the eastern coast of India as far as the ports at the mouth of the Ganges.[11]

No formal voyages of exploration were ever taken from there eastward, but Greek geographers were aware of lands that lay in that direction, thanks to reports from traders. By the middle of the first century A.D., the writer of a handbook for Greek merchants and skippers knew of a "Golden Region" that marked the eastern edge of the continent and a "Golden Island" that marked the eastern edge of the inhabited world. By the middle of the second century A.D., the Greek geographer Ptolemy knew of a "Golden Region" and a "Golden Peninsula" and lands beyond both. The "Golden Region," as most commentators agree, is Myanmar; as to the "Golden Peninsula," opinion is divided between Malay and Sumatra. Beyond this point, Ptolemy hypothesized the existence of a landmass that swept from Asia around the southern part of the Indian Ocean to connect with Africa, a misapprehension geographers were not fully disabused of until the voyages of Captain Cook.[12]

Ptolemy presents the ancients' knowledge of the world at its fullest, a world that stretched from the "Fortunate Isles"—the Canaries or Madeira—on the west eastward to Malay or Sumatra, and from the Shetlands on the north southward to some point between Zanzibar and Madagascar. Some of the information came from explorers' reports (Juba's expedition had discovered the western limit, and Pytheas's did the same for the northern range); the rest came from informal reports of traders or seamen.[13]

Notes

1. *Cambridge Ancient History*, 2:800 (arrival); 1:162–63 (overseas contacts).

2. *Oxford Classical Dictionary* s. vv. "Utica," "Gades," "Carthage."

3. Richard Stillwell et al., eds., *Princeton Encyclopedia of Classical Sites* (Princeton, 1976), s. vv. "Lixus," "Mogador."

4. Up-to-date text with a translation in French of Hanno's account is in Jehan Desanges, *Recherches sur l'activité des Méditerranéens aux confins de l'Afrique* (École française de Rome, 1978), 392–97.

5. For a discussion of Hanno's voyage, see Max Cary and Eric Warmington, *The Ancient Explorers* (Pelican, 1963), 63–68; James Thomson, *History of Ancient Geography* (Cambridge, England, 1948), 74–76. See Desanges, *Recherches*, 84–85, for the view that the portion of the narrative dealing with unknown waters was affected by Greek legend and the Greek schematic conception of the shape of Africa.

6. On the Canaries, Madeira, and Azores, see Cary and Warmington, *Ancient Explorers*, 69–71, and on the Azores, see also B.S.J. Isserlin in *Rivista di studi Fenici* 12 (1984): 32–46. For the finds of shipping jars, see Miguel Beltrán Lloris, *Las anforas romanas en España* (Zaragoza, 1970), 575–76.

7. Cary and Warmington, *Ancient Explorers*, 111–19, offers a full discussion of Herodotus's account.

8. On elephant hunting and the bases set up for it, see Lionel Casson in *Transactions of the American Philological Association* 123 (1993): 248–56. On trading posts as far as Dar es Salaam, see Lionel Casson, *The Periplus Maris Erythraei* (Princeton, 1989), 45, 51–61. On voyages beyond Dar es Salaam, see Thomson, *History of Ancient Geography*, 275.

9. On Pytheas, his voyage, and the various conjectures it has engendered, see Thomson, *History of Ancient Geography*, 143–50.

10. On Eudoxus, see Casson, *Periplus*, 11–12, 36, 224.

11. On the trade between Rome, Egypt, and India, see ibid., 21–27.

12. For the ancients' knowledge of lands east of the Bay of Bengal, see ibid., 235–36.

13. For Ptolemy's world, see Edward Herbert Bunbury, *A History of Ancient Geography* (1879; reprint, Amsterdam, 1979), ii, map opposite 568.

3

Maritime Exploration in the Middle Ages

WILLIAM D. PHILLIPS JR.

Some sixty years ago, when Samuel Eliot Morison wrote his still-influential biography of Christopher Columbus, it was common in the English-speaking world to consider scientific curiosity as the primary motivation for exploration.[1] The times in which Morison and others wrote no doubt influenced their views, which remained unchallenged for decades. The most spectacular of the exploratory ventures in the middle decades of the twentieth century were to places that were inhospitable to human life and offered little prospect of immediate and tangible rewards: balloon ascensions into the upper atmosphere, epic voyages under the north polar ice, scientific stations in the Antarctic, underwater probes, and the early phases of the space program. Looking back to the Middle Ages from their mid-twentieth-century perspectives, Morison and others could project twentieth-century concerns into the minds of medieval explorers and see similar motivations, especially when they could find contemporary sources that seemed to support their interpretations. Gomes Eanes de Zurara, as a famous example, listed curiosity as a factor that impelled Prince Henry of Portugal to support Portuguese exploration along the African Atlantic coast, even though a close reading of the sources showed that Henry's true motivations were very different and mixed crusading zeal with practical economics.[2]

For years, I have been reading the primary sources relating to European exploration in the medieval period, and my conclusion is that simple curiosity, though certainly present, was not a major motivation. Medieval venturers shared motivations and attitudes: a desire for economic advantage, whether through the acquisition of trade goods or lands for settlement; a belief that they knew where they were going or that past experience suggested what they might find, whether additional islands beyond the horizon or further extensions of continental coastlines; and a collateral desire to spread their spiritual values. Medieval explorers were curious, to be sure, but they were always apprehensive about venturing into the unknown. They all made scientific observations, according to the best practice of their day, but that was not their main impulse. Many of them had powerful backers, kings and popes, who sought spiritual reward, economic advantage, and geopolitical intelligence, often all at the same time. Individual explorers had similar motivations, frequently combined with aspirations for social advancement. Columbus's motivation, as is well known, easily blended religious and economic aims, while seeking and receiving noble status for himself and his family.[3]

In the early Middle Ages, with the end of the Roman Empire in the West and a concurrent Chinese decline in Asia, the trade that had linked the Mediterranean with India and China had collapsed.[4] Western Europe was backward, underdeveloped, and a poor cousin of the more sophisticated Byzantine Empire and the larger and vastly more wealthy world of Islam, which stretched from the Atlantic across North Africa, the Middle East, and into northern India. It effectively linked Europe, Africa, and Asia and blocked Europe from the easiest paths of access to Asia.[5]

Medieval western Europeans began to develop maritime trade in their own home waters. In the Mediterranean, Western Christian mariners came to know the winds and weather of the inland sea and to conduct regular trade with Egypt and other areas of North Africa, despite continual papal disapproval and frequent papal efforts at prohibition. In northern waters— the North Sea and the Baltic—regular trade patterns developed, first led by the Frisians and expanded greatly by the Scandinavians. For centuries, these two trading regions, one in the north and one in the south, had only a land connection, making use of rivers, river valleys, and Alpine passes, with the great nexus of trade fairs in the county of Champagne in France. By the thirteenth century, however, the land connections began to lose their importance as Italians established direct sea trade through the Strait of Gibraltar to Flanders and other parts of northwestern Europe.

In the meantime, Scandinavians had explored the North Atlantic in the ninth and tenth centuries and established bases in the islands north of the British Isles. When they reached Iceland, they found that Irish monks had preceded them, ample proof that Irish voyages in the Atlantic in search of souls were not all legendary. Scandinavians went on to Greenland, where they established colonies that lasted through the Middle Ages. Their existence was precarious at the end, due to the global cooling patterns in climate that accompanied the late Middle Ages. The Scandinavians also reached North America about the year 1000 A.D., in Labrador and Newfoundland,

FIGURE 7. Engraving from *Navigatio ac Itinerarium Iohannis Hugonis Linscotani in orientalem sive Lusitanorum Indiam* (Amsterdam, 1599) by Jan Huygen van Linschoten (1563–1611). This engraving is among the earliest visual representations of Asians to be widely published in Europe. Gift of Donald Angus. Peabody Essex Museum collections. 11½ x 13½ in.

but their North American colonies lasted only a short time. They were a long way from Scandinavia. They offered little of immediate economic worth, and the local Skraelings were hostile. Over the course of the later Middle Ages, the Viking outposts in North America were forgotten.[6]

By then, a much greater lure had come to occupy the imaginations of western Europeans: the wealth of Asia. At the very end of the eleventh century, western Europeans conquered a series of coastal enclaves in the eastern Mediterranean in what today is part of Syria, Lebanon, and Israel. They established the kingdom of Jerusalem, the principal polity, with a series of satellite states dependent on it. These Crusader states lasted for two centuries before the Muslims reconquered them. Historians still argue over whether the Crusades were the first stage of European overseas expansion or only failed precursors. For our purposes, the important thing is that the Crusades gave Westerners, for the first time in the Middle Ages, a window toward the world of Asia and a growing understanding of its wealth. Western Crusaders, some of whom were long-term residents in the eastern Mediterranean and others who went only for limited campaigns, came to appreciate spices, silks, porcelains, perfumes, and aromatics. Thus a demand arose in Europe for all these goods, which Europeans could only purchase from Muslim middlemen.[7]

What the Crusaders only partially perceived was that most of the Asian world lay beyond their precarious bases in the eastern Mediterranean. From the Red Sea and the Persian Gulf, well-developed trading routes led to India and China. Already in ancient times, Indian mariners were familiar with northern reaches of the Indian Ocean as far west as the Arabian Peninsula. They crossed the Bay of Bengal and established trade with Burma and Siam. To both the east and west, they established regular trade that flowed with the seasonal imperatives of the monsoons, in which the winds blew to the southwest for half the year and to the northeast for the other half. During their climate-enforced layovers in Siam, they introduced their culture and the religion of Buddhism. Gujarati and other Indian merchants and mariners traveled to Malacca, where they met Malayan mariners trading in the produce of the Spice Islands. Beyond Malacca also lay the South China Sea and the maritime routes to China.[8]

The Chinese imperial governments paid little attention to this far-reaching maritime trade. Throughout history, Chinese rulers, with some exceptions, have turned their attention inward, away from the sea. Their greatest threats always came from the nomadic peoples to the north; threats from the sea were negligible. Chinese sea trade was always a private venture, operated by individual Chinese merchants who traded in the South China Sea, and occasionally beyond the Strait of Malacca to India and points west. There were occasional voyages as far as the Persian Gulf and the Red Sea.[9]

Chinese imperial governments failed to maintain a navy and generally neglected the sea. The one exception to this rule took place in the early fifteenth century, when an extraordinary series of sea voyages left from China under imperial patronage and traveled as far as East Africa. Led by the eunuch admiral Cheng Ho, the fleet included a number of very large Chinese junks, though they were likely not nearly as large as has been claimed by Chinese enthusiasts from Joseph Needham onward.[10]

These voyages, spectacular as they were, do not qualify as voyages of exploration. The Chinese fleets went nowhere except along well-traveled and well-mapped lines of trade. Their motive was not curiosity, nor the search for new lands, nor even to spread religion. Rather, the prime motivations seem to have been to show the might of China and to bring back exotica for the sophisticated Chinese court. The voyages stopped abruptly in the early fifteenth century, and the new Ming Dynasty again turned its attention away from the sea and toward the northern frontiers. That did not mean, of course, that Chinese maritime trade ceased. Individual Chinese merchants and mariners, increasing numbers of them expatriates, conducted the trade, but always as private venturers.[11] The Indian Ocean, dominated but not entirely controlled by the Muslims, continued as a vital region of international trade, and Indian merchants and mariners sailed regularly to Southeast Asia.[12]

We should mention the migrations of the Polynesians in the Pacific, a series of great voyages in this same medieval period. As a consequence of their long-distance voyaging on the high seas, the Polynesians populated the islands of the mid-Pacific and maintained a sporadic inter-island trade. These voyages are not fully documented, but it seems that their prime motivation was a search for new lands to settle, perhaps impelled by overpopulation in Polynesia.[13]

Returning to Europe, we can see that from the time of the Crusades, western Europeans were fascinated with tales of Asia. For a time in the thirteenth and fourteenth centuries, the Mongols ruled Asia from the Black Sea to China. They imposed a Pax Mongolica that allowed secure travel throughout the lands they controlled.[14] Taking advantage of the opportunity, Western missionaries and merchants went to China and returned with newer and even more wondrous tales. The reports of the missionaries transmitted the knowledge they gained about Asia and the routes to China. The merchants, with Marco Polo most prominent among them, added their

FIGURE 8. *USS* Vincennes *of the United States Exploring Expedition in Disappointment Bay,* ca. 1842, after Captain Charles Wilkes (1798–1877), oil on canvas. Peabody Essex Museum collections, M265. 23½ x 35½ in.

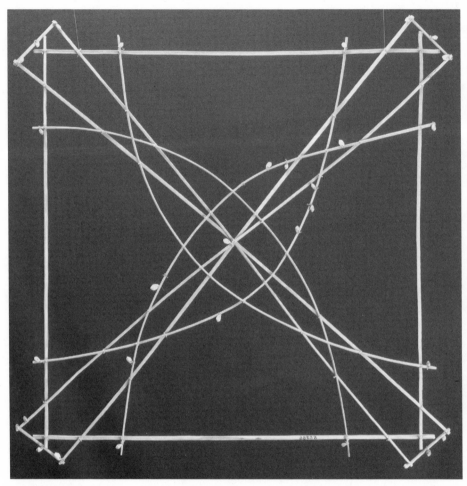

FIGURE 9. Stick chart from the Marshall Islands, ca. 1900, maker unknown. Stick charts present information about ocean waves, swells, and islands and were designed to teach navigation. This chart was collected by Alexander Agassiz on the *Albatross* Expedition. Gift of the Peabody Museum, Cambridge, Massachusetts. Peabody Essex Museum collections, E12210. 29½ x 29½ in.

own information. His famous book of adventures, commonly called *The Travels*, for all the scholarly arguments about the accuracy of its contents and the circumstances of its composition, provided as much information as any other source.[15] Even its errors were inspirational. Much later Columbus would base a crucial component of his view of the world on Polo's mistaken statement that Japan lay 1,500 miles off the coast of China. Columbus also excited both his royal backers and those who sailed with him when he related Polo's exaggeration about the availability of gold in Japan. Despite the incomplete and at times misleading accounts by merchants and missionaries, late medieval Europeans had sufficient information for Francesco Balducci Pegolotti to include an accurate guide to overland travel to China in his famous merchant's handbook, *La Practica della Mercatura*.[16]

By then, though, the Mongol empire was collapsing and with it the political unity of the regions from Russia to China. Thus an era of relatively secure, if enormously time-consuming, overland travel between Europe and Asia came to an end. Even if the Mongol empire had not broken apart and caused the silk routes to fragment, overland trade to Asia would have been limited at best. What Europeans needed were sea routes to Asia, but the Muslims still blocked Europeans from the Indian Ocean and the easy routes to India and beyond. The logical alternative was for Europeans to turn to the Atlantic.

They tried to find a sea route to Asia off and on for two centuries. The first known attempt was the 1291 voyage of the Vivaldi brothers, who took a fleet of galleys out through the Strait of Gibraltar and then turned southward around Africa. They disappeared.[17] Despite this failure, in the fourteenth and fifteenth centuries, Iberians, and to a lesser extent Italians, began to map the Atlantic, the coast of Africa, and—as it happened—the eventual sea route to the Indian Ocean.

Also in the fourteenth century, Europeans revisited the Canary Islands for the first time since the Roman era. They found the major islands in the Canaries inhabited by people at a Neolithic stage of development, and, throughout the fourteenth century, Christian missionaries (mostly Iberians from the Crown of Aragon) worked to convert them to Christianity. By the early fifteenth century, captains licensed by the kingdom of Castile began a series of military campaigns to conquer the Canaries, and by the end of the century the islands were Castilian colonies.[18]

Meanwhile, Portuguese and Castilians had begun to explore the African coast and to find ways to sail back north against the prevailing northeast trade winds. In the fifteenth century, the Portuguese settled the Madeira archipelago and the Azores. As they progressed farther down the African coast, they found the Cape Verde Islands. In a sense, they were making the Atlantic Ocean off the west coast of Africa into familiar maritime space, as they learned the coasts, the islands, and the wind and sea currents that enabled them to sail from point to point efficiently. They were setting the stage for the voyages that changed the history of the world: those of Columbus, Dias, da Gama, and the joint voyage of Magellan and Elcano.

Columbus, on his first voyage, sailed west from the Canaries and reached the Americas somewhere in the Bahama Islands. The voyage out was easy; he merely followed the trade winds with little variation in his westward course. On the way back, he tried to retrace his path, meeting failure until he turned north far enough to catch the prevailing westerly winds. This shows that Columbus did not have a complete idea of the Atlantic wind patterns when he began. Once he found the way, it was relatively simple for subsequent transatlantic voyagers to replicate his route.[19] On the eastern route to Asia in 1498, Vasco da Gama succeeded in reaching India from Portugal, following the pioneering route of Bartolomeu Dias as far as the southern tip of Africa and picking up a Muslim pilot to guide him across the Indian Ocean.[20] Then, between 1519 and 1522, Magellan and Elcano took a Castilian fleet around South America, across the Pacific, and back around Africa to Europe, giving Europeans their first idea of the vastness of the Pacific Ocean and some idea of the true size of the earth.[21]

Were these voyages of exploration in the rigorous sense of ventures into the unknown? They were probably not, although the best case could be made for Magellan as he started out across the Pacific. Columbus and da Gama were simply following in the steps of others who had plied the same waters but for shorter distances. The first southern Europeans who ventured into the unknown Atlantic were equally unknown fishermen, who followed schools of fish out to sea and came back to tell others about it. The same is true in the North Atlantic in the later Middle Ages, when Basque and British fishermen ventured farther and farther into mid-ocean and beyond.[22] The leaders of each Portuguese fleet that went south along the African coast were following the reports of their colleagues who had gone before, and they in turn would make detailed observations of their positions to aid those who followed. They all knew, or hoped, that at some point Africa would end and they would reach the Indian Ocean. Eventually their hopes were justified, but it took nearly a century of probing farther and farther south.

What about Columbus? He, after all, happened upon what no European had suspected: two continents previously unknown except to their inhabitants. We have to remind ourselves that America was not what Columbus was seeking, and that he died without acknowledging that what he found was anything other than a remote part of Asia that somehow Marco Polo had failed to describe. Using all the scientific tools and all the most up-to-date geographical knowledge at his disposal, Columbus persuaded himself that the globe was smaller than it is and that Africa and Eurasia covered much more of its surface than they do. That in turn enabled him to believe that what he found was the Asia he had sought, in exactly the place he expected to find it.

For the royal sponsors of both da Gama and Columbus, it almost goes without saying, the main goal was profitable economic enterprise. Two religious aims also were present: to outflank the Muslims in order to gain advantage in the long struggle between Christendom and the world of Islam and to bring Christianity to new peoples. The Castilian and Portuguese monarchs had political motivations and used overseas expansion to enhance the power of their kingdoms, if possible at the expense of their rivals. In this, they foreshadowed the place of maritime exploration and foreign conquest in the dynastic and national rivalries that dominated European concerns from the sixteenth century onward. For the explorers themselves, personal advancement, through the wealth and honor they hoped to obtain, was among their prime motivations. To accomplish their individual goals, they readily embraced the goals of their rulers. They were ready to fight and die to conquer in the name of their monarchs and to defend those conquests against European rivals. They believed that their religion was superior to all others and deserved to be spread, even though few were as obsessive about millenarianism as Columbus.

They and their contemporaries also took their accomplishments in a prosaic fashion. We tend to make too much of the novelty of the 1490s and early sixteenth century for Europeans. Europeans had, after all, been expanding for centuries, mainly one small step at a time along known or predictable paths.[23] They sailed the northern reaches of the Atlantic. They took back Mediterranean lands from the Muslims and conquered eastern European lands from pagan rulers. They mastered the sea routes of the Mediterranean and for two centuries maintained the crusader states. At the end of the Middle Ages, they began to learn the secrets of the Atlantic south and east of Iberia, and that led to contact with sub-Saharan Africa, India, and the Americas. All that was done in incremental stages, with each venturer using the accumulated knowledge of those who had gone before. Even the first circumnavigation by Magellan and Elcano, as arduous and harrowing as it was, merely proved what was obvious and well established among the educated: the world was a globe.

In conclusion, we can examine the testimony of a man who was well placed to contemplate the outcome of the medieval centuries of European maritime expansion and who found it less than revolutionary. The man was Sebastian Cabot, an expatriate Genoese like Columbus. In the 1530s, he was working in Seville as the chief royal pilot for the kingdom of Castile at a time when Castile was producing the *patrón real*, the master map of the trading centers of the world and the paths to them. In his deposition in a legal case, Cabot testified that he believed Columbus had found little that the classical world had not known. Most tellingly, he said that the classical geographer Solinus had written that westward from the Fortunate Islands, forty days away, were the Hesperides. Cabot asserted that the Fortunate Islands were the Canaries, an opinion widely shared among his contemporaries and by modern scholars. Moreover, he assumed, four decades after the first voyage of Columbus, that "those Hesperides islands are the islands that were discovered in the time of the Catholic Monarchs don Fernando and doña Isabel."[24] In other words, the true novelty of what Columbus found across the Atlantic only slowly entered the consciousness of early modern Europeans, even as they took advantage of their new maritime routes to Asia and the Americas.

Notes

1. Samuel Eliot Morison, *Admiral of the Ocean Sea: A Life of Christopher Columbus*, 2 vols. (Boston: Little, Brown, 1942). See also Morison's later writings: *Christopher Columbus, Mariner* (Boston: Little, Brown, 1955); *The European Discovery of America: The Southern Voyages, A.D. 1492–1616* (New York: Oxford University Press, 1974); and *The Great Explorers: The European Discovery of America* (New York: Oxford University Press, 1978).

2. Peter E. Russell, *Prince Henry "the Navigator": A Life* (New Haven: Yale University Press, 2000); and Ivana Elbl, "Man of His Time (and Peers): A New Look at Henry the Navigator," *Luso-Brazilian Review* 28 (1991): 73–89.

3. William D. Phillips Jr. and Carla Rahn Phillips, *The Worlds of Christopher Columbus* (Cambridge: Cambridge University Press, 1992).

4. Vimala Begley and Richard Daniel De Puma, eds., *Rome and India: The Ancient Sea Trade* (Madison: University of Wisconsin Press, 1991). Two classic works are Martin P. Charlesworth, *Trade Routes and Commerce of the Roman Empire* (Cambridge: Cambridge University Press, 1924) and Joseph T. Reinaud, *Relations politiques et commerciales de l'Empire romain avec l'Asie orientale (l'Hyrcanie, l'Indie, la Bactriane et la Chine) pendant les cinq premiers siècles de l'ère chrétienne* (Paris: Imprimerie impériale, 1863). For Rome's trade with the Near East, see Gary K. Young, *Rome's*

Eastern Trade: International Commerce and Imperial Policy, 31 B.C.–A.D. 305 (London: Routledge, 2001).

5. For an inclusive introduction, see Maurice Lombard, *The Golden Age of Islam*, trans. Joan Spenser (New York: American Elsevier, 1975). See also the classic work by Marshall Hodgson, *The Venture of Islam: Conscience and History in a World Civilization*, 3 vols. (Chicago: University of Chicago Press, 1974–77). See also Robert Mantran, *L'expansion musulmane: VIIe–XIe siècles* (Paris: Presses universitaires de France, 1991). For more recent studies, see Susan L. Douglass, ed., *The Rise and Spread of Islam* (Detroit: Gale Group, 2001) and Martin Sicker, *The Islamic World in Ascendancy: From the Arab Conquests to the Siege of Vienna* (Westport, Conn.: Praeger, 2000).

6. The historical literature on the Vikings is considerable. For places to begin, see John Haywood, *Encyclopedia of the Viking Age* (New York: Thames and Hudson, 2000) and Peter Sawyer, ed., *The Oxford Illustrated History of the Vikings* (New York: Oxford University Press, 1997).

7. The Crusades continue to attract the interest of historians and other scholars. For introductions, see Thomas F. Madden, *A Concise History of the Crusades* (Lanham, Md.: Rowman and Littlefield, 1999); Jean Richard, *The Crusades, c. 1071–c. 1291*, trans. Jean Birrell (Cambridge: Cambridge University Press, 1999); and Jonathan Riley-Smith, ed., *The Oxford History of the Crusades* (Oxford: Oxford University Press, 1999). For specific aspects, see Tomas Mastnak, *Crusading Peace: Christendom, the Muslim World, and Western Political Order* (Berkeley: University of California Press, 2002) and Carole Hillenbrand, *The Crusades: Islamic Perspectives* (Edinburgh: Edinburgh University Press, 1999).

8. Hsin-ju Liu, *Ancient India and Ancient China: Trade and Religious Exchanges, A.D. 1–600* (Delhi: Oxford University Press, 1988).

9. Moira Tampoe, *Maritime Trade between China and the West: An Archaeological Study of the Ceramics from Siraf (Persian Gulf), 8th to 15th Centuries A.D.*, BAR international series, 555 (Oxford: BAR, 1989); and John Noble Wilford, "Under Centuries of Sand, a Trading Hub," *New York Times*, 9 July 2002.

10. Robert Finlay, "The Treasure-Ships of Zheng He: Chinese Maritime Imperialism in the Age of Discovery," *Terrae Incognitae* 23 (1991): 1–12; Louise Levathes, *When China Ruled the Seas: The Treasure Fleet of the Dragon Throne, 1405–1433* (New York: Simon & Schuster, 1994); and André Wagener Sleeswyke, "The Liao and the Displacement of the Ships of the Ming Navy," *Mariner's Mirror* 82 (1996): 3–13. The Sleeswyke article shows how earlier writers exaggerated the size of the Chinese vessels.

11. For a starting point, see Roderich Ptak, *China's Seaborne Trade with South and Southeast Asia, 1200–1750* (Aldershot, England: Ashgate, 1999); and Hans Konrad Van Tilburg, *The Maritime History and Nautical Archaeology of China in Southeast Asia: Song to Early Ming Dynasties, 960–1435 B.C.* (master's thesis, East Carolina University, 1994).

12. Himanshu Prabha Ray and Jean-François Salles, eds., *Tradition and Archaeology: Early Maritime Contacts in the Indian Ocean* (New Delhi: Manohar, 1996); George Fadlo Hourani, *Arab Seafaring in the Indian Ocean in Ancient and Early Medieval Times* (Princeton, N.J.: Princeton University Press, 1995); Kuzhippalli S. Mathew, *Mariners, Merchants, and Oceans: Studies in Maritime History* (New Delhi: Manohar, 1995); Kuzhippalli S. Mathew and Satish Chandra, eds., *Shipbuilding and Navigation in the Indian Ocean Region, A.D. 1400–1800* (New Delhi: Munshiram Manoharlal, 1997); Patricia Risso, *Merchants and Faith: Muslim Commerce and Culture in the Indian Ocean* (Boulder, Colo.: Westview Press, 1995); Kenneth McPherson, *The Indian Ocean: A History of People and the Sea* (Delhi: Oxford University Press, 1993); Richard Seymour Hall, *Empires of the Monsoon: A History of the Indian Ocean and Its Invaders* (London: HarperCollins, 1996); and K. N. Chaudhuri, *Trade and Civilization in the Indian Ocean: An Economic History from the Rise of Islam to 1750* (Cambridge: Cambridge University Press, 1985).

13. Nicholas J. Goetzfridt, *Indigenous Navigation and Voyaging in the Pacific: A Reference Guide* (New York: Greenwood Press, 1992); and David Lewis, *We, the Navigators: The Ancient Art of Landfinding in the Pacific* (Honolulu: University Press of Hawaii, 1994).

14. David Morgan, *The Mongols* (Oxford: Blackwell, 1987); and Reuven Amitai-Preiss and David O. Morgan, eds., *The Mongol Empire and Its Legacy* (Leiden: Brill, 1999).

15. For the most recent study on Marco Polo, see John Larner, *Marco Polo and the Discovery of the World* (New Haven: Yale University Press, 1999). Larner comments extensively on the work of previous scholars.

16. Francesco Balducci Pegolotti, *La practica della mercatura* (Cambridge, Mass.: Mediaeval Academy of America, 1934).

17. J.R.S. Phillips, *The Medieval Expansion of Europe* (Oxford: Oxford University Press, 1988), 156–58.

18. Eduardo Aznar Vallejo, *La integración de las Islas Canarias en la Corona de Castilla, 1478–1526: Aspectos administrativos, sociales y económicos* (Seville: Universidad de Sevilla and Universidad de La Laguna, 1983); Felipe Fernández-Armesto, *The Canary Islands after the Conquest: The Making of a Colonial Society in the Early Sixteenth Century* (Oxford: Oxford University Press, 1982); and John Mercer, *The Canary Islanders: Their Prehistory, Conquest and Survival* (London: Collins, 1980).

19. Phillips and Phillips, *Worlds of Christopher Columbus*, 176.

20. Anthony Disney and Emily Booth, eds., *Vasco da Gama and the Linking of Europe and Asia* (Delhi: Oxford University Press, 2000); and Sanjay Subrahmanyam, *The Career and Legend of Vasco da Gama* (New York: Cambridge University Press, 1997).

21. Tim Joyner, *Magellan* (Camden, Maine: International Marine, 1992). Antonio Pigafetta, the Italian who accompanied Magellan and Elcano on the first circumnavigation, left an account that has been translated into English on several occasions.

One translation is by Paula Spurlin and is titled *The Voyage of Magellan: The Journal of Antonio Pigafetta* (Englewood Cliffs, N.J.: Prentice-Hall, 1969).

22. Mark Kurlansky, *The Basque History of the World* (New York: Walker, 1999); and Selma H. Barkham, *The Basque Coast of Newfoundland* (Plum Point, Newfoundland: Corporation, 1989).

23. The literature is vast. See Barry W. Cunliffe, *Facing the Ocean: The Atlantic and Its Peoples, 8000 B.C.–A.D. 1500* (Oxford: Oxford University Press, 2001); Vincent H. Cassidy, *The Sea around Them: The Atlantic Ocean, A.D. 1250* (Baton Rouge: Louisiana State University Press, 1968); Robert Bartlett, *The Making of Europe: Conquest, Colonization, and Cultural Change, 950–1350* (Princeton: Princeton University Press, 1993); and Felipe Fernández-Armesto, *Before Columbus: Exploration and Colonization from the Mediterranean to the Atlantic, 1229–1492* (Philadelphia: University of Pennsylvania Press, 1987).

24. William D. Phillips Jr., ed., *Testimonies from the Columbian Lawsuits* (Turnhout, Belgium: Brepols, 2000), 262.

⇥ 4 ⇤

Exploring from Early Modern to Modern Times

CARLA RAHN PHILLIPS

Many people see the urge to explore as a defining characteristic of human history, especially within Western civilization. It is a characteristic that has shaped some of the most dramatic periods in the human past and continues to motivate modern societies. To give just one example, many advertisements on television link exploration with an entrepreneurial spirit, responsible risk taking, and the personal ambition that were as important to historical exploration as they are to the modern business world.

I would argue that understanding the urge to explore and describing its consequences are some of the most important challenges for historical research in the humanities. By examining exploration over the expanse of two millennia, we can provide insights into the ways that human beings related to the world around them over the whole of recorded history. My focus encompasses the period from about 1500 to the present, with its vast range of venues and personalities. In trying to get a sense of the whole, I browsed through several encyclopedias of exploration as well as various scholarly works analyzing specific voyages.[1] Because encyclopedias are organized alphabetically, they can contain interesting juxtapositions. For example, the seventeenth-century buccaneers of the Caribbean might be sandwiched in between James Bruce, the eighteenth-century Scot who explored Abyssinia, and the sixteenth-century development of Buenos Aires. Saint Francis Xavier, the sixteenth-century Spanish Jesuit who first described Japan for Europeans from firsthand knowledge, precedes Sir John Franklin, the nineteenth-century English rear admiral who was one of a long line of seekers for a northwest passage through the Arctic ice between Europe and Asia.

Is it possible to understand their exploits as a whole, or are they so different because of nationality, chronology, technology, and venue as to make the exercise pointless? Can we locate a main narrative thread for the history of exploration in the last five centuries, or should we look for another metaphor, another image, that can help us to understand the whole?

If we make chronology the dominant variable, the standard history of seaborne exploration seems to follow a clear trajectory from the sixteenth century to the present. The story generally goes something like this: in the first generations after the transforming voyages of the late fifteenth century, Europeans circled the globe. This great age of exploration allowed European mapmakers to include a vast array of lands and peoples about which they were previously ignorant. From the late seventeenth and through the eighteenth centuries, with few new lands left to discover, the focus of European voyages shifted to scientific aims, as part of the scientific revolution and the Enlightenment that followed. In the nineteenth century, seaborne exploration caught the imagination of armchair travelers of the romantic era, who delighted in descriptions of perilous voyages and exotic destinations. Eventually, a fairly wide spectrum of travelers followed in the wake of the early discoverers, cruising all over the globe to explore lands that were known but still exotic to most of them. Some traveled for pleasure, and others traveled out of necessity or desperation.

From the early twentieth century, many would argue, true exploration shifted from the earth and the oceans to the skies, as humanity entered the age of flight. Once again, the early pioneers were followed by a flood of ordinary travelers who used airplanes as a common mode of transport. By the late twentieth century, seaborne travel saw a renaissance in the packaged-cruise industry, introducing an even broader spectrum of travelers to exploration. Voyages of discovery in the late twentieth century, strictly speaking, seem to have consisted largely of searches for shipwrecks from past centuries of glory. In short, if we proceed chronologically, the past five centuries carry us from the heroic age of seaborne exploration to seaborne exploration as history—a convenient shorthand term these days for whatever is dead and irrelevant to the present. Exploration beneath the seas is, of course, just entering its heroic age, but that is another story, discussed by Justin Manley. There is some truth to this chronological trajectory, with its neatly characterized centuries, but ultimately it does not do justice to historical reality.

A geographical approach might be more appealing because different areas of the globe served as the main focus for seaborne exploration at different times. Asia, its oceans and its islands, were the original goals of early modern European voyages and long continued to be their ultimate destination. Merchants and explorers were convinced that the potential for profit would be enormous if they could reach Asian markets and goods more easily. (Things have not changed much in 500 years.) The Americas, the legendary great southern continent, the Pacific Ocean, the interior of Africa, and the polar regions—each in its turn joined the list of goals for exploration over the past 500 years. In many ways, geography is the most logical organizing principle for an extended treatment of seaborne exploration, but a brief chapter cannot give proper attention to all the world's regions.

Another option would be to take a national approach, tracing the contributions of Spaniards and Frenchmen, Scots and Portuguese, Norwegians and Italians, Englishmen and Poles, among others, to the enterprise of exploration. That approach would make sense in certain contexts, but in a discussion of marine exploration, it does not. Some of the most astonishing and harrowing tales of exploration in all of recorded history took place largely on land. A few examples are the exploration of Siberia in the sixteenth century, the interior regions of North America and Africa in the nineteenth century, and the polar explorations of the late nineteenth and early twentieth centuries. The contributions of dozens of prominent individuals would be left out if we were to focus only on nations that contributed to maritime exploration.

Because we are looking at the sea as a highway for exploration, we should keep our eyes on the road, but taking that approach too literally would seriously distort our understanding of exploration over the past 500 years. To address at least some of the problems with the approaches mentioned above, I have chosen to focus on traditional themes related to exploration as a whole, but to view them largely through the lens of maritime expeditions. Writers have used many themes over the years to examine exploration, but I will rely on the classic trio of motives, means, and results. Under those headings, and without any pretense of comprehensiveness, what follows will be a series of questions and reflections on the phenomenon of exploration and its common characteristics over the past 500 years.

Let us begin with the motives. The classic urge for commercial possibilities generally ranks high on any list of motives for exploration, and this book includes a discussion of seaborne commerce. Did Europe, or China, or anywhere else with a seafaring capability really need all the commodities that exploration helped to provide? The answer is yes, no, and maybe. It is yes if we define needs as anything that was manifested as market demand and stimulated the home economy. It would be no if we exclude curiosities and status symbols of no clear value—stuffed lizards, tulips, brightly colored feathers, shrunken heads, and the like. We might answer with maybe if we include the books, maps, and even the above-mentioned exotica that

FIGURE 10. *Odyssey IIC*–class autonomous underwater vehicle. Courtesy of the MIT AUV Laboratory.

persuaded political leaders to claim particular locales and attract private investors and colonizers to consolidate their claims. My point is that the motives for exploration—even commercial motives—may not always be as rational as we might assume.

The search for new lands and new peoples has also been a powerful motive for exploration, but it is arguable, as J. H. Parry noted long ago, that many voyages of exploration were searches for lands and peoples that were known or believed to exist, not quests in search of the unknown. The discovery of unknown land in the Western Hemisphere was not only unexpected but also unwelcome in many ways; the preferred destination was Asia. If we accept Parry's argument, and I think we must, some of the most adventuresome voyages in history take on a more conservative or retrograde character than we often acknowledge. Even quests for the chimerical Fountain of Youth, or the great southern continent Terra Australis, or the Northwest Passage were launched in the belief that the destination existed, and expeditions to find them were ostensibly motivated by a practical calculation of potential profits. Despite repeated failure, generation after generation of explorers continued to believe that they would find the desired goal, if only they avoided the mistakes of their predecessors and looked in the right place. The fact that the same goals, and the same certainty of finding the elusive prize, persisted in some cases for centuries provides stunning evidence of the optimism that characterizes the impulse to explore. A similar attitude seems to define modern researchers looking for a cure for cancer or mapping the human genome. The belief that a goal, however remote and difficult, exists and is attainable may be the key to every increase in human knowledge since the dawn of time. In the short term, it may seem irrational; in the long term, it sometimes pays off.

This brings me to intellectual curiosity. Although many writers assume that eighteenth-century explorers invented scientific curiosity, it seems clear that the urge to map, collect, categorize, and describe was present from the earliest voyages of the age of discovery—and presumably long before that. From Columbus onward, explorers recorded and described winds, currents, plants, animals, people, and things, partly from a desire to find opportunities for profit and partly from what we can only call intellectual curiosity. A few expeditions, such as the six-year voyage of Francisco Hernández to Mexico in the late sixteenth century, were deliberately chartered to find new plants that might have medicinal properties.[2] Many eighteenth-century expeditions, including the extraordinary voyages of James Cook in the Pacific, perfectly exemplified the scientific spirit that helped to drive exploration, but scientific curiosity did not begin with those expeditions, nor were any of the eighteenth-century voyages, including Cook's, purely scientific.[3] They were motivated in part, sometimes in large part, by political rivalries.

Both Portugal and Castile found and claimed Atlantic islands in the fifteenth century and challenged one another in the exploration of West Africa, first in search of trade goods and later in search of a seaborne route to India. Claiming rituals in newly discovered lands were carefully staged to preempt rival claims, and they were recorded in meticulous detail.[4] The two monarchies settled their rivalry in a series of treaties during the late fifteenth century, with Portugal gaining exclusive rights to explore south and east of the Iberian Peninsula and Castile gaining exclusive rights to explore westward. The age of exploration, in other words, grew out of intense political rivalries in Europe, and it was not coincidental that Columbus's scheme to sail westward toward Asia found a warmer reception in Castile than in Portugal. Portuguese monarchs concentrated their efforts on developing the lucrative trade with India and East Asia and maintaining a chain of fortified trading posts around Africa to defend that trade.[5]

In general, European exploration in the late fifteenth and early sixteenth centuries set out to claim lands and trade routes in the name of the ruler who sponsored the expedition. In addition to land, subjects, and profit, the sponsors of the early expeditions clearly hoped that any discoveries made in their names would enhance their power and glory as well. Those same aims, I would argue, continued to motivate exploration for the next 500 years.

Building on the pivotal voyages of Columbus and others sponsored by Ferdinand and Isabel of Spain, the kingdom of Castile conquered vast territories in the Americas from the 1520s through the 1540s. They were claimed and organized into a colonial empire in the name of Charles I of Spain, the Hapsburg prince better known as Charles V of the Holy Roman Empire.[6] Extending his reach ever farther, Charles sponsored the first circumnavigation of the globe in an expedition that began in 1519 under Fernão de Magalhães (Magellan) and ended in 1522 under Juan Sebastián de Elcano.[7]

It was not by chance that serious French exploration of the Americas began in the same period during the reign of Francis I, the Valois prince whose foreign policy focused on challenging the Hapsburgs. Francis sponsored voyages by Giovanni da Verrazano in 1523 and 1527 and by Jacques Cartier in the 1530s and 1540s to explore the coast of North America in search of a northern route to Cathay (China). Another wave of French exploration flowed over North America in the late sixteenth century. Through those voyages, France established its presence in North America, but less as a venue for serious colonization than as a passageway through the American landmass toward Asia.[8]

England pursued similar goals from the late fifteenth century on, beginning several centuries of efforts to find either a northeast or a northwest passage to Asia. The main difference between English and French exploration in North America was that England simultaneously pursued a serious colonization strategy. Other northern nations, especially the Netherlands, Sweden, Denmark, and Norway, sooner or later joined in the chase for a northern passage to Asia that lasted well into the twentieth century and was more political than anything else.[9] Moreover, the cold war contention over control of the Arctic can be seen as an extension of that same quest.

In warmer climes, political rivalries also played a major role in most of the famous voyages of exploration over the past 500 years, from expeditions aiming for a specific destination to virtually every circumnavigation on record. That was as true of George Anson, Louis-Antoine de Bougainville, and Alessandro Malaspina in the eighteenth century as it was of Ferdinand Magellan and Francis Drake in the sixteenth. Explorers continued to stage claiming rituals in the eighteenth century—sometimes one after another on the same islands—as long as they thought they were the first outsiders to arrive. Jean-François de Galaup (the Count of La Pérouse), sailing for Louis XVI of France, did not claim the Hawaiian Islands, knowing that Cook had been there before him, and he also invoked the Enlightenment notion that such claiming would be an insult to the inhabitants. He did, however, claim other islands for France and bestowed French names on lands and geographical features throughout the Pacific, as long as he thought he was the first European to arrive.[10]

In the polar explorations of the nineteenth and twentieth centuries, the planting of national flags was often the defining moment of an expedition. Even in the era of airborne exploration, how else but politically do we explain why Neil Armstrong planted an American flag on the moon? Although the implications of such claiming rituals may have changed over time, their continuity nonetheless underscores the importance of political motives for exploration. I would argue that political motives provided such a strong impetus for voyages of exploration over the past 500 years that they probably outweigh all other motives combined.

The quest for fame and glory was personal as well as national, of course. Individual explorers over time clearly wanted to be rewarded for their exploits. From the earliest days of global exploration, many expedition leaders were mercenaries who went wherever they saw the best chance for personal advancement. If they abided by the terms of their contracts and brought glory to their sponsor, they could earn glory and riches of their own. Many later voyages of exploration retained a certain international character in their personnel, though we tend to define them in strictly national terms. They could also regard their fame as a form of immortality. James Cook's goal on his Pacific voyages was "not only to go farther than any man has ever been before but as far as it was possible for man to go."[11] His ambition echoes in the phrase that begins every episode of the old television series *Star Trek,* presumably by design: "To boldly go where no man has gone before." Cook stated one of the fundamental impulses of explorers—or at least of Western explorers—throughout history; his goal sounds entirely appropriate when transferred to the lure of deep space.

One could argue that in the late twentieth century, and in the absence of new lands to find and claim, the search for fame rediscovered exploration as a test of individuals trying to accomplish a great feat against high odds. Sir Francis Chichester's *Gypsy Moth* odyssey comes to mind, along with similar ventures by sea, land, and sky. Particularly interesting are attempts to re-create historic voyages, such as Thor Heyerdahl's various attempts to replicate ancient Egyptian and Polynesian voyages, or the efforts of Carlos Etayo or John Patrick Sarsfield to create and sail authentic replicas of Columbus's caravels.[12] In re-creating famous historical voyages, modern explorers clearly hope to claim their own place in history as well.

Spiritual motives for exploration over the past 500 years encompass not only formal religion but also a variety of aims that fit better under the heading of human spirituality than anything else. Sixteenth-century explorers often acted in the name of formal religion of one stripe or another, however they may have violated the tenets of those religions by their behavior. The urge to spread the knowledge of Christianity to all people in preparation for the Apocalypse is a difficult and uncomfortable concept for modern scholars to grasp. We must recognize, however, that many early explorers, not only missionaries, were motivated by that urge. We also know that many expeditions were undertaken by Christians hoping to find allies against Islam or against other forms of Christianity. Standard interpretations of later exploration tend to ignore the persistence of missionary urges, but they never really vanished.

A related sort of spiritual motivation resided in the quest, defined by the eighteenth-century Enlightenment, to find natural men and women, presumably pure and unsullied by civilization.[13] The idea in eighteenth-century Europe that civilization itself was responsible for all the ills of humanity predisposed explorers to see faraway societies as idyllic, but that idea was

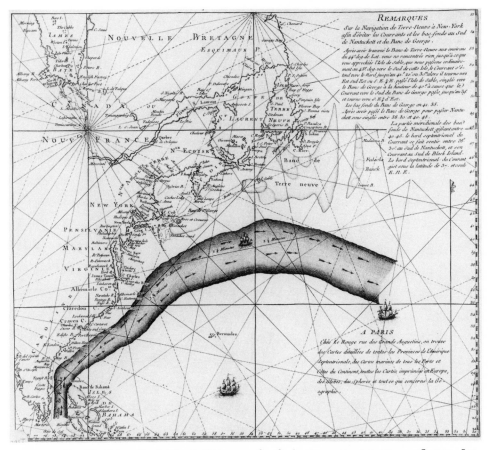

FIGURE 11. *Franklin-Folger Chart of the Gulf Stream, 1780–83*, by George Louis Le Rouge (fl. 1740–80), after Timothy Folger. Benjamin Franklin commissioned the first chart to show the flow of the Gulf Stream based on information he received from the Nantucket captain Timothy Folger. Peabody Essex Museum collections, C5778. 15 x 17 in.

hardly invented by Rousseau and his contemporaries. Early explorers often described the peoples they encountered as if they and their surroundings represented the unspoiled earthly Paradise described in Scripture and reinforced by late medieval and early Renaissance travel books.[14] It is instructive in this regard to compare the diary of Columbus's first voyage with some of the early descriptions of Tahiti in the eighteenth century or even with some romantic travelers in the nineteenth and twentieth centuries.[15] Think of the French painter Paul Gauguin, to give just one example. Initial encounters throughout the past 500 years were shaped by prior experience and by the hopeful expectation that somewhere civilized humanity could revisit, if only as spectators, the innocence that had marked human life before the fall into sin. If humanity ever encounters intelligent life elsewhere in the cosmos, our initial reaction will probably be similarly optimistic. In historical encounters, reality usually seeped in sooner or later with the realization that Paradise already knew violence, hierarchy, private property, despotism, and various other ills, long before European civilization evolved. Whether this led explorers to feelings of revulsion and betrayal or simply to a more honest appraisal and analysis, the trajectory was often strikingly similar over time.

I would argue that all of the motives discussed here—politics, nationalism, personal ambition, intellectual curiosity, and spiritual yearning—were present in one form or another on every voyage of exploration during the past 500 years. They were combined in different ways at different times, of course, but they were present throughout, however different the voyages may appear at first glance.

Many of the obvious differences in the voyages from one century to another had to do with the logistics, or means, through which they were undertaken. To launch a voyage of exploration in any century required a wide range of technical, financial, and bureaucratic support, as well as leadership and personnel. The means had to exist, and they had to be marshaled and assigned to the enterprise, or it simply would not take place. We cannot understand why seaborne exploration occurred merely by tracing the evolution of shipping, banking, finance, or the structure of centralized states. On the other hand, the means available at any given time helped to define what sorts of exploratory voyages would be undertaken, if and when someone decided to undertake them. Despite Leonardo da Vinci's fascinating designs, airborne exploration was not a possibility in the sixteenth century. Extreme polar exploration became feasible only in the late nineteenth century, and it was not practical even then. Exploration of the cosmos, or of the deep oceans, has become possible only very recently. Yet the mere existence of appropriate technology does not explain why exploration is undertaken—or why it is not. These are obvious points, but they bear mentioning, nonetheless, because technology has often been viewed as cause, means, and effect, sufficient unto itself.

The most important technical requirements for seaborne exploration include appropriate vessels, navigational devices, information technology, and weaponry. I would argue that these requirements varied over the centuries only in the details. The sophisticated vehicles, devices, and sources of information available today are different in degree but not in kind from the full-rigged ship, mariner's astrolabe, compass, sailing charts, and artillery of the late Renaissance that were in their day state of the art.[16] Whichever inventions inhabited the far horizon of available technology at a given time and place defined what was possible for voyages of exploration. I suspect that the initial sense of wonder that new technology inspires would be much the same in any age. Over time, the new becomes commonplace and then antiquated as invention moves toward a new horizon. Then the cycle begins again, but always starting from the most distant frontiers of current possibilities.

A large part of the scholarship about exploration in the past 500 years has been devoted to technological issues broadly defined, but there is no time to consider them here. I will simply mention that maps—part of the "information technology" available to explorers—could serve as motives, means, and results for historical voyages. They were sometimes accurate depictions of reality, sometimes projections of political ambitions or wishful thinking, and sometimes a hodgepodge of various impulses.[17] Like other forms of technology—computer software, to take a modern example—every new development in mapping did not necessarily represent an improvement in reliability. The fanciful projections of legendary continents, geographical features, or peoples on many historical maps inspired individuals and governments to undertake a long list of foolhardy enterprises, some of which, such as Columbus's voyages, unexpectedly paid off.

This brings me to the results of voyages of exploration over the past 500 years. The development of trade was perhaps the most immediate and far-reaching result, and it is discussed in detail by others. I will mention only the striking fact that trade appeared in every aspect of seaborne exploration—motives, means, and results—from the beginning.[18] Long before Spaniards in Columbus's time knew exactly where they were going, they still engaged in trade. We often read that Vasco Núñez de Balboa's discovery of the Pacific Ocean in 1513 brought about the realization that North and South America were separate continents, and that Asia was two oceans away from Europe. That realization did not dawn immediately, however, nor was it necessary for the development of trade. At the time, not even Spaniards knew the full implications of Balboa's discovery, and no one else even had a clue. It would be generations before the full contours of the Americas and their relationship with Asia were widely known and accurately mapped. By then, hundreds of ships a year carried the trade between Spain and America, and there were regular voyages between America and Asia as well.

There is no doubt, however, that geographical knowledge, often in the form of new maps, was one of the most important results of voyages of exploration. Whether or not that knowledge was disseminated immediately or fully is another issue. Rulers who sponsored voyages of exploration were anxious to claim the glory of new conquests but reluctant to provide accurate maps for their rivals. As a result, early maps and sailing directions were often state secrets in the sixteenth and seventeenth centuries, jealously guarded and anxiously sought after, so that new knowledge spread unevenly and erratically. Once a nation's claims had been acknowledged by its rivals, at least temporarily, the value of publicity could mediate the need for secrecy.

Exploration resulted in new knowledge about peoples as well as places. I already discussed the quest for unspoiled human societies as one of the motivations for exploration throughout the modern period. Descriptions of those societies were also an important result of exploration and eventually evolved into the modern science of ethnography. Some authors mistakenly attribute the beginning of an ethnographic sensibility to the so-called scientific voyages of the eighteenth century, but it was unmistakably present as early as the Spanish missionaries of the sixteenth century and arguably present far earlier.[19] Throughout the modern period, explorers and travelers often included surprisingly analytical and respectful descriptions of the peoples they encountered along the way.

Memoirs and travel accounts were already an important literary genre in the Renaissance, although they often recognized no boundary between reality and fantasy. The reports of early explorers, like their maps, provided a record for posterity. It is hardly surprising that they viewed their exploits through the distorting filter of self-justification, especially if they hoped to attract future sponsors or escape blame for past failures. Hernán Cortés's letters to the emperor Charles V provide classic examples of such distortions, but there are dozens of others throughout the modern history of exploration.[20]

We might argue that publicity itself became a primary result of seaborne exploration in the eighteenth century. The general characteristics of many parts of the globe were widely known by then, but the rigors of ocean voyages discouraged casual travel. The growing literate elite in Europe, with its culture of salons, intellectual societies, and bourgeois dabbling in the sciences, gloried in reports of exploration and exotic destinations. They were especially charmed by tales of unspoiled island paradises in the Pacific Ocean. James Cook was the first to map many stretches of the Pacific accurately, because he carried chronometers that allowed him to measure longitude precisely. The result was exhilarating to the reading public in eighteenth-century Europe, as if Cook had finally mapped the "new heaven and new earth" of Saint John's Book of Revelation. The maps and posthumous accounts of Cook's voyages became best sellers in Europe and rapidly spread knowledge of a vast area of the globe previously known more in legend than in fact. In the nineteenth and twentieth centuries, a broad range of more ordinary travelers explored the globe and marketed their journals or artwork to an interested public.

Another portion of this book deals with the sea as a source of inspiration, but a few words are in order here. The record of modern exploration by sea and land can usefully be analyzed as a commodity. Whether produced by legitimate travelers or by rogues and charlatans, it supplied a public demand for vicarious adventure and continues to do so today, as demonstrated by the continued popularity of travel stories in print and other media. The popular television show *The Crocodile Hunter* has more in common with the adventures of Marco Polo than we might like to admit. These days, the potential to profit from publicizing an unusual voyage or exotic adventure often seems to be the main reason for undertaking it.

I have already noted the political motives behind seaborne exploration. Did enhanced state power and wealth result from those efforts? I would argue that it did in enough cases to inspire successive waves of state-sponsored exploration throughout the modern period. The tangible rewards became more difficult to demonstrate as the costs of the efforts rose—for example, in polar exploration—but the expense could still be justified solely in terms of global political rivalries. That is also true of space exploration in our own times, of course. There are various other potential results of exploration over the past five centuries that might be mentioned, both tangible and intangible, but these should be sufficient to indicate the ways in which voyages of exploration have helped to shape the modern world.

In surveying seaborne exploration over the past 500 years, I was looking for common characteristics, so it is not surprising that I have found them. The scholar's mind is remarkably accommodating in that regard. Nonetheless, I think that the patterns I have noted are real, rather than illusory. The

FIGURE 12. Sketch of men offloading cargo, 1801, by Ange-Joseph Antoine Roux (1765–1835), watercolor on paper. Peabody Essex Museum collections, M3359. 9 x 12 in.

most striking characteristic that seems to define virtually all of the major efforts at exploration I have read about, whatever the century, is their persistence, to put it positively, or obsession, to put it more harshly. Once a goal such as a new route to a particular place was defined as worthwhile, voyage after voyage pursued that goal. Major voyages were launched with no other purpose than to find traces of earlier voyages that had disappeared. When Sir John Franklin's 1845 expedition in search of the elusive Northwest Passage vanished, as many as thirty voyages in eleven years were sent out in search of it, without any realistic hope that anyone had survived. That extraordinary quest, sometimes known as the "white passion" of the British Royal Navy, was extreme but hardly unique. In other words, in the history of exploration, it took a long time to write off failed efforts and move on to something else.

That persistence or obsession, often driven by national or personal rivalries, bestowed bragging rights on whomever arrived at the objective first. In the case of foreign expedition leaders, the country where an explorer was born and the sponsoring country could each claim a share of the glory. Perhaps inadvertently, modern scholars perpetuate these rivalries into the present. We need only recall the ongoing arguments about Francis Drake's discoveries and purported discoveries on the west coast of North America and about whether Robert Peary or Frederick Cook first reached the North Pole.[21] There are, of course, many similar arguments about exploration elsewhere, just as there are perennial arguments about the nationality of several of the early explorers. If human nature is any guide, we are likely to extend similar controversies into the cosmos.

What interests me is that virtually all of the individuals who became explorers, at least in the past 500 years, shared certain characteristics. Above all, they were risk takers and adventure seekers. Sometimes, though not always, taking risks in faraway places seemed to be easier for them than managing the day-to-day challenges of human relationships at home. They seemed to thrive on adversity, and if they were blocked by circumstance or preempted by rivals, many found a way to pursue the same or similar ends by other means, or in other places. Here again, the word obsession comes to mind. Although there were often sharp rivalries among explorers from different nations, and even from the same nation, there are also hints that they recognized a shared identity. That helps to explain why former rivals would volunteer for dangerous rescue missions when a competitor went missing.

The public fascination with exploration—with its successes and perhaps even more with its failures—shows no sign of abating. The Portuguese series of publications about "disasters at sea" in the seventeenth century is echoed in our own times by the popular fascination with shipwrecks, including the recent *Titanic* phenomenon. In this survey, I have dealt exclusively with Western civilization because the Western world seems to have dominated seaborne exploration during the past 500 years, but I suspect that the urge to explore, defined very broadly, knows no geographical or ethnic boundaries. Rather, it is shared by select individuals who recognize no limits to their imagination.

Notes

1. The notes to this chapter can do no more than provide a few points of entry into the vast quantity of published work available. Good overviews include Felipe Fernández-Armesto, ed., *The Times Atlas of World Exploration* (London: Times Books, 1991); Patricia D. Netzley, *The Encyclopedia of Women's Travel and Exploration* (Phoenix, Ariz.: Oryz Press, 2001); *The Encyclopedia of Discovery and Exploration* (Garden City, N.Y.: Doubleday, 1973); Jean Riverain, *Concise Encyclopedia of Explorations* (Chicago: Follett, 1966); Helen Delpar, ed., *The Discoverers: An Encyclopedia of Explorers and Exploration* (New York: McGraw-Hill, 1980); Eric Newby, *The Rand McNally World Atlas of Exploration* (New York: Rand McNally, 1975); Daniel B. Baker, ed., *Explorers and Discoverers of the World* (Detroit: Gale Research, 1993); Paolo Novaresio, *The Explorers: From the Ancient World to the Present* (New York: Stewart, Tabori & Chang, 1996); and William H. Goetzmann, *The Atlas of North American Exploration from the Norse Voyages to the Race to the Pole* (New York: Prentice Hall General Reference, 1992).

2. Francisco Hernández, *The Mexican Treasury: Writings by Dr. Francisco Hernández* (Palo Alto, Calif.: Stanford University Press, 2001); and Simon Varey, Rafael Chabrán, and Dora Weiner, eds., *Searching for the Secrets of Nature: The Life and Works of Dr. Francisco Hernández* (Palo Alto, Calif.: Stanford University Press, 2001).

3. James Cook, *The Journals of Captain James Cook on His Voyages of Discovery: The Voyage of the Resolution and Discovery, 1776–1780*, ed. J. C. Beaglehole, Hakluyt Society, extra series, no. 34–37 (Cambridge: Cambridge University Press for the Hakluyt Society, 1955–74). The set has recently been reprinted by Boydell and Brewer.

4. Patricia Seed, *Ceremonies of Possession in Europe's Conquest of the New World, 1492–1640* (Cambridge: Cambridge University Press, 1995).

5. William D. Phillips Jr. and Carla Rahn Phillips, *The Worlds of Christopher Columbus* (Cambridge: Cambridge University Press, 1992), 51–63.

6. A good introduction to current scholarship on Spain's American conquests appears in Mark A. Burkholder and Lyman L. Johnson, *Colonial Latin America* (Oxford: Oxford University Press, 2001), 1–78.

7. Tim Joyner, *Magellan* (Camden, Maine: International Marine, 1992).

8. Samuel Eliot Morison, *The European Discovery of America*, vol. 1, *The Northern Voyages A.D. 500–1600* (Oxford: Oxford University Press, 1971).

9. Ann Savours, *The Search for the North West Passage* (New York: St. Martin's, 1999); and Clive Holland, *Arctic Exploration and Development, c. 500 B.C. to 1915: An Encyclopedia*, Garland Reference Library of the Humanities, 930 (New York: Garland, 1994).

10. Jean-François de Galaup de La Pérouse, *The Journals of Jean-François de Galaup de La Pérouse*, 2d. ser. (London: Hakluyt Society, 1994–95), 179–80.

11. This was quoted in Fernández-Armesto, *Times Atlas*, 177.

12. Roger C. Smith, *Vanguard of Empire: Ships of Exploration in the Age of Columbus* (Oxford: Oxford University Press, 1993).

13. Anthony Pagden, *European Encounters with the New World: From Renaissance to Romanticism* (New Haven: Yale University Press, 1992); and Peter J. Marshall and Glyndwr Williams, *The Great Map of Mankind: Perceptions of the World in the Age of Enlightenment* (Cambridge: Harvard University Press, 1982).

14. Boies Penrose, *Travel and Discovery in the Age of the Renaissance, 1420–1620* (Cambridge: Harvard University Press, 1952); Mary Campbell, *The Witness and the Other World: Exotic European Travel Writing, 1400–1600* (Ithaca: Cornell University Press, 1988); and Chloe Chard and Helen Langdon, eds., *Transports: Travel, Pleasure, and Imaginative Geography, 1600–1830* (New Haven: Yale University Press, 1996).

15. Oliver Dunn and James E. Kelley Jr., eds. and trans., *The "Diario" of Christopher Columbus's First Voyage to America, 1492–1493, Abstracted by Bartolomé de las Casas* (Norman: University of Oklahoma Press, 1989).

16. Carlo M. Cipolla, *Guns and Sails in the Early Phase of European Expansion* (London: Collins, 1965); and John H. Parry, *The Discovery of the Sea* (Berkeley: University of California Press, 1974).

17. John Brian Harley, *The New Nature of Maps: Essays in the History of Cartography* (Baltimore: Johns Hopkins University Press, 2001); Jerry Brotten, *Trading Territories: Mapping in the Early Modern World* (Ithaca: Cornell University Press, 1998); David Buisseret, ed., *Monarchs, Ministers, and Maps: The Emergence of Cartography as a Tool of Government in Early Modern Europe* (Chicago: University of Chicago Press, 1992); Frank Lestringant, *Mapping the Renaissance World: The Geographical Imagination in the Age of Discovery* (Berkeley: University of California Press, 1994).

18. Charles Corn, *The Scents of Eden: A Narrative of the Spice Trade* (New York: Kodansha International, 1998).

19. Anthony Pagden, *The Fall of Natural Man: The American Indian and the Origins of Comparative Ethnology* (Cambridge: Cambridge University Press, 1982).

20. Hernán Cortés, *Letters from Mexico* (New Haven: Yale University Press, 1987).

21. Harry Kelsey, *Sir Francis Drake: The Queen's Pirate* (New Haven: Yale University Press, 1998).

5

Deep Frontiers

Ocean Exploration in the Twentieth Century

JUSTIN E. MANLEY AND BRENDAN FOLEY

Earth is an ocean planet, but humans live on land, and they have explored, charted, and sought to understand the terrestrial world. Until quite recently, most ocean exploration has been confined to sailing the surface of the waves and navigating to the next landmass. Forays into the undersea realm were limited to the shallows until the second half of the twentieth century, but the past fifty years have witnessed fantastic discoveries in the deep sea. We take our inspiration and part of the title for this chapter from the "Deep Frontiers: Ocean Engineering at MIT" exhibit at the Hart Nautical Gallery of the Massachusetts Institute of Technology Museum. That exhibit focuses on the research and development activities of MIT, but here we attempt to summarize some developments in exploration of the ocean depths during the twentieth century, underscoring technological advancements and how they have facilitated ever-deeper excursions into the ocean. Similar to the microcomputing industry on which so much of its recent development is founded, marine exploration technology is improving at a rapid rate. Much of this chapter leans toward the post–World War II era and the most recent evolutions of modern ocean engineering.

The Ocean and Its Depths

The ocean covers 360 million square kilometers and 71 percent of the earth's surface. The seven seas of literary reference notwithstanding, all oceans are connected and form one continuous body of saltwater. The ocean contains 97 percent of the planet's water, a total volume of 1,365,336,000, 000,000,000,000 liters. To put it in perspective, if the borders of the United States formed a giant bathtub, the sides would have to be 140 kilo-

FIGURE 13. *View of Liverpool from Cheshire,* 1840, by Robert Salmon (ca. 1775–1850), oil on panel. Gift of William L. Parker in memory of Charles Hamilton Parker. Peabody Essex Museum collections, M15320. 15½ x 33 in.

meters high to hold that volume of water. As a final comment on ocean size, the Pacific Ocean alone has a larger surface area than all seven continents combined.

The storms and vast distances faced by contemporary sailors are only two facets of the ocean's challenge. The chemical and physical properties of the ocean also present obstacles to human exploration. Sunlight penetrates only a few hundred meters, so the depths are inky black. The deep ocean is cold, too; its average temperature is 3.8 degrees Celsius, just a few degrees above freezing. Other daunting factors present obstacles to exploration. The average salinity of the ocean is thirty-five parts per thousand. If all of the ocean's salt were distilled and piled on land, it would cover the continents with a layer 4.9 feet (1.5 meters) deep. Salt makes the marine environment unfriendly to ferrous metals, which presents a problem for exploration in the deep, as metal vessels provide protection for humans against the pressure of ocean depths.

With each ten meters of depth, the pressure increases by one atmosphere, and the average depth of the ocean is 4,000 meters. Its deepest point is 6.8 miles (10.9 kilometers) in the Mariana Trench off Guam in the western Pacific. If Mount Everest were sunk in this trench, its peak would still lie a full kilometer below the waves. The pressure at the bottom of the Mariana Trench is 15,136 pounds per square inch (1,109 kilograms per cubic centimeter), about the same pressure you would feel on the palm of your hand if you tried to balance a stack of fifty jumbo jets. The deep ocean's extreme pressure, low temperature, darkness, and corrosive effects on metals make it as inhospitable to humans as outer space.[1]

Divers: Direct Human Exploration

Despite the challenges of ocean exploration, humans have been interested in it for most of our history. Often the impetus for undersea investigation has been the retrieval of lost goods. The first record of a diving project under the sea comes from the writings of the Greek historian Herodotus in the fifth century B.C., when the Persian king Xerxes employed a diver to recover sunken treasure. By the first century B.C., salvage diving was so common in the eastern Mediterranean that a codified pay scale existed; divers' remuneration increased with operating depth. These early attempts were breath-hold dives. To extend operations, divers needed a source of air so they could stay under water longer.

Around 1530, salvors developed one solution to this problem, the diving bell. This was an old idea, dating at least to the time of Alexander the Great in the fourth century B.C. These bell-shaped, open-bottomed tubs were low-ered into the water on a cable. Air trapped in the bell permitted divers to breathe while working in the water below the device. A diver could also swim out from the bell to perform tasks while holding his breath, and then duck back inside to replenish the air in his lungs. This was an improvement over simple breath-hold diving, but dive duration was limited by the amount of air in the small chambers. Despite the limitations, salvage divers using these devices recovered valuables from scores of wrecks.

In 1690, the English astronomer Edmund Halley devised a system of air replenishment for diving bells. Weighted air-filled barrels sent from the sur-face refilled the working compartment of the bell. In a 1706 demonstration, Halley reportedly was able to spend four hours submerged in a bell at a depth of sixty-six feet (twenty-two meters). A decade later, another English inventor, John Lethbridge, reshaped the diving bell into another configura-tion. His diving dress consisted of a leather-covered barrel fitted with a glass view port and watertight sleeves. Using this apparatus a diver could work at sixty feet (twenty meters) for a little more than half an hour, but since the dress ostensibly was watertight, Halley's air replenishment system was not compatible with it. It took inventors another hundred years to configure a diving dress with a constantly replenished air supply.

In the early nineteenth century, several men connected diving apparati to air pumps on the surface. The English brothers John and Charles Deane patented early designs in 1828 consisting of an air hose running from a surface pump to the diver's helmet. The diver wore a heavy suit for thermal protection. The helmet rested on his shoulders, held in place by its own weight and straps connected to a waist belt. The gear was not yet perfected; if the diver tipped far enough forward, the helmet could fill with water. A few years later Augustus Siebe refined the design, incorporating an exhaust valve into the helmet and sealing it to a full-length waterproof suit. With a handful of modifications, the equipment used today in standard surface-supplied diving is based on the Siebe outfit.

The helmet suit extended divers' capabilities, but in Siebe's time, divers were still tethered to the surface. Siebe and his contemporaries envisioned a self-contained underwater breathing apparatus (SCUBA), but manufactur-ers were not capable of producing either tanks of sufficient strength to hold compressed air or high-pressure compressors to fill them. Another century passed before the introduction of a workable SCUBA. During World War II, Jacques-Yves Cousteau and Émile Gagnan, a naval officer and an engineer from France, built on the centuries of diving technology that preceded them and combined a demand regulator with high-pressure air tanks. Their

Aqua-Lung was the first successful self-contained apparatus. SCUBA allowed humans to swim untethered to at least 200 feet (70 meters) in depth. With more exotic gas recipes, including helium-oxygen mixes, divers can achieve even greater depths.[2]

Taking Explorers Deeper

Early divers made terrific strides, and those following in their footsteps sought to go even deeper. Between the two world wars, a few submersible devices emerged to carry humans far beyond diver depth. The most difficult challenge faced by designers of such systems was the immense pressure of the deep. Eventually innovators settled on a spherical vessel to withstand the crushing force and shield fragile human occupants. After many years of ocean engineering research and development, the sphere remains the most effective shape for deepwater pressure vessels.

One pioneer of ocean exploration took his journeys to the deep in little more than a giant metal sphere on a cable. William Beebe led an effort to develop and test the bathysphere, a device that consisted of a metal sphere 1.5 inches (3.8 centimeters) thick. The only disturbance of the spherical shell was a hatch and a quartz window of 3 inches (7.6 centimeters). Inside this tiny compartment of 4.5 feet (1.4 meters) in diameter, Beebe descended to a depth of 800 feet (244 meters) on June 6, 1930. Later, in 1934, he pushed to a record depth of 3,028 feet (922 meters). Since the bathysphere was attached directly to the support ship, it would experience all of the wave action from the surface. Bouncing about in the cold dark waters off Bermuda, Beebe demonstrated his commitment to ocean exploration. Glimpses of the ocean depths never before witnessed by human eyes rewarded his perseverance, and the observations and sketches of marine life made during these deep plunges opened new vistas for ocean explorers.

In the years just before World War II, an innovative Swiss physicist named Auguste Piccard sketched out an initial design for a tool that would take explorers deeper than Beebe's bathysphere. Taking a design hint from such lighter-than-air vessels as dirigibles, Piccard used a giant bag of gasoline, which is lighter than water, to form an underwater balloon. With bags of lead shot for ballast, a small spherical pressure chamber slung beneath the gasoline balloon could sink to the bottom of the ocean and then float back to the surface. He called this unique underwater vessel a bathyscaph, and in it he slowly maneuvered about at great depth pushed by small propellers. The bathyscaph freed Piccard from the huge lengths of cable required to lower the earlier bathysphere. In early 1960, an improved version of

Piccard's bathyscaph, *Trieste*, took his son, Jacques, and a U.S. Navy officer, Don Walsh, down to 35,800 feet (10,911 meters). That depth record still stands unbroken.

Both the bathyscaph and bathysphere were far from ideal tools for exploration, but the achievements made in them paved the way for further excursions into the ocean depths. The bathysphere was limited by its cable; *Trieste*'s limited maneuverability was an improvement, but she still was not a suitable platform for extensive work on the ocean floor. These shortcomings of the vehicles were highlighted dramatically when the USS *Thresher*, a nuclear submarine, was lost with all hands in 1963. A crew in *Trieste* found the wreckage, but beyond a visual inspection they were unable to provide much assistance. The *Thresher* tragedy and other events during the cold war fueled the development of additional technologies for ocean exploration.[3]

The Cold War

Cold war fears translated into billions of dollars for basic research in the deep ocean. Engineers working for the U.S. Navy developed nuclear-powered submarines in order to travel farther, faster, and quieter under the waves. Conventionally powered submarines must run their diesel engines on or near the surface to recharge their batteries, making them easy to detect. Nuclear submarines do not rely on batteries to power their dives, so they can remain stealthily submerged for months at a time. The first American nuclear-powered submarine, *Nautilus*, slid down the ways in 1954. Others followed closely behind, and submariners used the virtually unlimited endurance of the new vessels to pry open unexplored regions of the oceans. In 1958, an American nuclear submarine performed the first underwater transit of the polar ice cap. The Soviet Union launched nuclear submarines in 1957, and gathering intelligence about this new threat became a high priority. Since the vessels stayed submerged for most of their deployment, airborne or surface radar could not locate them. Listening was the best way to find them, as sound waves propagate well through water. To isolate the acoustic signature of submarines through the background noise of the ocean, the U.S. Navy had to learn more about the environment. A longtime benefactor of ocean science, the navy channeled cold war funds to scientists investigating physical oceanography. Navy researchers soon discovered that layers of water with dissimilar temperatures or salinity could produce a phenomenon known as a sound channel. These channels carried sound waves over hundreds or even thousands of miles. The navy took advantage of this by building a sensitive network of hydrophones called Sound Ocean Surveillance System, or SOSUS. As SOSUS informed its operators about the maneuverings of the Soviet fleet, it also prompted new inquiries into the biology and geology of the oceans.

In addition to listening to their adversaries and plying the depths in nuclear submarines, the U.S. military and intelligence community took some extraordinary steps to reach into the deep sea. In the late 1960s, navy hydrophones in the Pacific detected the violent demise of a Soviet submarine. Soon a secret U.S. navy submarine, *Halibut,* hovered over the site of the Soviet submarine. *Halibut'*s depth rating was limited, but the boat was rigged with cables to dangle cameras, lights, and manipulator devices far below the submerged submarine. Not content with the intelligence gathered by the spy sub, the Central Intelligence Agency hatched a plan to recover the entire Soviet vessel. The result was the *Glomar Explorer,* a ship capable of extending miles of pipe in sixty-foot lengths to the sea floor. At the end of the pipe was a set of enormous claws, intended to grapple the wrecked submarine and cradle it to the surface where it could be closely scrutinized. Ultimately, *Glomar Explorer* did recover a small portion of the submarine, badly damaged during the process. Since the grappling claws were directly connected to the surface ship, every wave lifting or rolling the ship translated into movement of the manipulator and put tremendous stresses on the connecting pipe. After this single mission, *Glomar Explorer* was retired.[4]

Scientific Frontiers

The defense community was not the only beneficiary of cold war investment in ocean exploration and research. New technology became available to scientific users asking fundamental questions about the nature of the earth. Deep submergence systems allow geologists to see and investigate the bottom of the ocean. Geologists began to probe the bottom of the ocean and discovered the Mid-Atlantic Ridge, a chain of submerged mountains that runs down the middle of the Atlantic Ocean. This prompted them to revive a hypothesis first broached in the early decades of the twentieth century: plate tectonics. Analysis of the Mid-Atlantic Ridge showed it to be a boundary between continental plates. Geologic mechanisms discovered there conclusively proved that the earth's surface is in very slow but constant motion. Plate tectonics are now accepted in the scientific canon, but it was only the drive into deep-ocean exploration during the cold war that brought the theory to the scientific mainstream.[5]

Biologists have also benefited from ocean exploration, and for them, the oceans are still the scientific frontier. More than 99 percent of the biosphere, or living space, on the planet is within the ocean. It should contain huge numbers of plant and animal species. Currently, only one-quarter of the roughly 1.7 million known species are aquatic. Estimates run as high as ten million possible aquatic species. If correct, that leaves vast numbers of creatures yet to be discovered. Following in the footsteps of geologists, biologists have begun to fill in the some of the gaps in our knowledge about life in the ocean depths.[6]

One of the most startling finds in the deep ocean was the discovery in 1977 of hydrothermal vents. These areas of intense geologic activity spew hot gas and molten rock into the ocean. Found at great depth, these vents provided evidence for the origins of chemical and mineral balances in the ocean. Even more momentous was the discovery of life in the superheated water around these vents. At the vents' depth, there is no sunlight; life based on photosynthesis cannot exist. Scientists discovered in the vent communities life forms that converted the products of the vents into energy by a process called chemosynthesis. This discovery is now providing clues to the evolution of life on Earth and possibly elsewhere in the cosmos. After less than a quarter-century of study, it is expected that deep-ocean hydrothermal vents will harbor more ground-breaking discoveries for both biology and geology.[7]

Research Submersibles

The tool that allowed scientists to reach the bottom of the ocean in the late 1960s and early 1970s was the submersible. Small submarines optimized for nonmilitary applications were a novelty, but a vital tool for science and exploration. One of the most well known examples is the deep submergence vessel (DSV) *Alvin*. Championed by Allyn Vine of the Woods Hole Oceanographic Institution (WHOI), built by General Mills (of cereal fame), and funded largely by the U.S. Navy, *Alvin* was delivered to WHOI on June 5, 1964.

Alvin is yet another vehicle based on a spherical pressure hull. The sphere's diameter of 7 feet (2.13 meters) was first built of high-strength steel, giving *Alvin* an operating depth of 6,000 feet (1,828 meters). Ten years later, it was replaced with a titanium sphere that allowed *Alvin* to dive to 10,000 feet (3,048 meters). The personnel sphere is surrounded by an exoskeleton including mechanical arms, propellers, batteries, and all other vehicle systems. The pilot and scientists aboard *Alvin* see out through four plastic portholes. A variety of cameras, lights, and instruments is carried to help scientists make maximum use of *Alvin*'s deep-diving abilities.

Before serious scientific application of *Alvin* could get under way, it was called upon to complete one of its most challenging, and famous, early missions. On January 17, 1966, a U.S. B-52 bomber collided in midair with a refueling tanker. Both aircraft disintegrated, and a hydrogen bomb fell into the sea off Palomares, Spain. *Alvin* was called in to aid in the search for the missing weapon, performing thirty-four dives and successfully locating the missing bomb. (The navy recovered the bomb using another new technology, ROVs, remotely operated vehicles, to be discussed later.) Since the late 1960s, *Alvin* has participated in science dives, including the 1977 French-American Mid-Ocean Undersea Study (FAMOUS), which examined the Mid-Atlantic Ridge and discovered deep sea hydrothermal vents. In the twenty-five years since that expedition, *Alvin* has continued to perform for the ocean science and exploration community, recently completing her 3,500th dive.[8]

Alvin is one of the best-known research submersibles, but there are now several others. Notable examples are the *NR-1* operated by the U.S. Navy and the Russian *MIR I* and *II*. The *MIR* submersibles are familiar to the public as they were used in the filming of an IMAX movie about the *Titanic*. The *NR-1* is a nuclear-powered submarine that has played a significant role in ocean exploration, providing target sites for further investigation by ROVs. Several of these sites have turned out to be intriguing ancient shipwrecks.

Acoustics

The *NR-1* is a one-of-a-kind vessel. Nuclear power gives the boat extended duration under water. Its hull can sustain dives to 3,000 feet, and it is equipped with view ports that allow scientists to see the sea floor and a manipulator arm capable of retrieving objects from it. The submarine also carries video and still cameras and illumination lights. The combination of this technology is enough to set *NR-1* apart from other deep submersibles, but its most important assets are its sonar systems.

Light energy attenuates over very short distances in water. For instance, *NR-1*'s purpose-built thallium iodide floodlights pierce the blackness of the deep sea only to a range of about fifty feet. Sound energy, on the other hand, can travel very long distances under water. Lower frequencies travel farther than higher frequencies, but at the cost of better resolution. High frequency sonar has a shorter range, but it can identify smaller objects. Depending on the frequency of the sonar pulse, targets can be detected at ranges of hundreds of meters. Mounted on *NR-1* are two varieties of sonar capable of searching large swaths of the sea floor. The submarine is equipped with an Obstacle Avoidance Sonar (OAS) that sweeps a cone ahead of the vessel. The details of this system are classified, but an anecdote from a recent deployment gives a glimpse of its utility. During a 1997 survey of the deep Mediterranean, the OAS detected a target at a range of approximately 800 meters. When *NR-1* reached the object, it turned out to be a soda can. Sonar of this extraordinary resolving power and range is not commonly available to researchers outside of military circles, but *NR-1*'s other survey sonar can be purchased off the shelf.[9]

Complementing the OAS is side-scan sonar, a technology pioneered by MIT's Harold "Doc" Edgerton in the 1960s. As the name suggests, side-scan works by transmitting short serial pulses of sound energy laterally into the water. The sonar then listens for the echoes as the sound bounces off objects on the bottom or in the water column. Sonar targets appear as bright reflectors in the data, and any object standing above the sea floor casts an acoustic shadow behind the reflection. Side-scan sonar systems rigged on tow fish are routinely deployed from surface vessels and are used by a variety of ocean researchers. The task of locating objects under water is eased tremendously by side-scan sonar, but the data are often very difficult to interpret. Sonar targets must be "ground truthed" by optical inspection before a researcher can conclusively identify an object. One way of ground truthing targets is to observe them with cameras attached to submersible robots.[10]

Remotely Operated Vehicles

Remotely operated vehicles developed in parallel with manned submersible systems beginning in the 1960s. The navy deployed an early ROV during its mission to recover the lost hydrogen bomb off Spain, the same mission in which *Alvin* proved so useful. That robotic system was called CURV, for cable-controlled underwater research vehicle. After *Alvin* located the bomb, there was a danger of the manned submersible becoming trapped in the weapon's parachute and shrouds. CURV offered a safer alternative for the recovery operation since its operators were kept safely on the surface. The team planned to use CURV to attach lines to the bomb so the device could be hauled to the surface. During the operation, the billowing parachute and shrouds ensnared CURV, exactly as *Alvin*'s crew feared would happen to their vehicle. The navy salvage team tried to free CURV by winching it away

FIGURE 14. *Battle at Sea* by Montague Dawson (ca. 1895–1973), oil on canvas. Gift of Mrs. Joan J. Dubin. Peabody Essex Museum collections, M18145. 24 x 20 in.

from the bottom, and to their surprise the bomb stayed with the bundle all the way to the surface.[11]

ROVs possess several advantages over manned systems. As the H-bomb mission illustrated, keeping people comfortably on the surface instead of in vehicles below the surface clearly increases the safety of deep operations. ROVs have operational benefits compared to manned systems. Human endurance limits are not a constraint, as the vehicle can be lowered to the bottom to perform its duties while crews rotate through watches in the control van on the surface. The vehicle transmits data up the coaxial or fiber optic tether, so scientists can monitor the sea floor in real time. Electrical power is sent from the surface down the cable, so dive duration is not limited by battery power. Once launched, an ROV does not have to be recovered until the mission is complete or some malfunction necessitates its retrieval. Further, ROVs can be much smaller than systems like *Alvin* since no people have to fit inside the vehicles. This allows them into tighter spaces.

Specially designed ROVs have worked in very confined areas, occasionally in tandem with manned systems. During the 1986 *Alvin* dives on the *Titanic,* a miniature ROV called *Jason Jr.* was tethered to the manned submersible. After *Alvin* reached the wreck, a highly skilled ROV pilot flew *Jason Jr.* down the grand staircase of the ship. The tiny vehicle brought back captivating pictures from the interior of the great liner without disturbing its repose. No manned system would have been capable of the feat.

Jason Jr. was specifically designed for its *Titanic* task. Its larger namesake, *Jason,* is a flexible system designed to accomplish a much wider variety of scientific missions. Developed in the late 1980s and 1990s largely with funding from the Office of Naval Research, *Jason* has performed missions for the navy, biologists, geologists, and oceanographers. It is capable of reaching depths of 19,685 feet (6,000 meters) and has been employed to document shipwrecks in deep water. Some of these wrecks have been recent, such as the 1980 loss of the British bulk carrier *Derbyshire* in 14,107 feet (4,300 meters) of water. Other sites investigated by *Jason* have been much older. In 1990, *Jason* participated in its first archaeological application, photographing the perfectly preserved War of 1812 wrecks *Hamilton* and *Scourge* in Lake Ontario. During the 1997 Skerki Bank archaeological project in the Mediterranean Sea, the ROV collected data from five Roman-era shipwrecks at a relatively shallow depth of 2,788 feet (850 meters). For that project, the vehicle was equipped with lights, video and still cameras, and sensitive acoustic gear capable of mapping the sites with centimetric precision. It also had a manipulator arm dexterous enough to recover delicate glass objects. *Jason* is one of the most advanced remotely operated vehicle systems in the world and is the only vehicle currently capable of performing archaeological surveys to the professional standards of that field.[12] *Jason* represents the cutting edge of ROV technology, and planning for the construction of an even more advanced version is under way now. Several commercial companies build less sophisticated vehicles, available for a multitude of underwater tasks.[13]

Technology Evolves

As the *Jason* entered the ocean exploration scene in the late 1980s, other technologies had a wide impact. A fundamental problem of ocean exploration, both above and below the waves, has always been navigation. Recognizing this, the U.S. Department of Defense set out to develop a navigation system that would allow its military forces to pinpoint their locations around the globe. Using a network of twenty-four orbiting satellites, the Global Positioning System (GPS) provides navigation accuracies approaching ten meters. Initially, this accuracy was reserved for military users, but even then civilian systems could provide 100-meter positioning.

Global Positioning System

The GPS greatly improved the ability of mariners to locate their vessels on the ocean surface, but the system cannot provide submarine positioning. Even so, refined surface navigation makes it easier for submarine explorers to relocate sites of interest and to perform systematic and accurate surveys of the bottom. New acoustic navigation systems, made possible by electronic improvements, combined with GPS to put deep-ocean explorers in much better command of their positions. Slowly, the technologies evolved until high-precision surveys of the ocean floor became a reality.

A discussion of technical evolution would not be complete without some mention of the personal computing revolution. As computers' size and cost diminished while their power increased, they facilitated developments in ocean exploration. Computer-aided design supported ever more precisely engineered machines. Embedded microprocessors gave even simple systems "brains." New methods of communication, including the Internet, facilitated the sharing of knowledge. All of these productivity and technology enhancements can be seen in the new tools of ocean exploration. Without advances in microcomputing, the development of autonomous underwater vehicles (AUV) would not have been possible.

Autonomous Underwater Vehicles

Although ROVs provide a level of service beyond manned submersibles, they are limited by their tethers. A new technology in ocean exploration eliminates that tether. The autonomous underwater vehicle is a small submersible carrying its own electrical power and control processor. Using rudimentary computer intelligence, AUVs can be programmed to navigate the ocean depths, react to changes in their environment, and collect scientific data. The advantage presented by AUVs is the ability to work without being cabled to a ship. This reduces cost, simplifies deployment, and improves the performance of the system, as it is not limited by weather or influenced by wave action while submerged. Initially, the military developed large, expensive prototype AUVs, but the scientific community did not have access to the technology. It was only in the late 1980s that progress was made in moving the AUV into the hands of scientists.

The AUV Lab at MIT Sea Grant pioneered development of small, low-cost AUVs. By 1992, the AUV *Odyssey* was built and being tested in New England. In 1993, it performed its first scientific work exploring the waters of Antarctica. Building on this success, the Office of Naval Research funded construction of several improved *Odyssey II*–class vehicles. These serve scientists in a variety of missions around the globe from New Zealand to Italy. MIT AUVs have supported missions for oceanography and biology and tested new methods of acoustically identifying and visualizing objects buried under ocean sediments.

The versatility of the *Odyssey*-class AUV is a result of its flexible design. Like its antecedents *Alvin, Trieste,* and the bathysphere, *Odyssey* uses spherical pressure vessels to protect its fragile components. This allows the AUV to dive to 19,685 feet (6,000 thousand meters) and reach more than 90 percent of the ocean's depths. However, unlike its manned predecessors, *Odyssey*'s spheres are made of glass. These spheres are lighter and less expensive than metal versions and much easier to fabricate. Most of *Odyssey*'s control electronics, the main vehicle computer, and batteries are housed inside the spheres. All other systems on the AUV are designed to operate at depth and are placed within the outer fairing of 6.5 feet (2 meters) and a diameter of 23.6 inches (60 centimeters). The outer fairing is similar to *Alvin*'s exoskeletal design concept. It enhances the vehicle's hydrodynamics and protects the systems mounted to the inner structural fairing. This approach makes *Odyssey*-class AUVs highly capable, reasonably priced, and able to deploy different sensors tailored to specific mission requirements.

The AUV Lab at MIT pioneered the development of this technology, but the products of other AUV laboratories have made important contributions to ocean exploration. At WHOI, two AUVs have been significant. The autonomous benthic explorer (ABE) has been used to study deep-ocean geology and oceanography in environments that were unsuitable for *Alvin* or *Jason*. ABE is about three times as large as *Odyssey*. A much smaller WHOI autonomous vehicle class is the remote environmental monitoring units (REMUS) that can be lifted and deployed by one individual. REMUS is used primarily in coastal areas where its short range is not a significant handicap. The Norwegian Kongsberg-Simrad group has used another large AUV, the Hugin system, to perform surveys of the ocean floor for the offshore oil industry. Although such applications of AUVs for ocean exploration are in their infancy, AUVs promise to be a valuable element in future efforts.

Back to the Past

Herodotus's histories illustrate that sunken ships have drawn us to the deep for thousands of years. Improvements in technology, however, allow us access to sites in increasingly extreme environments. The diving bells of the sixteenth, seventeenth, and eighteenth centuries allowed divers to salvage warships and commercial vessels down to thirty meters. The equipment assembled by the Deane brothers and Siebe in the nineteenth century increased the capabilities of divers, and their gear was tested during Royal Navy salvage operations on the sunken *Royal George*. Archaeologists learned to use the Aqua-Lung in the 1960s and began to study ancient shipwrecks as archaeological sites. The U.S. Navy commandeered Piccard's *Trieste* to solve the puzzle of *Thresher*'s loss. *Alvin* dived to the *Titanic*. *NR-1* carried us to the bottom of the Mediterranean Sea to witness the remains of Phoenician and Roman vessels. *Jason* has prowled the decks of warships in Lake Ontario, documented the twisted wreckage of *Derbyshire*, and transported us telerobotically to the Mediterranean wrecks located by *NR-1*. Each generation quickly employs its submergence technology to access the sunken maritime technology of its own and earlier times.

The technologies discussed here have arrived at a perfect time for archaeologists. Since the late 1950s, scholars in that field have been excavating and documenting shipwrecks from various times in history and in most of the oceans of the world. A sizable database of comparative reports now sits in libraries, derived from wrecks studied within diver depth. The remains of ships sunk near land teach us a great deal about our past, but because they are in such shallow waters, some of their information has been lost over the centuries. Storms disturb the sites; salvage divers and treasure hunters can remove objects from them. In some areas, trawl fishing activity smashes wrecks, destroying the spatial relationships between objects and carrying them away from the wreck. Wrecks in deeper water tend to be undisturbed and are a trove for archaeology.

Already, deepwater archaeology has shifted our perception of the past. Historians used to believe that ancient mariners hugged the coast, avoiding passages across the open sea. Skerki Bank and subsequent projects have shattered that misconception. As advanced technology brings more wrecks to light across broad areas of the sea floor, a better picture of trade and exchange in the ancient world is emerging. New tools are changing the face of archaeology in the deep sea. Shallow-water archaeology is identical to land archaeology, with the addition of diving gear. In the deep water, complex technical systems take over survey tasks, freeing archaeologists for the intellectual rigors of site interpretation.

Among the new instruments on deep-submergence vehicles aiding the deepwater archaeologist are a variety of acoustic and optical sensors. In ROV operations, a constant stream of broadcast-quality video imagery passes up the cable from the vehicle. Precisely navigated along acoustic survey track lines, the vehicle collects electronic still photographs that are then consolidated into overall site images. At the same time, two high-frequency narrow beam sonars sweep the site. One collects topographical information, producing a relief map accurate to a few millimeters. The other sonar sends pulses of acoustic energy into the wreck itself, receiving returns from below the sediments and artifacts evident on the surface. After a few short hours of survey, the archaeology team has information that would require several field seasons to collect by traditional survey methods. All of this data is collected nondestructively. No physical contact is made with the site, leaving the material record of the past intact. Most ancient wrecks carried ceramic storage jars to hold the trade goods, and the style of the jars often tells archaeologists points of origins and sometimes even the likely contents of the jars. Given enough wrecks, the economies of ancient cultures can be glimpsed from these investigations.

Although a tremendous amount of information can be retrieved from deepwater sites by remote sensing, some questions can only be answered by intrusive methods. The personal belongings of the crew and objects relating to their accommodations, food, and recreation activities may lie beneath the blanket of sediment covering a wreck. On the few deepwater projects accomplished to date, a robotic manipulator arm was used to recover a few surface objects designated by the chief archaeologist. Selective sampling of objects produces more information, but more extensive excavation could deliver more. Robotic excavation is difficult and time consuming, but engineers and archaeologists are working together to create the tools to do it. Within a few years, deepwater archaeologists may be able to excavate a site thousands of meters below them to the exacting standards of the profession.

Conclusions

The twentieth century saw tremendous progress in exploring the ocean depths. A rapid technological evolution, especially fueled by the cold war, was a key facilitator of this progress. A notable trend through most of the century was the drive to send humans to the ocean bottom. This yielded impressive feats of engineering, like the bathyscaph and the DSV *Alvin,* as well as astonishing breakthroughs in science. New ecosystems and unique biology at hydrothermal vents and geologic evidence for plate tectonics were the result of this human-centered exploratory drive. These incredible results, and many others, fueled a new round of technological development.

With the growth of computers and technologies based on the space program, underwater exploration became the province of robotic systems during the last few decades of the century. Rapidly, tethered unmanned submersibles like *Jason* took over from the few deep-diving submersibles like *Alvin.* By the end of the century, ROVs outnumbered manned submersibles roughly 100 to 1. This incredible multiplication of resources for ocean exploration has driven even more exciting discoveries. The location and detailed study of the *Titanic* and discovery of ancient Mediterranean shipwrecks far from shore are just two notable examples.

The twentieth century has seen the opening of a truly new frontier. While outer space beckons, the vastness of our own planetary oceans is largely unexplored. Clearly, this is an area ripe for further efforts. There is immense potential in new deep-sea tools, such as the *Odyssey* and other AUVs, fueled by the supporting technologies of computing and networked communications. The next century is sure to yield ever more fascinating results in ocean exploration. Lest we take too much pride in our accomplishments in this field, we close with the sobering fact that we have touched only a drop in the proverbial bucket. The surface of Venus has been more extensively explored than the earth's oceans.[14] The twentieth century was but the first step into the deep frontier.

Notes

1. *Sustainable Seas Expeditions: Teacher Resource Book* (Santa Barbara, Calif., 1999), 82–83.

2. *U.S. Navy Diving Manual*, vol. 1 (San Pedro, Calif.: Best Publishing Company, 1985), 1–10.

3. William J. Broad, *The Universe Below: Discovering the Secrets of the Deep Sea* (New York: Touchstone, 1997), 38–42, 71, 73, 79.

4. Sherry Sontag and Christopher Drew, *Blind Man's Bluff: The Untold Story of American Submarine Espionage* (New York: Public Affairs, 1998), 28, 217.

5. Richard Ellis, *Deep Atlantic: Life, Death, and Exploration in the Abyss* (New York: Alfred A. Knopf, 1996), 31–50, 110–29.

6. *Sustainable Seas Expeditions*, 82–83.

7. Ellis, *Deep Atlantic*, 31–50, 110–29.

8. "DSV *Alvin:* 25 Years of Discovery," *Oceanus* 31 (1988/89): 10–17, 22–28, 34–47.

9. *NR-1 Submarine: Nuclear-Powered Research and Ocean Engineering Vehicle*, Department of the Navy Sea Systems Command, 1992.

10. For more on side-scan sonar, see John Perry Fish and H. Arnold Carr, *Sound Underwater Images: A Guide to the Generation and Interpretation of Side-Scan Sonar Data* (Orleans, Mass.: Lower Cape, 1990).

11. Flora Lewis, *One of Our H-Bombs Is Missing* (New York: McGraw-Hill, 1967), 226–29.

12. James P. Delgado, ed., *Encyclopedia of Underwater and Maritime Archaeology* (New Haven: Yale University Press, 1997), 187.

13. R. D. Ballard et al., "The Discovery of Ancient History in the Deep Sea Using Advanced Deep Submergence Technology," *Deep-Sea Research* 47 (2000): 1591–1620.

14. *Sustainable Seas Expeditions*, 82–83.

➤ 6 ➤

A World-Embracing Sea

The Oceans as Highways, 1604–1815

OLAF U. JANZEN

From the passing of the Elizabethan Age at the beginning of the seventeenth century to the end of the Napoleonic Wars just after the close of the eighteenth century, European commerce flowed along oceanic highways that were truly global in extent. The oceans provided highways for Dutch, French, Spanish, Portuguese, and English maritime experiences, as well as those of Sweden, Denmark, Russia, the United States, and a host of smaller nationalities, city-states, and principalities. It was an age characterized by what historians today refer to as "mercantilism," in which maritime trade was dominated by a rapidly expanding volume of such luxury and consumer commodities as sugar, coffee, tobacco, fish, and grain. It was equally an age when oceanic highways permitted the rapid growth of traffic in African slaves to the New World and when European powers struggled increasingly—not only on land but also on the sea itself—to control and use the wealth that traveled on these oceanic highways. To say something reasonably coherent about such a diversity of material within a brief chapter is a daunting challenge. Therefore, I will explore several themes within the narrow framework of the Newfoundland fishery, fisher society, and fish trade during the eighteenth century. Like so many other oceanic activities, this is one in which all aspects of oceanic commerce are manifest: oceans as highways; the struggle for control of the commerce on those highways; the national and ethnic diversity of the shipping, markets, and individuals engaged in oceanic commerce; and, above all, the strategies and considerations necessary to succeed in oceanic commerce. Through this admittedly narrow window into the past, it is possible to explore the way in which the oceans functioned as highways for ships, people, and commodities during the seventeenth and eighteenth centuries.

Before the seventeenth century, Europeans had already developed significant maritime highways as they engaged in commerce within and beyond Europe. The Baltic, the Mediterranean, the English Channel, and the Atlantic seaboard had all become busy with shipping and trade. During the sixteenth century, Europeans exploded beyond the confines of their homelands as they extended their reach to Africa, Asia, and the New World. By the seventeenth and eighteenth centuries, trade was expanding along well-established routes across the Atlantic to North and South America, south to Africa, across the Indian Ocean to India, Southeast Asia, and the Far East, and then back again on homeward voyages. A broad range of commodities flowed to Europe along these oceanic highways—sugar from the West Indies; tobacco from the Chesapeake; fish from Newfoundland; tea, silks, and porcelain from China; and spices from the East Indies. A great diversity of manufactured goods went to overseas colonial destinations as well as thousands of migrants in search of new opportunities and new homes, and slaves were carried by the millions out of Africa to both the New and Old Worlds. The ships engaged in these trades were as diverse in size and appearance as the cargoes they carried, from large, well-manned ships of the British East India Company to the small fifty- or seventy-ton vessels employed in the fisheries. Nevertheless, for the most part, they evolved very little after 1700, the major refinements having been worked out in the course of the seventeenth century—a mariner of 1700 would have had no difficulty working a ship of 1800. He might have observed that the prominent quarterdecks and fo'c'sles characteristic of ship profiles in the seventeenth century had gradually diminished, so that a great many vessels were flush-decked by the late eighteenth century. He would have noticed that the seventeenth-century tiller had given way to the wheel, and he might have realized that copper sheathing had begun to appear on the bottoms of ships that ventured into the tropics, particularly on those ships that specialized in the slave trade.[1]

Until well into the seventeenth century, most ships engaged in oceanic shipping were Dutch. By one calculation, the Dutch owned more tonnage than the rest of Atlantic Europe combined. This domination is typically explained with reference to the development of the fluit late in the sixteenth century, which gave the Dutch the ideal oceanic cargo carriers—ships that, according to one observer, "measure little and stow much."[2] It is, on the face of it, a reasonable argument; the fluit may not have been designed for speed, but it was ideally suited for the movement of bulk cargoes, where transportation costs were generally greater than the costs of production. Its small crew enabled the Dutch to earn more profit per ton of vessel than anyone else. Yet surely all this begs the question of what enabled the Dutch provinces to build so many ships. Clearly, innovations in shipping technology are not, in and of themselves, sufficient explanation to account for predominance on the oceanic highways.

Eventually, other nations acquired Dutch fluits or developed designs of their own that were patterned in part on the fluit.[3] By the middle of the seventeenth century, they were also introducing policies designed to liberate themselves from the Dutch stranglehold on shipping and commerce, policies to which historians later attached the word *mercantilism*. By the eighteenth century, both France and England were relying far more on their own shipbuilding capabilities than on those of the Dutch, who, in a relative sense at least, began to fade as the dominant maritime commercial power. Yet this, too, suggests that the key to understanding changing patterns of trade and domination at sea rests with our ability to recognize the significance of what was happening ashore.

Because this was an age of sail, shipping routes and even schedules were determined in considerable measure by factors over which ships had little control, but to which they had instead to adapt, such as oceanic currents or prevailing patterns of winds. Europeans had learned by experience that in order to cross the Atlantic as expeditiously as possible, the best route did not necessarily follow the shortest line on the chart. Indeed, the winds that blew from Europe to the West Indies and the northern coast of South America did so with such predictability that maritime trade could depend on these winds for a reliable and reasonably predictable passage—hence the name *trade winds*. The course followed by a merchantman making its way from the West Indies to Europe took it north to the latitude of Bermuda, then northeast until it reached the great fishing banks south of Newfoundland, where the ship would catch the westerlies for the Atlantic crossing. For a merchantman making its way from Europe to North America, however, the westerlies were a costly inconvenience that required tacking and wearing on a zig-zag course for several weeks. Consider, for instance, the seventy-ton *Christian*, which departed Leith in Scotland in June 1726 on a voyage to Newfoundland with a load of biscuit. The passage across the Atlantic to St. John's took six weeks, roughly twice the time taken by English West Country ships that had made the crossing earlier in the season, before the prevailing westerlies of summer could hinder their crossing.[4] In 1746, also in the month of June, a naval expedition that made its way from France to Nova Scotia followed a course that was longer in distance than the *Christian*'s route. However, by sailing south from its home ports before venturing across the Atlantic, the expedition attempted to catch the trade winds so that

OLAF U. JANZEN

the sail-handling skills of its inexperienced crews would not be overly challenged.[5]

Winds were not, however, the only consideration in selecting a course on the oceanic highways of the day. There were also ocean currents such as the Gulf Stream. While their precise nature was not then fully understood, their effect on the movement of ships on the oceanic highways was known to all, and ships either avoided a course that would oblige them to sail against the current or chose one that enabled them to pick up additional speed by sailing with the current. The capabilities of the ship itself also mattered—its ability to sail well into the wind, carry cargo, and be worked by an economically sized crew. The anticipated length of the voyage was also a consideration.

By reason of the roundabout routes that the oceanic highways followed, as well as for very sensible reasons relating to the constant search to maximize the profits of a voyage, ships and vessels engaged in Atlantic trades developed distinct three-point voyages that gave rise to the idea of "triangle trades." The term is a simplification of the way in which ships found it more profitable to add legs to their voyage pattern. For instance, a ship might carry a cargo of wines and fabrics from France to the West Indies, then transport rum and molasses—and perhaps a reserved portion of the wine and fabrics—to Louisbourg or Canada before proceeding back to France with furs, fish, or timber. Conversely, a ship might carry manufactured goods and wines from France to Canada, and then pick up a cargo of fish and wood and deliver it to the West Indies before returning to France with sugar. Ideally, each leg of the voyage should make a profit. With three legs per year, a ship would generate more profit than a vessel engaged in a bilateral trading pattern. It was this kind of logic that inspired the Scottish merchants who chartered the *Christian* of Leith to venture into the Newfoundland trade in 1726. They already had some experience exporting Scottish fish to pay for the Iberian wines they imported. The idea of selling Scottish biscuit in Newfoundland in exchange for fish that could then be carried to Spain and exchanged for cork and wine seemed a reasonable and profitable extension of their trade.[6]

The notion that many ships followed a three-point pattern over the course of a year can be something of an oversimplification. For instance, in the Newfoundland trade, the vessels that carried men from England to the fishery were not necessarily the same vessels that carried the fish from Newfoundland to southern Europe. By the late sixteenth century, vessels that played no role in catching or curing fish but instead did nothing more than move cargoes of fish to market had made their appearance.[7] Moreover, a merchant-venturer engaged in the Newfoundland trade did not necessarily confine his activity to fish. Rather, he might invest in several commodities, so that his ship might carry several cargoes to various destinations before it made its way back to its point of origin in Europe. For instance, a ship arriving in Spain with a cargo of Newfoundland fish might take on a mixed cargo of Iberian fruit, wines, ironwork, and silks to be sent to America and exchanged for a cargo that might take the ship back to Newfoundland, or that might take it on to the West Indies before heading home. The term "triangle trade" should not, therefore, suggest that the precise movement of a given ship in a particular commodity trade can be predicted. Nevertheless, there is some validity to the term, for it accurately describes the principal directions in which investment capital in the form of shipping and cargoes moved.[8]

One advantage of such a shipping pattern is that it put a ship to profitable use practically the entire year round. The drawback was that a triangular voyage pattern also took more time than a bilateral one, with the result that oceanic trades were constantly dominated by deadlines that must have contributed significantly to the anxiety of the merchant-venturer. Failure to meet those deadlines could defeat the voyage, perhaps even discourage investors from venturing further onto the oceanic highways. This, too, can be demonstrated with reference to the voyage of the *Christian* in 1726, although it must be understood that the same concerns existed in most trades. The *Christian* was fitted out in May and departed in June. It should have made Newfoundland in July but arrived instead in August, by which time the purchase price of fish had been set at a higher level than would had been the case with an earlier arrival. The ship acquired its cargo of fish quickly enough to make its departure for Spain in September, but it was a slow sailer, so that by the time it reached Barcelona, the demand for its fish had already been satisfied by those who arrived before. This made it difficult to dispose of *Christian*'s cargo and therefore imposed additional delays on the ship. By the time a return cargo of wine had been secured, the season was so advanced that the prevailing Mediterranean winds now blew contrary, denying the crew an easy return voyage to Gibraltar. Just as *Christian* arrived there, longstanding tensions between Spain and England caused hostilities to break out; the *Christian* and all other shipping at Gibraltar were forced to wait nearly a month before a convoy could be arranged for their safety. More than a year passed between the *Christian*'s departure from Leith and its return home. Whether the voyage earned a profit at all is moot; there is certainly no evidence that the merchants who chartered the *Christian* ever tried to invest in the Newfoundland trade again.[9] There may have been a pronounced rhythm to many of the commodity trades that employed the oceanic highways, but none could be described as a simple business.[10]

Given their duration, oceanic voyages could present a ship with many risks and hazards, so that those who ventured forth onto the oceanic highways were understandably preoccupied with finding ways to reduce risks. In 1604, the *Hopewell* of London took out insurance against the following hazards of the Newfoundland trade: "the seas men of warre, Fire, enemies, Pirates, Robers, Theeves, Jettesons, Letters of Mark and counter Mark, Arrestes, Restraintes, and detaynements . . . barratrye of the Master and Marriners of all other perilles, losses and misfortunes whatsoever they be."[11] The nature of most trades generally, and the gaps in the communication between the owner and the master of the merchantman in particular, meant that the master had to be given considerable freedom to exercise independent judgment. Trust was, therefore, an essential ingredient in the working relationship between shipmaster and merchant in oceanic trades. Many merchants encouraged younger members of the family to serve as shipmasters, in part to assure themselves of a reliable servant or to apprentice a possible heir in the business. A particularly successful shipmaster might be invited into a partnership role, a relationship that might then be further cemented by a carefully arranged marriage into the family.

In France, for instance, an important business practice was *la société familiale*. This refers to the intricate network of shared investment and vessel ownership by which family connections were used to secure French businesses against the many risks of eighteenth-century commerce.[12] Under this arrangement, all members of a family would contribute their personal capital into a common family fund for purposes of owning, outfitting, and crewing several vessels and ships. Business capital and family fortunes blended and became indistinguishable. The family, in effect, became a joint shareholding venture, with the profits of the voyages distributed among the members of the family according to the amount each had contributed. In this way, the security of share ownership and business partnership was cemented by blood ties and kinship. The participants in this kind of family business might relocate in several seaports, and specialize in different activities, all to ensure the well-being of a family involvement in oceanic commerce.

An excellent example of the way family and kinship were used to secure investment in oceanic commerce is provided by the brothers Chenu of Saint-Malo during the first half of the eighteenth century: Claude Chenu, Sieur Boismory (ca. 1678–17?); Pierre Chenu, Sieur Dubourg (ca. 1683–1769); Jacques Chenu, Sieur Duchenôt (ca. 1687–1758); and Louis Chenu,

Sieur Duclos (ca. 1694–1774). A fifth Chenu, Jerôme, Sieur Dupré (ca. 1698–17?), may have been a cousin.[13] The Chenus did not belong to the top rank of Saint-Malo's *négociants*; they lacked the wealth, the diversity of commercial activity, and the international associations that were definitive characteristics of the great merchants.[14] Rather, their business dealings were limited to the French North American cod fishery and its related activities— outfitting, ship owning, and trade. As young men, they all served as captains of fishing or trading vessels that they either owned themselves or that were owned by a brother. This in itself was fairly typical of all levels of merchants engaged in overseas commerce, though Louis Chenu appears to have been content to remain a captain-owner throughout his later years, even as his brothers were establishing themselves as merchants of Saint-Malo or its suburb Saint Servan. Claude Chenu was the most mobile of the four; at various times, he was identified as a resident of Granville, Saint-Malo, and La Rochelle, although he always maintained both the business and personal sides of his relationship with his brothers. Together, the Chenus maintained fishing stations, owned vessels (sometimes as individuals but usually in partnership with one another), and participated in the truck trade at Île Royale (as Cape Breton Island was known to the French). Their sons provided them with a large labor pool from which were drawn the captains and junior officers of the Chenu vessels and the next generation of merchants. In short, they were a fairly typical example of a phenomenon visible within both the French and the West Country English–Newfoundland fisheries: a family trying to emerge out of the ranks of shipmasters and become merchants, shipowners, and outfitters determined to emulate those in their community who, through their own success, had demonstrated that it was possible to rise from equally modest means to the highest ranks of Malouin commercial society.[15]

The reduction of risks and the safeguarding of investment in oceanic commerce were enhanced by factors and methods other than the bond of family—religion, for instance. Throughout the world of European oceanic trade, examples abound in which religious fellowship combined with family ties cemented through marriage to create powerful business alliances—for example, the Huguenots of seventeenth-century La Rochelle or eighteenth-century Carolina or the Quakers of eighteenth-century Newfoundland.[16] The element of trust, on which commercial credit depended so absolutely, was thus ensured in many informal ways.

Yet trust only went so far. Good old-fashioned influence was an essential ingredient in securing one's investments on the oceanic highways of the seventeenth and eighteenth centuries. Alan Pearsall has recently demon-

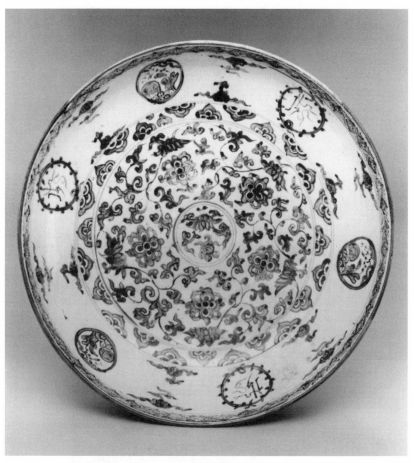

FIGURE 15. Chinese porcelain charger, 1522–66, decorated with typical lotus scrolls and roundels containing carp, interspersed with roundels representing a crown of thorns containing the monogram IHS, the symbol of the Jesuit order. Such dishes were among the very first to be decorated with European-specific designs, in this case possibly made for the Portuguese market. Peabody Essex Museum collections, AE85730. 20⅜ in.

FIGURE 16. *De galezen van Frederick Spinola door's Landts oorlogs Scheepen overseilt in den Yaere 1602* by Jan Luyken (1649–1712). This illustration from *Nederlandtsche Jaerboeken en Historien* (Amsterdam, 1681) by Hugo Grotius depicts the Spanish fleet under Frederico Spinola being overtaken by Dutch men-of-war. Peabody Essex Museum collections. 12¼ x 14 in.

strated the way in which the Russia Company pressed the British Admiralty for warships to escort and protect their trade with Archangel during the War of the Spanish Succession.[17] Merchants of the English West Country who engaged in the Newfoundland trade used their positions as mayors and aldermen of their communities to petition London for measures to protect their commercial interests. Of course, it can be difficult to determine precisely how effective such pressure actually was. Historians often assume that lobbying by the Newfoundland fishing interests was effective because the policies adopted by government seemed to match the policies desired by the trade. Yet government perceptions and priorities could differ significantly from those of the fishing interests, making it necessary for the merchants to word their petitions in such a way that their real objectives were disguised in order to assure themselves of a favorable response from government. Thus, the view that the Newfoundland fishery was a "nursery for seamen" has been challenged on the grounds that the fishery provided the navy with relatively few mariners, and that its image as a "nursery" was an illusion maintained by the merchants to justify their resistance to government regulation of their industry.[18]

Nevertheless, there is little doubt that one of the most striking developments in oceanic trade during this period is the degree to which government legal, diplomatic, and military measures shaped mercantile opportunities. This was made abundantly clear at a recent conference session on the theme "merchant organization and maritime trade in the North Atlantic, 1660–1815." Several historians explored a diversity of examples, including government-encouraged penetration of trade with Iceland by British merchants during the Anglo-Danish war of 1807–14, the success of local merchants in wresting control over commerce in the Spanish port of Bilbao from foreign merchants in the late 1600s, and the sudden opportunity presented by the Act of Union of 1707 for Scottish merchants to break into British Atlantic trades that had been previously denied them by virtue of mercantilistic restrictions.[19] What is also striking throughout this period is the degree to which oceanic trade in the Atlantic, as opposed to the commerce with the Far East, the East Indies, Africa, and even the West Indies, did not depend on large-scale, corporate organization. There was no equivalent in the Atlantic trades to great merchant companies like the British, French, and Dutch East India Companies, the Royal African Company, or the Hudson's Bay Company. Was this because the state was better able to provide the measure of security that companies had to provide themselves in more remote or disputed waters? It is clear that more work is needed before the full complexity of the "oceanic highways" can be understood.

To conclude, there were many considerations that shaped behavior on those highways—risk, trust, access to reliable information, and an understanding of the nature and the limitations of government regulation, to name but a few. One thing is evident. Effective analysis of the use to which the oceanic highways were put during this period requires that we understand more than just the obvious needs of maritime commerce—a ship, a cargo, and a crew. What takes place on land has as much bearing on maritime history as what takes place at sea. To put it in other words, while it is undeniable that the oceans served as profoundly important highways during the seventeenth and eighteenth centuries, an understanding of the land-sea relationship is vital to our attempts to comprehend the nature of the oceanic highways.

Notes

1. David Williams, "The Shipping of the British Slave Trade in its Final Years, 1798–1807," *International Journal of Maritime History* 12, no. 2 (December 2000): 20, esp. table 7. Using a sampling of ships employed in the slave trade at the turn of the nineteenth century, Williams determined that more than 93 percent were sheathed, most with copper. In contrast, in other trades, only 10 percent were copper-sheathed in 1806.

2. Cited in Ralph Davis, *The Rise of the English Shipping Industry in the Seventeenth and Eighteenth Centuries* (Newton Abbot, England: David and Charles, 1972), 49.

3. Roger Morris, *Atlantic Seafaring: Ten Centuries of Exploration and Trade in the North Atlantic* (Camden, Maine: International Marine, 1992), 112–13. The lineage of eighteenth-century pinks and cats can be traced back to the fluit, according to Morris.

4. Olaf U. Janzen, "A Scottish Venture in the Newfoundland Fish Trade, 1726–1727," in *Merchant Organization and Maritime Trade in the North Atlantic, 1660–1815*, ed. Olaf U. Janzen, Research in Maritime History, vol. 15 (St. John's, Newfoundland: International Maritime Economic History Association, 1998), 140.

5. James Pritchard, *Anatomy of a Naval Disaster: The 1746 French Expedition to North America* (Montreal: McGill-Queen's University Press, 1995), chap. 4. The expedition sailed south to catch the Portuguese trade winds that carried them to the northeast trades as far as the mid-Atlantic, where a change in course could be made to Nova Scotia. Unfortunately, contrary and variable winds dragged the voyage out; the expedition was at sea three months instead of the expected seven weeks before it could anchor in Nova Scotia.

6. Janzen, "Scottish Venture," 136–39.

7. Peter Pope, "Sack Ships in the Seventeenth-Century Newfoundland Trade," *Northern Seas 1999*, Yearbook of the Association for the History of the Northern Seas (St. John's, Newfoundland: AHNS, 2001), 33–46.

8. Pauline Croft, "English Mariners Trading to Spain and Portugal, 1558–1625," *Mariner's Mirror* 69 (1983): 257. Croft identifies the *Parnell* of London (1579–80) as "one of the earliest ships to have completed the new triangular voyage from England to . . . Newfoundland . . . and thence down to the Mediterranean." Gillian Cell describes the triangular trade in *English Enterprise in Newfoundland, 1577–1660* (Toronto: University of Toronto Press, 1969), 31–32.

9. Janzen, "Scottish Venture," 140–53.

10. A very perceptive analysis of the deadlines that had to be met by a French ship engaged in the Newfoundland fishery and trade is provided in Jean-François Brière, "Le commerce triangulaire entre les ports terre-neuviers français, les pêcheries d'Amérique du nord et Marseille au 18e siècle: nouvelles perspectives," *Revue d'histoire de l'Amérique française* 40 (1986): 193–214.

11. Cell, *English Enterprise*, 12. "Barratrye" or "barratry" refers to fraud or gross negligence of a ship's officer or seamen against a ship's owners or insurers.

12. The importance of family in eighteenth-century French business is discussed in André Lespagnol, "Une dynastie marchande malouine: Les Picot de Clos-Rivière," Société d'histoire et d'archéologie de l'arrondissement de Saint-Malo, *Annales 1985*, 233; Laurier Turgeon, *Les échanges francocanadiens: Bayonne, les ports basques, et Louisbourg, Île Royale (1713–1758)* (mémoire de maitrise, Université de Pau, 1977), 86.

13. Information on the family has been compiled from various registers, reports, declarations, and other manuscripts housed in the Archives of Fortress Louisbourg National Historic Park, Louisbourg, Nova Scotia, the Archives départementales de l'Ille-et-Vilaine, Rennes, the Archives de l'arrondissement maritime de Rochefort, Rochefort, and the Archives départementales de la Charente-maritime, La Rochelle. Also of great use was L'Abbé Paul Paris-Jallobert, *Anciens registres paroissiaux de Bretagne (Baptêmes—Mariages—Sépultures): Saint-Malo-de-Phily; Evêché de Saint-Malo—Baronnie de Lohéac—Sénéchaussée de Rennes* (Rennes, 1902), and L'Abbé Paul Paris-Jallobert, *Anciens registres paroissiaux de Bretagne (Baptêmes—Mariages—Sépultures): Saint-Malo (Evêché—Seigneurie commune—Sénéchaussée de Dinan)*, vol. I (Rennes, 1898). The parents of the Chenu brothers were Jean Chenu and Margueritte Porée.

14. André Lespagnol et al., *Histoire de Saint-Malo et du pays malouin* (Toulouse: Privat, 1984), 152–53.

15. Lespagnol, *Histoire de Saint-Malo*, 131–32. One such model of success was Noël Danycan, Sieur de l'Epine (1656–1734), the son of a small outfitter who began his own career as a captain-outfitter of a Newfoundland fishing vessel. Worth only 15,000 livres at the time of his marriage in 1685, he was worth millions twenty years later, thanks to investments in the South Seas trade.

16. J. F. Bosher, "The Gaigneur Clan in the Seventeenth-Century Canada Trade," and R. C. Nash, "The Huguenot Diaspora and the Development of the Atlantic Economy: Huguenots and the Growth of the South Carolina Economy, 1680–1775," both in Janzen, *Merchant Organization and Maritime Trade*, 15–51 and 75–105; W. Gordon

Handcock, "The Poole Mercantile Community and the Growth of Trinity, 1700–1839," *Newfoundland Quarterly* 80 (1985): 19–30.

17. Alan Pearsall, "The Royal Navy and the Archangel Trade, 1702–14," *Northern Seas 1996*, yearbook of the Association for the History of the Northern Seas (Esbjerg, Denmark: Fiskeri- og Søfartsmuseet, 1996), 64.

18. See Gerald Graham, "Fisheries and Sea Power," *Canadian Historical Association Annual Report for 1941*, 24–31, reprinted in *Historical Essays on the Atlantic Provinces*, ed. G. A. Rawlyk (Ottawa: Carleton University Press, 1967), 716; and David J. Starkey, "The West Country–Newfoundland Fishery and the Manning of the Royal Navy," in *Security and Defence in South-West England before 1800*, ed. Robert Higham (Exeter: University of Exeter Press, 1987), 93–101.

19. Anna Agnarsdóttir, "The Challenge of War on Maritime Trade in the North Atlantic: The Case of the British Trade to Iceland during the Napoleonic Wars," and Aingeru Zabala Uriarte, "The Consolidation of Bilbao as a Trade Centre in the Second Half of the Seventeenth Century," both in Janzen, *Merchant Organization and Maritime Trade;* 221–58 and 155–73; Janzen, "Scottish Venture," 133–53.

7

The Role of Short-Sea, Coastal, and Riverine Traffic in Economic Development since 1750

JOHN ARMSTRONG

For many years, coastal and short-sea trade was larger in scale and more important than overseas trade, and it was crucial in the development of industrialization and urbanization that took place from the late eighteenth to the middle twentieth centuries in Europe, the United States, and, later, elsewhere. Despite this, the amount of scholarship devoted to coastal and short-sea trade has been negligible, and the role of this form of transportation was either ignored or played down. Perhaps by airing here some of the important contributions the coaster made to British and European economic growth, and by indicating where there seem to be parallels in the American experience, further research into this topic will be stimulated.

By coastal trade, I mean internal trade; that is, the movement of goods within the boundaries of a country. The form of transport that might have competed most clearly with the coaster was the railway. If we want support for the argument that the coaster has been ignored, we only have to look at the vast number of tomes, both popular and academic, on the railways and compare that to the few books on coasting. There is no comparison. Consider the furor of the late 1960s and 1970s over the role of railways in U.S. economic growth, sparked by Robert Fogel's work.[1] It spawned a whole raft of derivative studies in most developed countries and a minor industry in counterfactual studies. Nothing similar has been attempted for the coastal trade. No one has tried to calculate its impact by working out what would have happened if it had not existed. Study of the coastal trade is neglected in almost every country in Europe as well as the United States and other developed countries. It is also instructive to look at the amount of literature on overseas trade and compare that to the quantity written on coastal trade.

Again, there is no real comparison. Whether it be U.S. exports of cotton or corn, or British imports of rice, sugar, and tobacco, much more has been written on the trade, the ships, and the companies involved in overseas commerce. Shipping lines such as Cunard, Collins, Black Ball, and White Star have become household names. By comparison, most people could not name a single coastal or short-sea company.

Consider the treatment given to the two types of trade in that compendium of maritime history, Robert G. Albion's pioneering *Naval and Maritime History: An Annotated Bibliography,* ably continued by Benjamin Labaree.[2] Overseas trade receives ten alphabetical codes, whereas there is no separate heading for coastal trade, and that topic does not even appear in the subject index. There are six codes for United States shipping, but most entries are about overseas trade, trading houses, or shipping lines. Piracy, whaling, and marine disasters have their own sections, but not coastal shipping or trade. Albion and Labaree do mention in their annotations works that deal with the coastal trade, and, to be fair to them, there are not that many. This is not a criticism of their work; the balance of their entries probably reflects reasonably accurately the amount of research done. In terms of volume of output, the coastal trade did not deserve a separate alphabetical code. This supports my point that it is an underresearched field.

If anyone doubts that contemporary governments believed that the coastal trade was important, they have only to recall that the U.S. government, like virtually all European states, protected its domestic shipping from foreign competition. Well before the Jones Act of 1920, coastal trade was confined to U.S.-built ships owned by American nationals.[3] From 1789, Congress monitored ships operating in the coastwise trade by insisting that they obtain a clearance from the coast guard, and only domestically built and operated vessels were granted this document. Later, they insisted that the ships be fully crewed by American citizens, and, in 1817, the Navigation Act was passed, specifically excluding foreign shipping. This act was based on the English Navigation Acts of ancient lineage and has been in force ever since 1817. This was the condition for cargo-carrying ships, and in 1838, an act was passed to require the same conditions for ships in the coastal passenger trades. This act was difficult to enforce, and it was not until 1886 that a fine of two dollars was imposed for each passenger landing from a foreign-owned vessel. If this put teeth into the act, they were only of the milk-teeth variety. True incisors came a little later in 1898, when the fine was increased to $200 per head.

These details are not very important. What matters is that virtually from the birth of the Republic, the United States excluded foreign vessels from

FIGURE 17. *View of Nootka Sound with the Spanish Settlement in Nov. 1792*, attributed to H. Humphries; inscribed "For Lord Hood," ink and wash on paper. Bequest of Stephen Phillips. Peabody Essex Museum collections, M14953. 10 x 17½ in.

the coastal trade, and during the nineteenth century, that trade was not freed up. Rather, the grip was tightened. The United States was no different from most European countries. The only exceptions in Europe were countries that were too small to have any appreciable internal coastal trade, such as Belgium, which had a coastline of only about forty miles, or Great Britain after 1856, which repealed its navigation acts.[4] In the latter case, Great Britain was moving toward free trade based on a massive lead in technology in steam engineering, iron (and later steel) production, shipbuilding techniques, and shipping operations. As a result, it anticipated very little effective opposition from any foreign nationality in its coastal trade and thus needed no protection.

The logic of protection for the coastal trade was largely based upon the "nursery of seamen" argument.[5] The theory was that sailors might learn their trade on coasters and then move on to deepwater ships, having mastered the basic skills of handling lines, sails, and navigation. Needless to say, not all coastal sailors graduated into deep water, and not all deepwater sailors commenced in coasters. Indeed, there has been much doubt cast on the whole idea of the coastal trade acting as a nursery of seamen in a number of countries. However, the theory of the nursery of seamen argued that sailors in the coastal trade could be recruited into the fighting navy when war threatened or broke out. Given that efficient warship operation depended on experienced and skilled men, and that, contrary to popular mythology, the press-gang did not recruit indiscriminately but sought out those who knew their way around a ship, the logic of recruiting men from the coastal trade was obvious. Since the wartime navy grew in the number of ships, experienced mariners were vital to this expansion, and the coastal trade may have played its part.

A second type of evidence—the statistics—emphasizes the importance of the coastal trade. In the late nineteenth century, the United States lost her place as a major ship-operating nation as far as foreign trade was concerned. Ben Wattenberg notes that the tonnage of U.S. ships in the foreign trade declined between 1870 and 1910 from 1.4 million registered tons to 0.8 million.[6] Ronald Hope is less generous regarding absolute size but less pessimistic about the trend, suggesting that the overseas fleet of the United States stagnated at about 0.6 million net tons from 1870 to 1910.[7] Whatever the actual statistics, there is no doubt that the transition from wood and sail to iron and steam benefited the United Kingdom. The natural advantages of the United States, such as its abundant supplies of timber, tar, and turpentine, were no longer relevant. This decline is even more marked when we look at the league table. Hope places the United States in 1870 second in the world after only the United Kingdom in fleet size. By 1910, the United States was ninth after many European countries and Japan. Most fleets had expanded in size, while the American had, at best, been stagnating.

Compare this dismal performance in overseas shipping with what was happening in the coastal trade. There the tonnage of shipping rose one and a half times between 1870 and 1910, according to Wattenberg, from about 2.6 million tons to over 6.5 million. This is the opposite of the foreign-going shipping trend and represents an annual growth rate of about 3 percent over forty years, a steady, if unspectacular, growth over a long time period. It provides evidence of the continuing importance of the coastal trade, not just to carry goods but also in its demand for U.S.-built ships since, apart from rebuilt foreign wrecks, coasters had to be of U.S. construction.

The westward movement in the United States is commonly seen as the preserve of the horse and covered wagon and later of the railroad. Hence the westward-moving frontier and its final demise might be seen as having nothing to do with the coastal trade. I suggest that that is incorrect in several regards. There were communities on the Pacific coast before the transcontinental railways reached there and before the westward-moving frontier had rolled across the continent.[8] These settlements were established largely as a result of what has been called "the longest domestic trade route in the world," that from the Atlantic coast around Cape Horn to San Francisco. The gold rush of 1849 depended on such coasters, as did the growth of the urban centers on the Pacific coast. As the population moved away from the coast into the inland valleys, the maintenance of these Pacific coast settlements depended on the coasters. From the Atlantic coast, they brought the many different types of manufactured goods necessary for building towns and exploiting the land, such as steam engines, circular saws, and hand tools. In addition, these communities needed large quantities of coal for domestic heat, light, and power, as well as for the boilers of steam locomotives and other engines. To bring it from the Atlantic would be exorbitantly expensive, and local supplies were then unknown. As a result, a regular coaster trade was established from Puget Sound to San Francisco.[9]

Francis Jenkins, who wrote about the Saginaw Steel Steamship Company, shows that coal production in Vancouver rose sharply in the late nineteenth century from 400,000 tons to more than 1 million, as the growth of San Francisco and other inland towns was fueled.[10] Saginaw Steel ships carried 3,500 to 4,000 tons of coal at around eleven knots, often completing three round trips in a month and earning about $20,000 gross per month. Coal was only the second largest output from the Pacific Northwest; lumber was the largest. Again, coasters were crucial in carrying this cargo down the coast and to the East because the economics of the coaster were specially suited to the long haul and large loads, where time was not at a premium. The coaster enjoyed economies of scale, because it could carry a large load, and the costs were very little different for a full or partial load. It also benefited from economies of the long haul, since many of its costs were incurred on entering, being in, or leaving port. By comparison, operating costs once at sea were relatively light. Port dues, cargo-handling costs, pilotage, and ballast acquisition and discharge were a large proportion of total costs and were incurred regardless of the length of haul. Normally, this made short trips uneconomic, but rewarded long hauls by giving low costs per mile traveled. Until the transcontinental railways were built and their feeder lines completed, some communities were dependent on seaborne trade, just as some rural Welsh and Scottish villages depended upon the coastal ship to service their needs until late in the nineteenth century. The capital costs of building railroads to some of these remote communities would have been excessive and the traffic insufficient to provide a reasonable return on the capital expended. Hence, shipborne trade remained crucial to these communities, especially for low-value, high-bulk cargoes such as coal, limestone, corn, bricks, and timber.

A similar phenomenon can be seen in Australia, where railways tended to be built at right angles to the coast rather than parallel to it. This allowed settlement and exploitation of the coastal belt and provided a means of bringing agricultural produce and mineral products out of the interior to the coast. The cost of building railways to link the small coastal townships was prohibitive, especially in a country with such a large landmass and a relative shortage of capital. Thus, the coaster played a vital part, providing a regular service, especially once steam was adopted, linking these coastal communities to more populous urban centers.[11] This allowed the assembly of goods for export. The coaster provided a feeder service, collecting large numbers of small parcels of grain, wool, hides, or minerals and aggregating them at a major port for export. Similarly, coasters distributed the imported goods that came into the major ports in large consignments, breaking bulk into smaller parcels as required by each community. The combination of railway, coaster, and deepwater ship acted like a hub-and-spoke system, as exemplified by modern airlines and truck operations. The export port was a hub, and the coasters provided the spokes, while the railways were the landward extension of these spokes. This allowed the most efficient use of all three modes of transport.

The assembling of export cargoes and the distribution of imports was one of the functions of the British coaster as well. Many large oceangoing ships came into Liverpool or Hull and discharged their cargoes—often over the side so as to avoid some harbor dues—into coastal schooners or steamships, which then proceeded to a number of smaller ports. For example, grain came into Liverpool's Huskisson Dock and was loaded directly into small steamers for the short journey around the coast to the tiny port of Connah's Quay, which boasted its own flour mill.[12] On the return trip, the same coaster might well pick up goods destined for export.

The coaster played an important role within the industrial revolution. A number of industries used bulky raw materials, including iron ore and limestone to manufacture pig iron; china clay for porcelain; coal for power, light, and heat; and cotton and wool for the textile industries. Various forms of manufactured iron for railway construction and shipbuilding and such large pieces of machinery as locomotives, textile machinery, and steam engines also needed to be transported. In Britain, the process of industrialization commenced before the construction of the mainline railways, and hence the only economical way to move large quantities of low-value, bulky goods over any real distance was by water. This meant using the coast, rivers, estuaries, and—since the late eighteenth century—the growing network of canals.[13] Plenty of examples can be found. In 1875, Middlesbrough sent more than 150,000 tons of pig iron to Grangemouth. From there, it probably went along the Forth and Clyde Canal to feed Glasgow's thriving heavy engineering and shipbuilding industries. In the same year, Liverpool sent coastwise more than 100,000 tons of salt, of which 33,000 went to support Newcastle's chemical industry and another 27,000 were destined for Leith, perhaps to produce sulfuric acid. In that same year, Garston, near Liverpool, received more than 15,000 tons of pit wood, much of it coming from Ireland, and probably for use as pit props in the coal industry.[14]

Exceeding all of these was the coastal trade in coal that by 1913 amounted to about 20 million tons around the coasts of Britain, of which nearly a half went to London.[15] The United States, too, despite its much greater endowment of timber (and thus wood to use as a fuel), also grew increasingly dependent on coal, and much of this was carried in wooden sailing coasters.[16] Later on, steel steamers were used, as Jenkins has shown. Without the coastal and fluvial transport of these heavy, low-value cargoes, Britain's industrialization would have been markedly slower and possibly even stifled at birth. Nor could the railways have saved the day. If we reverse Robert Fogel's counterfactual argument and move it to Britain, we would need to imagine that there was no coastal shipping and that the railways were introduced rather earlier than was the case, in order to fill the gap that the removal of the coaster left. Even this is difficult to imagine. The construction of the earliest railways depended upon coastal transport to shift heavy and bulky goods such as rails, chairs, and locomotives. Also, the main line railways were direct descendants of the wagon ways that proliferated in the northeast of England to carry the coal from the mines to the banks of the river Tyne where it could be loaded into collier brigs for despatch coastwise.[17] If there had been no coastal fleet to receive the coal, there would have been no need to innovate the wagon ways. Then there would have been no basis for the proper railways like the Stockton and Darlington or the Liverpool to Manchester. Rather than a lack of coasters speeding up the advent of the railways, it was likely to be delayed.

Even if we ignore these complications and assume the railways would have been built in the absence of the coaster, they would not have been able to carry the traffic that was in practice carried by the coaster. The rail network was already overloaded and the subject of many complaints from the local merchant community.[18] Trains with cargo were delayed as they had to give way to passenger trains, and they were slow. Freight sent in partial train loads contributed to further delays because trains were constantly being disassembled and reassembled. Thus, the late-nineteenth-century British railway system was in no shape to carry much extra tonnage of goods, and the coaster was crucial to British industrialization. A similar conclusion could be drawn for many of the European countries with long coastlines, such as France, Italy, Norway, and Spain.

If the coaster was crucial to industrialization, it was no less so to the associated process of urbanization. When people began to live in large groups in towns rather than on farms, they stopped or severely curtailed producing their own food. However, regular hours of work all year and a scarcity of land for personal plots and hedgerows meant that urban populations had to depend on commercial supplies of food, fuel, and drink. Home brewing, jam or soap making, and keeping chickens or pigs were rural activities that were not possible in towns. Hence, to feed their growing populations, towns needed to import increasingly large quantities of foodstuffs from agricultural areas. Cheshire cheese came all the way around the coast to London, as did salmon from Scotland, eggs from Berwick, and grain from East Anglia.[19] A whole variety of foodstuffs was moved by coaster into the major urban centers. In 1850, 2,000 tons of turnips and nearly that amount of potatoes entered Glasgow on coastal ships.[20] The former came mostly from Stranraer, Berwick, and Campbeltown, the latter from Newburgh and Inverness. In 1881, Newcastle-upon-Tyne received coastwise 9,000 tons of potatoes and 14,000 tons of flour. Liverpool in 1875 imported coastwise 10,000 tons of potatoes, all from Irish ports, and 12,000 tons of butter, also from Ireland. Whether it was grains, livestock, flour, meal, vegetables, or cheeses, the coaster played a large part in moving these foodstuffs from rural areas into the towns and cities.

The coaster provided a similar service in the supply of raw materials to towns to quench the citizens' thirsts. It carried large quantities of barley, malt, and hops to brewers. Without cheap water transport, the cost of the Englishman's pint would have been much higher. Once brewed, some types of beer were capable of being moved considerable distances without spoiling, especially stouts, porters, and ales. These were carried on coastal ships, especially across the Irish Sea. Nor were there only human foodstuffs needed in the towns. Short-distance transport was done almost entirely by horsepower, and the horse needed feeding. Given that each working animal ate about twenty pounds of corn and ten pounds of chaff each day, large imports of maize and, especially, oats were needed to feed the growing population of urban horses.[21] These, too, were carried by the coaster. For example, in 1849, Bristol received 15,000 tons of oats coastwise, mostly from Ireland. London in 1890 received 22,500 tons, mostly from Aberdeen, and Bristol 18,500 tons, largely from Ireland.[22] The equine population also needed hay and straw, partly to eat and partly as bedding. This also needed to be brought into the towns from farming areas. It was a classic example of high bulk but low value, and as such, it needed water transport for its low cost. In London, much came from Essex and Kent by means of flat-bottomed barges, called "stackies," specially suited to shallow harbors. These were usually grossly overladen, to the extent that the mate stood on top of the stack and shouted directions down to the skipper at the tiller. They were essential to the horse economy of the towns.[23]

Urban growth required large-scale inflows of heavy, low-value, building materials to expand the urban infrastructure. House and factory construction in Britain required bricks, slates, timber, sand, and lime. All of these were high in weight but low in unit value. Some of them, like slates, tiles, and bricks, were also easily chipped or broken if incorrectly stowed or handled and so needed slow and careful loading.[24] Despite the United States's much greater reliance on lumber for house building, the making and transporting of bricks occupied some of the coastal ships of the Northeast.[25] In addition to these materials, commercial buildings and factories often used stone; streets needed paving slabs and cobbles as well as granite setts for curbs. Granite was found in Aberdeen in Scotland, slate in northern Wales, and Portland stone from the southern coast was popular in London.[26] All of these were carried into the heart of cities by small coasters coming up the rivers to deliver, and all were long-distance trades.

The cities were not merely consumers; they were also producers of waste products. At the most unpleasant level, the growing human population produced large quantities of human waste. Before main drainage and piped water were widely available, this waste was allowed to accumulate and shoveled into horse-drawn carts by "night soil" collectors. From there, it needed onward transmission, to be either dumped at sea or delivered to a sewage farm to be treated and used as an agricultural fertilizer. Similar treatment was needed for the tons of horse droppings that accumulated in stables and fouled the roads to such an extent that crossing sweepers were needed to brush a path through them for the respectable classes. This waste, too, was usually carried by barge or coaster downriver or coastwise to corn-growing areas, there to be used to improve soil fertility.[27] Thus, the coaster was essential in removing noxious waste products that, if not taken away, would have added to the unhealthy state of the towns and further increased their high death rates.

Towns created many other waste products that were not wanted in the towns but that could be recycled elsewhere. Domestic heating in most English towns in the nineteenth century was achieved almost entirely by burning coal in open hearths. This was an inefficient method, and, among the ash and clinker, there was much unburnt or partly burnt fuel. Both the ash and the residual fuel could be used by brickmakers, the ash to bulk out the clay and the fuel to help in the burning process. This waste was known as "breeze," and with the growth of the urban population, vast quantities were created.[28] From most large cities, it was barged down the river or canal into the surrounding countryside where brick making occurred. These sites needed a combination of suitable clay, cheap water transport to bring in breeze and small coal and to take the bricks to their users, and no close habitations because of the unpleasant smell and fumes from brick burning. River, canal, coastal, and short-sea shipping played an essential part in this. Other bulky waste products included cullett—broken glass bottles—which was taken back to the glass furnaces to be melted down and reused. This was another low-value cargo. London, being an area of conspicuous consumption, created much of this waste, and most of it was shipped downriver and up the coast to Newcastle-upon-Tyne, a city that had a number of large firms making glass bottles.

Another important contribution to economic growth made by the coaster was as the test bed for many ideas that, once found effective in the coasting trade, were introduced more widely into the mercantile fleet. J. Grahame Bruce wrote an important article on this several decades ago.[29] In it, he stressed that most of the significant technological innovations in ship design were pioneered in river or coastal craft. In terms of propulsion, the early experiments with steam engines—whether of William Symington in Grangemouth in 1801 or Robert Fulton on the Hudson River in 1807—took place on rivers or in estuarial and coastal waters. Similarly, the first commercial services, such as Henry Bell's *Comet* of 1812, ran on rivers. Later, when greater economy was looked for and compound engines tried out, the earliest in the United Kingdom were in the Thames ferries of the 1840s. Much later, when Charles Parson had developed the turbine engine and tried it out in his *Turbinia,* the first commercial application was in the *King Edward* of 1901, a Clyde steamer trading across the Irish Sea. The turbine gave it much greater speed—twenty miles per hour—that was appreciated by its passengers. The point is that the turbine was first tried in the coastal trade before it went on to be important for large, deepwater ships. Similarly, developments in boiler shape and type were pioneered on coastal or river vessels.

Boiler design was crucial to raising steam pressures from around twenty-five pounds to well over 100 pounds by 1900. The higher pressure allowed compounding and later triple expansion that significantly reduced coal consumption for any given power output and hence reduced operating costs and increased the range of the steamer. Bruce also makes a case for suggesting that screw propulsion was pioneered on coastal or short-sea vessels on the Thames in 1837 by John Ericsson, who later emigrated to the United States and carried on his experiments there. Water ballast was tried out in a number of forms, but the *Bedlington,* an iron-hulled screw collier built in 1841 and employed in the trade from the northeast to London and the south coast, was the first in the United Kingdom. Steel for the hull was first used in the United Kingdom on the *Columba* in 1878. The ship was built for David MacBrayne and ran in the Scottish coastal and island trade. Later it went to the United States. To cite further examples would become tedious. The point that Bruce is making, and that is borne out by his examples, is that the drive to innovate came often in the coastal, river, or short-sea trades. Here the cost and danger of failure was lower than in blue-water trades, and once the idea was ironed out and made reliable, it was adopted by the owners of larger vessels.

To conclude, this chapter has stressed the long and continuing role of short-sea, coastal, and river traffic. It was vital to the transport of goods a thousand years ago and grew in importance down to the twentieth century. It was crucial to moving people and commodities around in the early modern period and in industrialization and urbanization, both of which required the movement of large quantities of low-value but high-bulk raw materials. Other forms of transport, such as horse-drawn road transport, could not have coped with the quantities, and the cost would have been prohibitive. The main drawback of the sailing ship—its unpredictability—was overcome by the application of steam, which also speeded up journeys. Although initially used for post, parcels, passengers, and livestock, the steam coaster soon moved into bulk trades, such as the coal trade from the Newcastle area, because, despite its higher capital costs, it could cram in many more voyages in a given period than the collier brig and hence earn more revenue. Nor should passenger traffic be ignored. Steamers provided regularity and certainty on short-sea crossings that sailing packets were never able to have, and steamboats also offered one of the earlier forms of mass leisure—the boat trip down the river, along the coast, or to an attractive island. The waters of the Clyde and its estuary, the Bristol Channel, the Solent, and the Thames were crowded with pleasure boats in the summer months carrying commuters in the week and holiday makers at the weekend. Thus, the coastal and short-sea trader played a vital role. There is enormous scope for exploring this, given the paucity of published work on the topic.

Notes

1. Robert W. Fogel, *Railroads and American Economic Growth: Essays in Econometric Growth* (Baltimore: Johns Hopkins Press, 1964); Gary R. Hawke, *Railways and Economic Growth in England and Wales, 1840–1870* (Oxford: Oxford University Press, 1970); and Patrick K. O'Brien, *The New Economic History of the Railways* (London: Croom Helm, 1977).

2. Robert G. Albion, *Naval and Maritime History: An Annotated Bibliography* (Mystic, Conn.: Marine Historical Association, 1963–72); and Benjamin Labaree, *A Supplement (1971–1986) to Robert G. Albion's Naval and Maritime History: An Annotated Bibliography* (Mystic, Conn.: Munson Institute of American Maritime Studies, Mystic Seaport Museum, 1988).

3. Mark D. Aspinwall, "Passenger Ships in the Coastwise Trade: American Public Policy since 1789," *American Neptune* 48 (1988): 173–77.

4. Sarah Palmer, *Politics, Shipping and the Repeal of the Navigation Laws* (Manchester, England: Manchester University Press, 1990).

5. John Armstrong, "The Crewing of British Coastal Colliers, 1870–1914," *Great Circle* 20 (1998): 77.

6. Ben J. Wattenberg, *The Statistical History of the United States from Colonial Times to the Present* (New York: Basic Books, 1976), 749–50.

7. Ronald Hope, *A New History of British Shipping* (London: John Murray, 1990), 308.

8. Francis G. Jenkins, "The Saginaw Steel Steamship Company and Its Steamers," *American Neptune* 42 (1982): 245–75.

9. Giles T. Brown, *Ships That Sail No More: Maritime Transportation from San Diego to Puget Sound, 1910–1940* (Lexington: University of Kentucky Press, 1966).

10. Jenkins, "Saginaw Steel," 245–75.

11. John Bach, "Sea Transport in Australia: The Rise and Fall of the Intrastate Shipping Industry of New South Wales," *Maritime History* 2 (1972): 5–30; and Graydon R. Henning, "Competition in the Australian Coastal Shipping Industry during the 1880s," *International Journal of Maritime History* 5 (1993): 157–73.

12. John Armstrong and David Fowler, "The Coastal Trade of Connah's Quay in the Early Twentieth Century: A Preliminary Investigation," *Flintshire Historical Society Journal* 34 (1996): 113–33.

13. See John Armstrong and Philip Bagwell, "Coastal Shipping," in *Transport in the Industrial Revolution*, ed. Derek Aldcroft and Michael Freeman (Manchester, England: Manchester University Press, 1983), 142–76.

14. Clyde Bill of Entry for 1875 and also Liverpool Bill of Entry for 1875.

15. *Coal Merchant and Shipper* 26 (1913): 111.

16. Basil Greenhill and Sam Manning, *The Schooner "Bertha L. Downs"* (London: Conway, 1995); and Robert H. I. Goddard Jr., *"Anna R. Heidritter,"* *American Neptune* 21 (1961): 23–27.

17. M.J.T. Lewis, *Early Wooden Railways* (London: Routledge, 1970); and Maurice W. Kirby, *The Origins of Railway Enterprise: The Stockton and Darlington Railway, 1821–1863* (Cambridge, England: Cambridge University Press, 1993).

18. See John Armstrong and Julie Stevenson, "Liverpool to Hull—by Sea?" *Mariner's Mirror* 83 (1997): 160–62.

19. Walter M. Stern, "Cheese Shipped Coastwise to London towards the Middle of the Eighteenth Century," *Guildhall Miscellany* 4 (1973): 207–11; and Tony Barrow, "Corn Carriers and Coastal Shipping: The Shipping and Trade of Berwick and the Borders, 1730–1830," *Journal of Transport History*, 3d ser., 21 (2000): 6–27.

20. Clyde Bill of Entry for 1850, Newcastle-upon-Tyne Central Library, River Tyne Improvement Commission, Table of Sundry Goods Imported Coastwise, 1881; and Customs Bills of Entry for Liverpool for 1875.

21. John Tilling, *Kings of the Highway* (London: Hutchinson, 1957), 80; and Hervey Benham, *Down Tops'l* (London: Harrap, 1951), 111, 126.

22. Customs Bills of Entry for various years.

23. Hervey Benham, *Last Stronghold of Sail* (London: Harrap, 1948), 178; and Benham, *Down Tops'l*, 111–12, 116–27.

24. Jean Lindsay, *A History of the North Wales Slate Industry* (Newton Abbot, England: David and Charles, 1974), 188–94.

25. Philip P. Chase, "Schooner *William Jewell*, 1853–1947," *American Neptune* 19 (1959): 120–22; and Ernest S. Dodge, "The Last Days of Coasting on Union River Bay," *American Neptune* 9 (1949): 169–79.

26. Benham, *Down Tops'l*, 53–54.

27. Benham, *Last Stronghold*, 77, 96.

28. Frank G. Willmott, *Bricks and Brickies* (Rainham, England: Meresborough, 1972), 21–22.

29. J. Grahame Bruce, "The Contribution of Cross-Channel and Coastal Vessels to Developments in Marine Practice," *Journal of Transport History* 4 (1959): 65–80.

8

The Sea as an Arena for Conflict

JOHN B. HATTENDORF

If we were to look out from an Olympian mountaintop to the sea below, a global picture would emerge in which a large percentage of the world's population lies in coastal areas. This number is estimated to range today from 35 to 50 percent of the world population and is much higher (reaching 90 percent) in specific geographical areas such as Greece.[1]

Affairs at sea, particularly the conduct of warfare at sea, involve a body of very specialized knowledge and professional practice. Indeed, for many years, specialized historical scholarship on the naval aspects of maritime affairs took this same approach. Authors and their readers viewed affairs at sea in a similar way, isolated from the mainstream of life ashore: a kind of exciting and exotic spectacle. Such analytical works, often cast in the traditional language of professional seamen, appeared remote, and the creation of an even more specialized naval patois and professional jargon in modern times has added to this sense of separateness. Despite this, activities at sea, and particularly the issues of war at sea, are closely tied to the mainstream of history ashore. The title of this chapter, "The Sea as an Arena for Conflict," however useful it is in drawing attention to the subject and in representing a traditional view of it, is misleading for some portions of what one can expect to read in the following pages.

As far back as the Bronze Age Minoans on the island of Crete, beginning about 2000 B.C., a network of sea trade began to develop in the Aegean and eastern Mediterranean, as by-products of an agricultural economy. By 1700 B.C., these merchant traders had to arm themselves for protection against sea raiders and pirates. Perhaps they even went on to capture rival islands. As Chester Starr asked rhetorically, "What does this evidence of maritime activity, especially in the second millennium, have to do with the conscious utilization of sea power? The answer must be very little."[2] While underwater archaeological evidence suggests that manmade violence at sea existed very early on, "the deliberate exercise of sea power was dependent upon the rise of firm political units with sufficient resources to support navies" and vessels purposely built for conflict at sea.[3] It is important to underscore the point that conflict at sea is not always characterized by the presence of state-supported navies with vessels especially configured for war. Particularly in the Mediterranean and in Asia, the traditions of piracy and corsairing go far back.

Even if it is not the whole story of conflict at sea, the rise of navies is the matter of central and continuing interest, generating a specific subspecialty within the broader field of maritime history. Along these lines, much has been written on the technical side of such developments, the designs of the ships produced, the tactics employed in battle, and the types and characteristics of the weapons used in battle. The discussion among historians of ancient naval history has often centered on the trireme as the first ship built expressly for war, along with its variants, such as the ships with five, six, and even forty tiers of oars that followed.

The importance of maritime affairs in ancient history and, particularly the importance of conflict at sea, was intermittent, but, from time to time, war at sea did have an impact at occasional critical moments. As examples of this, Carthage and Athens both became states whose primary power rested at sea, but both lost in wars to states that were more fully developed in fighting land warfare.[4] When this observation is seen within an overly narrow perspective, one too easily reaches a wrong-headed conclusion. It is not that one form of warfare is superior to another; it is that they are interrelated. Here we find the relevance for navies of the capacities for finance, acquisition of supplies, shipbuilding, government organization, and direction. What is equally true is that it is not merely the shore component that is important to sea operations. Operations in battles at sea have relationships that are often complementary, either directly or indirectly, to the results of events that occur entirely within the sphere of land warfare.

In our modern understanding of conflict at sea, this interrelationship can be clearly seen in a study of ancient history. Yet as warfare at sea became a more dominant feature in later centuries, the context and the issues changed from period to period. For the Romans, the Mediterranean was their mare nostrum. Their reference to the sea in this phrase was to not only its centrality in the geography of the Roman Empire but also its commerce, Roman political and military strength gathered along the shores of that sea, and the role of the sea as a medium of transportation and communication in the transmission of ideas, religion, and culture. Security at sea—the heart of what naval affairs is all about—and, in particular, the security of travel on the Mediterranean was a central issue for the Romans. Above all, the sea was central to translating political and military power into the economic, social, institutional, and linguistic order that survived both the shift of political power from Rome to Constantinople in the fourth century and the Germanic invasions that followed.

More than sixty years ago, Belgian historian Henri Pirenne argued that the end of antiquity and the beginning of the Middle Ages could be traced to the period in which the Mediterranean ceased to be a Roman's mare nostrum. As maritime centers developed along the European and North African shores, Pirenne explained, "The sea which had hitherto been the centre of Christianity became its frontier."[5] Both before and after this change, the nature of conflict at sea reflected fundamental shifts involving cultural encounters as well as trade and political rivalries.

Today, in the twenty-first century, sea power and sea control have a new context.[6] Navies have changed, both superficially and fundamentally. Compared to the situation a mere fifty years ago, ships look different and have different propulsion systems; aircraft are faster and have a wider variety of capabilities. Naval weapons are much more accurate and more devastating in their effects. Communications have proliferated in every imaginable way. Each of us now can have in our homes global communications through the Internet, while navies have vastly more complex means to obtain, share, store, sort, and present information to decision makers at various levels of command. The art of navigation and our very understanding of "the way of a ship" have changed through the use of satellites and global positioning systems.

The pace of change in navies is remarkable. Virtually every day, navies are faced with some technological innovation. One of the most difficult and fundamental questions for naval leaders is how to deal with this type of change. While new technological ideas appear every day, it takes time to bring them to fruition—time during which a whole range of other ideas could appear. The practical problem involves identifying the most important new technologies, selecting them for testing and development, and then deciding which new technologies to distribute widely to the fleet.

To deal with the widespread technological nature of navies, there has been a fundamental change among sailors. We can no longer personify them as the bluff and hearty line-haulers who were so essential to the sailing-ship navy. Today, men and women in navies around the world are sophisticated in science and deeply educated in technology.

While navies were once separate, autonomous entities within a government structure, they are no longer so today. One of the most telling lessons of World War II was the need to coordinate more closely the joint operations of all the armed services. Throughout the world, over the past half a century, ministries of defense have slowly unified admiralties and naval ministries with war departments, ministries of the army, and air ministries, often adding to them in the same defense ministry or department, the munitions and logistics support agencies involved with armed forces. Moreover, naval officers have had to learn to talk with colleagues in other armed forces using the same terms and the same approaches to planning and budgeting and sharing the same appropriations of tax dollars. Each of the services is increasingly becoming part of this same process, dependent upon one another and essential to one another in planning, budgeting, and operations.

At the same time that this lengthy process of unifying armed forces is occurring within nations, another process of integration is developing beyond and across national borders. While once we could think of a navy entirely in terms of one country and one country's maritime concerns, today we are learning to think of navies operating as part of United Nations forces, in terms of regional alliances, or even in terms of ad hoc coalitions gathered together to undertake some particular, mutually agreed-upon task. Additionally, one is no longer just concerned about coordinating the ships and aircraft of one country, but now increasingly in finding ways by which the forces of one country can operate effectively with those from another. This is an immensely difficult task that involves not only the obvious differences in language, culture, and tradition but also the basic patterns of solving practical problems and carrying out routine tasks. Moreover, it means sharing a certain number of procedures and certain types of information that were once state secrets.

In recent years, ships of various navies have operated together very successfully under the United Nations as well as under NATO and under other regional organizations and agreements. We have seen them during the Gulf War, in Somalia, in the Adriatic, and off Haiti. Our recent experience with such multilateral naval forces has emphasized the common concerns and natural ties that exist among sailors around the world.

It was these fundamental ties, found in the shared heritage of centuries of naval tradition and the mutual understanding of ships and the sea, that NATO built upon in the late 1940s in bringing together the naval forces of many European countries. It was the basis that helped to form the still-continuing Inter-American Naval Symposia in 1959. It was the starting point for the successful initiative in 1967 to create the NATO Standing Naval Force, Atlantic, and in 1969 to establish the first worldwide gathering of chiefs of navies at the International Seapower Symposium.

In subsequent years, the Standing Naval Force has become a model for several other multinational naval forces. The International Seapower Symposium continues to meet each odd-numbered year and has proliferated into regional meetings, in the even-numbered years, with the Western Pacific Naval Symposium in 1988, and the West African Naval Symposium in 1992. Further initiatives along these lines continue to develop.

Old ideas seem to be disappearing. Among them are the traditional view that navies are a nation's "first line of defense," that a navy and its battle fleet exists to fight a huge battle with a similar kind of enemy battle fleet, and that a navy is somehow always connected to the growth of imperial power.

In large countries, some citizens wonder why they need naval forces at all, when there is no aggressive naval force threatening them. Large navies are becoming much smaller. In terms of its ships, for example, the U.S. Navy is 40 percent of the size it was five years ago; the Royal Navy, today, is one-tenth of the size of the U.S. Navy. Yet small- and medium-sized naval forces are proliferating. There are more countries in the world today, and there are more naval forces in the world today. In 1946, the editor of the authoritative reference work, *Jane's Fighting Ships,* listed fifty-two navies.[7] Fifty years later, in 1996, there were 166 listed.[8]

Today the range and power of naval weapons have increased. Some equipment can detect ships and aircraft at ranges of thousands of miles, merging strategic and tactical considerations. In this, the uses and the analysis of the full range of the electromagnetic spectrum have become as important in modern warfare as the weapons that electronics control and guide. In facing a difficult, fast-moving environment, responsible commanders in maritime areas depend upon fast and reliable transmission of large amounts of data. While essential to one's own exercise of command and control over forces, the situation also provides another area for manipulation, blocking, and interfering with an enemy's essential needs. In short, warfare in coastal areas requires the close interaction of army, air force, and amphibious landing forces. The interaction of forces with the intensity and speed of operations have shifted emphasis from the craft carrying weapons and the color of the uniform behind them to the effectiveness and countering of the weapon itself.

A larger matter of maritime interest that also emphasizes coastal regions parallels this change in the character and in the focus of contemporary naval warfare. The 1982 United Nations Convention on the Law of the Sea has now come into effect and has been ratified by the majority of the world's states. This development in international law has granted coastal states specific rights and responsibilities in offshore waters.

JOHN B. HATTENDORF

These changes include the extension of territorial waters to twelve nautical miles from shore and the extension of some rights to an exclusive economic zone 200 nautical miles from shore to the continental shelf. These responsibilities and rights in these areas cover the establishment of artificial islands, the conduct of maritime scientific research, and the protection and conservation of the natural marine environment, including control of the catch of fish and exploitation of other natural underwater resources on and under the continental shelf.

This extension of a coastal state's jurisdiction at sea has placed certain limitations on the freedom that the great naval powers have traditionally and exclusively exercised. In effect, it has transferred these jurisdictions, in many cases, to small- and medium-sized coastal states, at a time when those offshore resources are becoming increasingly important, both economically and politically. This situation demands that coastal states have the adequate power to manage their responsibilities. This fact, combined with the capabilities of modern naval weapons, has made small- and medium-sized navies into major actors. This position is enhanced even further as the world's major naval powers reduce their size. Today, we must take seriously an entirely new dimension in naval affairs: the sea power of the coastal state.[9]

If we look at this new development from another perspective, however, it suggests new possibilities that could spark a crisis or even a war. As coastal states extend their sovereignty outward on the open sea, they may easily create friction with neighboring states that have conflicting interpretations of the facts or overlapping claims in a region. Additionally, the new interest of coastal states in maintaining control in offshore areas puts them potentially in opposition to large naval powers that have traditionally maintained the right of warships to pass on the high seas. It creates potential restrictions for major maritime powers that would like to use their navies as direct adjuncts to diplomacy. At the very least, it moves a coastal state's naval forces farther offshore, into positions where a misunderstanding could take place and create a conflict or crisis.

Here we see the possibility of a major problem for contemporary sea power and sea control. The increase in areas under sovereign control, the increase in range and capabilities of naval armaments, and the increase in the number of nations with navies heightens the potential for conflict.

The parallel rise in the use of multinational naval forces, however, suggests one possible antidote to the situation. While multinational naval cooperation is one very practical means to augment one's limited resources, by complementing one nation's naval capabilities with those of another, it also requires close cooperation and interaction between the participating navies. This interaction builds understanding between nations, providing direct links of communication and discussion.

As we try to peer into the future of naval power and imagine how navies will look at the end of the twenty-first century, however inadequately and limited we are in our powers to do so, we already believe that the Internet revolution will have a profound effect on any future conflict at sea as well as on the structure and organization of navies and armed forces in general. This change is not entirely about the technological means by which forces exchange information rapidly and try to control and dominate it; the change involves organizational as well as technological issues. Thus, thinking about this area of future naval warfare is less about the advance of information technology than about the challenges it implies for organization and for the interactions between technology and organizational changes for navies.

The so-called information revolution favors and strengthens network forms of organization based on a variety of links and communications at various levels. This is a method of operation that directly challenges hierarchical forms of organization and, certainly, navies have long been structured in a hierarchical way. In the political, economic, social, and military area, the recent rise and move to develop network forms of organization is one of the most significant developments with implications for the future. Networks in which every connection point or node can communicate with every other are one of the single most important aspects of this new development, a development that implies that all the armed forces and police forces will soon be, if they are not already, forced to formulate new concepts for organization, doctrine, strategy, and tactics. Advanced thinkers in the navy today suspect that there will be two general types of future conflict: "cyberwar" and "netwar." Both terms refer to comprehensive approaches to conflict based on the centrality of information. They are comprehensive, in that they combine organizational, doctrinal, strategic, tactical, and technological innovations, for both offense and defense.[10] In this regard, many of the nascent ideas that we hear about today suggest even closer links between events at sea and those ashore.

In conclusion, then, as we look back across the wide range of issues addressed by those interested in the sea as an arena for conflict, one can begin to understand more clearly that activities at sea, particularly the issues of war at sea, are closely tied to the mainstream of history ashore. The latest developments in this area lead us to examine more closely the fact that this interrelationship has always been there, despite our longstanding habit of seeing maritime affairs as a different world.

When seen from the broadest perspective, from the first sporadic incidents in which maritime affairs played an important role through more recent history, it seems that the importance of maritime affairs ebbs and flows in relation to the context of events. Today, as we look toward the sea in the light of both history and current developments, we can grasp that the new influences that tie maritime affairs more closely to events ashore help us to understand that similar factors have existed all along. Our earlier tendency to place maritime events into a private and separate arena has allowed us to miss some important insights.

We can see, too, that maritime issues are increasingly important factors in contemporary affairs, but the context surrounding them, as well as their nature, has changed. Navies, themselves, have changed, as have many of their most important future missions and tasks. Yet because of the increased scale of naval proliferation and the expansion of maritime interests among coastal states, as well as by the very mobility of naval forces and their multidimensional capabilities, the issues surrounding the use of armed force at sea continue to be important. There is every indication that they will become even more important in the future, but the character of their organizational relationships ashore are very much open to question. The impact of change in so many areas—ranging from new developments in international law and the character and effectiveness of weapons to the joint-service and multinational employment of naval forces, as well as the organizational and technological implications coming through innovation—stresses the need to see conflict at sea in a much wider perspective.

To put this another way, the point in this chapter about conflict is the same one that has been made in each of the other chapters of this volume. The events and issues of sea history need to be seen in the light of events and developments ashore at the same time that events ashore need to be complemented by the perspective from the sea. Linked in this way, maritime history becomes the vehicle of true global history.

Notes

1. IPCC 1996b, 294. Contrary to a common assertion, according to which "it is estimated that 50–70% of the global human population lives in the coastal zone," the population is rather land-bound.

2. Chester Starr, *The Influence of Sea Power on Ancient History* (Oxford: Oxford University Press, 1989), 11.

3. Ibid., 5.

4. Ibid., 6, 84.

5. This is adapted from the introduction in *Naval Policy and Strategy in the Mediterranean: Past, Present and Future,* ed. John Hattendorf (London: Frank Cass, 2000), xxi.

6. This section is adapted from chapter 15 of *Naval History and Maritime Strategy: Collected Essays,* ed. John Hattendorf (Malabar, Fla.: Robert Krieger, 2000), 253–66.

7. *Jane's Fighting Ships, 1946–47* (London: Jane's, 1947).

8. Captain Richard Sharpe, ed., *Jane's Fighting Ships, 1996–97* (London: Jane's, 1997).

9. See Jacob Børresen, "The Seapower of the Coastal State," *Journal of Strategic Studies* 17 (1994): 148–75.

10. Major J. P. Harvey, "Circumstance and Technology: The Effective Tasking and Use of Network-Based Assets," JMO course, Naval War College, February 2000.

→ 9 ←

Power and Domination

Europe and the Sea in the Middle Ages and the Renaissance

RICHARD W. UNGER

Europeans emphatically did not have command of the sea in the Middle Ages and the Renaissance, but that did not stop them from fighting at sea and fighting over the sea. The history of conflict at sea before the seventeenth century forms at the very least an informative backdrop to the appearance of navies. It also indicates the continuity that did exist, and, even more important, it shows which forces were at work to give navies the form that they finally developed. Traditionally, European naval history began in the seventeenth century, when there were navies and naval battles among European states. Starting with the naval wars in the waters around Britain among the English, Dutch, and French, though, ignores the long series of events that set the stage for the fighting between and among states.

The appropriation of the sea, the establishment of boundaries on the water, was something done by European governments in the High Middle Ages and reached a peak at the time of the Treaty of Tordesillas in 1494. In 1493, the pope, with little if any basis for his claimed authority, divided the world between Iberian colonizers with the bull *Dudum Siquidem*, a division recognized in the treaty between Castile and Portugal a year later.[1] Even in the thirteenth century, if not before, claims to power over bays and straits and seas around the continent of Europe led almost invariably to conflict among competing forces. European expansion predated 1492, and not just by a few decades. Even in the ninth century, people from the European continent pressed out from the mainland by sea. The various forays to other parts of the world, nearby or distant, were preceded by and based firmly on success at sea.

The second Christian millennium started with a European naval resurgence in the Mediterranean. By the end of the Middle Ages, and so halfway through that millennium, forays had become state-sponsored expeditions to dominate other lands and peoples. Maps reflected the change. The transformation was the basis for subsequent maritime developments and found its roots in the first effort at domination of the world's oceans.

No comprehensive theory of naval power in the Middle Ages exists.[2] The variety of conflicts at sea over time and in different parts of Europe and the paucity of sources about such conflicts makes the task of organizing such a theory daunting if not impossible. Obviously, modern views of naval power do not apply to those early attacks along the shores of the Mediterranean in the five centuries after the first signs of European expansion. Any appreciation of conflict at sea in the Middle Ages has to be derived from an understanding of the Europeans' concept of the sea and of the unique character of medieval naval forces and how they were used.

Any list of the principal factors influencing European naval practice in the Middle Ages must of necessity be speculative and probably inadequate since there was always a great variety in the actions of soldiers and sailors at sea. Such a list, however, would almost certainly describe the nature and evolution of politics on land in all of the European states, including the level and methods of taxation. Also listed would be the state of the economy; its growth, and the patterns of any such growth in production; and the ideas about the sea held by those in positions of political power. Since developments in the technology of ship design created new possibilities as well as placed constraints on what could be done at sea, this factor belongs on the list. Lastly, in the list would be a discussion of the environment—the terrain and the winds and currents at sea. Each of the factors on the list would influence all the others.

The list of factors shaping and driving the development of conflict at sea from 1000 to 1500 (or, more precisely, the span of time from the Scandinavian colonization of Iceland beginning in 870 and the departure of Columbus on his first voyage of discovery in 1492) is certainly a long one. Because of the differing physical environments and differing technological traditions, there was always a great difference between changes in the Mediterranean area and those in the Scandinavian area of Europe. In both parts of Europe, political, social, and economic chaos typified the late first millennium. The Roman Empire had controlled the Mediterranean Sea and even the Atlantic and North Sea shores of western Europe well into the fifth century. In the north, the withdrawal of the Romans left the seas open to anyone interested in exploiting them—and by any means. In the south, the Byzantine Empire tried to carry on the Roman practice of maintaining rule over the sea.

RICHARD W. UNGER

The emperor at Constantinople created a system of naval levies and taxes to support the navy, similar to what was in place to sustain land forces. The Byzantine Empire needed ships and sailors to fend off the powerful Muslim empire and needed them to protect commerce. Piracy, more or less well organized and more or less supported by governments, was always a part of medieval life at sea. The Byzantines took their role of providing security at sea seriously, including defense against pirates, at least in the eastern Mediterranean. Succeeding emperors set up fleets with bases spread around the shores of the empire, each fleet being responsible for a region but also available for major campaigns. Skilled seamen were to be kept in readiness, and salaried government officials, though few in number, were to see that the fleets were available when needed. Pressure at sea from Muslims to the south and east and later from the Kievan Russians to the north forced the Byzantines to expand their naval role. Commitment to naval forces varied with the emperors and with internal politics and the fortunes of the empire.[3] There was a series of successes in the tenth century, most notably retaking the island of Crete from Muslim pirates in 960 and 961, but those successes evaporated, largely because of bad government and internal dissension, by the late eleventh century.

At the same time in the north, Scandinavian pirates who called themselves Vikings proved a terror to people living near any sea or river anywhere in northern Europe, from Spain to Russia to Iceland. Those sailors employed ships of superior design to get them to many different places to trade and to raid. The distinction between the two was often lost on them. They pushed farther afield, along the rivers of eastern Europe and out into the Atlantic Ocean, than any of their predecessors. In the eleventh century, most Scandinavians joined Europe, at least nominally, by becoming Christians.[4] It was a very clear sign of their incorporation into what was becoming an increasingly European cultural identity. As their ties with Rome and with other centers of Latin Christendom increased, they brought with them the aggressive maritime expansion and overseas and overland colonization that had typified the late first Christian millennium in the northern parts of the continent.

There was greater stability at sea from the eleventh century on, but that did not mean an absence of violence. Naval primacy in the Mediterranean shifted to the mercantile centers of Italy.[5] Many of those towns were successful in piracy to start and used that success as a foundation for commercial expansion and for prosperity. The piratical raids, when they were successful, served to promote a pattern of investment in warships with the anticipation of gain. Putting funds into fighting was perceived as legitimate and, if the attacks were directed against Muslims, even laudable. Pisa and Genoa might be the best known of the aggressors, but they were by no means unique, among either Christians or Muslims. Just as in the north, violent acts could go on side by side with peaceful exchange. Both served to increase interest in the sea and expansion of the naval potential in Italian towns.

At about the same time, Danish kings set up a form of naval levy to supply fighting ships from different districts along their coasts. The militia was to keep the sea lanes open. The Scandinavian system was hardly well organized and did not prove durable. It was much more a product of a policy of conquest in the late twelfth and early thirteenth centuries when the kings of Denmark found themselves with an empire.[6] For expeditions at some distance from their shores, the kings relied on hired ships or independent suppliers of ships, that is, naval entrepreneurs. Such entrepreneurial warfare was a pattern that was to be common in the High and even into the Late Middle Ages and even more in the south than in the north. The suppliers were often nobles or aristocrats, men like the ones who supplied forces on land to their governments. While governments would find private operators to supply ships and men in wartime, in the years without overt conflict, those same governments would protect their coasts, trying to stop theft at sea and to prevent smuggling. For the concept of smuggling to exist at all, there had to be government taxes on goods taken in or out of the jurisdiction. Governments had to have authority to levy duties and had to have some ability to enforce their will. More important, though, there had to be some trade for governments to tax. A growing volume of trade, governments powerful enough and well organized enough to levy taxes on it, and taxes that individuals wanted to avoid characterized the early years of the second Christian millennium. Trade and taxes on trade became common in both northern and southern Europe by the High Middle Ages.

The naval forces of Italian towns, especially from Genoa and Venice, came to dominate the Mediterranean by the late thirteenth century. As the design of ships changed, towns created their own naval shipyards that produced and maintained purpose-built naval vessels. The arsenal at Venice dates from 1104. The one at Barcelona from 1284. One even appeared in the north at Rouen in 1294 to supply galleys for the French king to use in wars against England.[7] Galleys were one of the principal driving forces for the building of arsenals. As they became more specialized and as they evolved, sacrificing cargo space for manpower to get greater speed and maneuverability, they became less useful in trade. If governments of Italian towns, and for that matter the king of France, wanted to deploy galleys, they had in the thirteenth century and beyond to build and maintain such vessels themselves. Private individuals could and still did supply warships just so long as those vessels could be used for trade and earn a return to owners in peacetime. Governments still turned to cargo vessels in time of war, renting them or impressing them. That was true as much in England and France as it was along the shores of the Mediterranean.

Probably from 1294 and certainly after 1353, the wars between Venice and Genoa took on different attributes. The arsenal at Venice began to produce bigger galleys, while the private shipyards in both city-states produced larger sailing ships. In the wars of the thirteenth century, each side set out to destroy the fleets, naval and commercial, of the other. Blockading took the place of piracy. Sporadic individual attacks were replaced by actions of fleets, mobilized at great expense, to attack enemy strong points or engage enemy fleets. The wars became battles over control of strategic points. Those sites, well known to contemporaries, were created by geography and, by definition, by the trade that passed the strategic points. The design of trading ships had an influence as well, since the type of ship and its capabilities had a determining effect on the routes chosen. The greater intensity of trade tended to concentrate exchange and so limit the number of strategic points. The greater variety of ships and improvements in navigation in the thirteenth century tended to increase the number of strategic points as shippers found themselves with greater flexibility.[8] Though both contestants tried to find allies on land, the outcome of the contests between Genoa and Venice depended completely on naval victory or defeat. Venice would prevail in the end because Venice won on the water.

In both the south and the north in the High Middle Ages, the volume of trade grew. The long-term development of the economy meant a rise in demand for goods. Technical improvements in transportation made it profitable to move even such relatively bulky goods as timber, grain, and salt. At sea, the cog, a vessel of Celtic design originating in northern Europe, evolved by the late thirteenth century into an effective bulk carrier. It was roomy and capable of long voyages on the open ocean. In fact, the size and handling qualities of the cog made standing out to sea and avoiding the coasts a good idea. By 1300, the cog was known in the Mediterranean, where it would be subject over time to extensive modification. While it took a considerable crew to handle its single large square sail, the cog still could carry a broad range of commodities economically, commodities that typically had not entered trade before. The cog was not the only efficient bulk carrier, and shippers found themselves with an expanding variety of options to move trade goods. For merchants and shippers of cargoes with lower value per unit of volume, it was necessary to move significantly larger quantities of the goods along fixed routes at fixed times in order to make a profit. As trade moved away from the coasts, there was a tendency for naval warfare to move as well.

Northern Europe in the thirteenth and fourteenth centuries knew virtually no naval organization. Naval forces were made up, with few exceptions, of impressed cargo ships that served as transports and also as fighting ships, many of them cogs. Any arrangements to deploy naval forces were temporary. Battles were few, and piracy and reprisals were common. The new and bigger ships such as the cog made naval warfare even more like land warfare on floating platforms. The establishment in the fourteenth century of the Hanseatic League, a group of trading towns banded together to protect their interests at sea, failed to generate any sort of permanent administrative structures. It would be in the emerging kingdoms of western Europe that such institutions were to be first found.

The differing patterns in the North and Baltic Seas and in the Mediterranean converged, creating common naval practice with common goals in the fifteenth and sixteenth centuries. The emergence of very similar policies and institutions throughout Europe was mirrored by the emergence of a new and common understanding about the sea and policies that governments should hold toward the sea. The merging of European practice arose from changes in the technology of shipbuilding, related developments in weapons technology, a cross-fertilization with easier and more extensive exchange of information, and some new ways of discussing and understanding what governments were to do. All of these changes were worked out, as always, in an interplay with the environment.

In a series of steps, European shipwrights developed the full-rigged ship, a vessel with a hull similar to a cog but with a rig that combined square sails with a triangular lateen one. The hull built in the Mediterranean style, with planks abutting and strength coming from the interior frame, made the vessel lighter than a cog of similar size. The rig gave greater maneuverability and an ability to negotiate in less favorable winds. Over little more than a century, the full-rigged ship became the generic deep-sea sailing vessel of the entire region. It drove oar-powered vessels, galleys, out of naval warfare, at least on the rough North Sea and Atlantic Ocean and sharply diminished their role in the Baltic and Mediterranean. The exception was the use of galleys in amphibious operations.[9] Amphibious warfare was always a part of medieval naval warfare, but it declined in the fifteenth and sixteenth centuries with the evolution of the sailing fighting ship.

The greater maneuverability and carrying capacity made the full-rigged ship superior for combat. If that was not enough, such vessels were soon equipped with gunpowder arms. The development of ever more reliable, lighter, and cheaper cannons was certainly a slow process, one not really complete until after 1600, when big warships carried dozens of iron guns that could be fired rapidly. Even by the 1540s, though, the change in ship design and the addition of guns created a ship suited to war, able to stay at sea much longer than its predecessors, and one capable of inflicting much greater damage on any enemy. The new types of vessels made it possible to conceive a plan to protect domestic shipping by eliminating the naval forces of a potential enemy. From that new power, and from the growing power of self-conscious sovereign states, emerged the idea of domination of the sea.

Even in the fourteenth century, there had been mention of the kings of England as *roys des mer*. It was only a passing comment and seems to have had no impact on any policy.[10] At about the same time, there were claims from a Catalan chronicler about his king needing to rule the sea.[11] In the early fifteenth century, an English government bureaucrat wrote a long poem about the need to defend the island kingdom on the seas.[12] It was in the mid-sixteenth century, however, that a senior official in the Low Countries recommended that his ruler, Charles V, gain mastery of the sea as the proper goal of government policy on trade, shipping, and commerce. The author, Cornelis De Scepper, was a humanist with the advantage of a classical education and a knowledge of and facility with language to express the novel concept. He was also an old soldier who perhaps brought ideas of territorial domination from land warfare to bear on matters to do with the sea. His thoughts and his expression of them were also the product of new possibilities created in the sixteenth century by the loosening of the constraints of political organization, the technology of shipbuilding, the economy, and the relationship of shipping with the environment.[13] By 1600, naval warfare was not yet that of the eighteenth century, but in some places, most notably in the Baltic, there were all of the features of the titanic naval struggles between Britain and France of 200 years later.[14] There was also extensive convoying of lightly armed or unarmed fishing vessels and cargo ships by specialized warships, another typical pattern of later naval and maritime practice. The change in thinking was mirrored once again in maps, with cartographers populating their charts with ships, vessels that might dominate the sea.

The examination of changes in and interaction of various forces impinging on conflict at sea in the Middle Ages suggests rather loose groupings of medieval naval warfare. Though by no means precise, in either dating or their common features, there still seem to have been roughly three periods.

The first period began around 1000, with the counterattack by Europeans against Muslims and the incorporation of Vikings into what was being called by contemporaries "Europe." It was marked by expansion at sea preceding expansion on land and by the use of geography in combination with technology to gain an advantage over the elements as well as potential enemies.

The second phase or period began around 1250 in the Mediterranean but also to some degree in the north as well. Bases began to appear to meet supply problems. Supply was always critical for naval forces. The increase in the scale of naval conflict alone pushed forward such developments. In the north, naval wars (typically with few if any pitched battles) were largely wars of supply. In the south, wars were fought more for the control of strategic points for trade. The agents in the wars, the Italian maritime republics and the other protagonists, generated large naval forces and programs for maintaining those forces and revitalizing them in peacetime. Venice even went so far as to establish a complex structure for a state-owned fleet of trading galleys in order to promote trade and create a naval force that could be pressed into service when needed.[15] The towns produced something that looked very much like standing navies with bases to support them. There was throughout Europe, and more obviously in the south, an interdependence of trade and naval power. Venice was the most extreme example, but Venice was not alone.

The third period began around 1500. The voyages of discovery from Iberia down the coast of Africa and on to India and to the New World are a clear indication of a new era in the history of naval conflict. It was much more the ability of Europeans to win naval battles and to supply outposts at great distances in hostile surroundings and often among hostile people that distinguishes the sixteenth century and separates Renaissance naval warfare from that of the Middle Ages. The naval victories won in the Indian Ocean in the first decade of the sixteenth century by small Portuguese squadrons against overwhelming odds were a dramatic sign of the change in conflict at sea.[16] Ships would no longer grapple with each other to create something like a land battle but would stand off and exchange gunfire, trying to disable or destroy each other without having to board. Naval warfare took on a whole new character. A new understanding of sea power emerged in northern Europe in the Renaissance. The circumstances of conflict at sea had changed. With the new conditions also came a novel interpretation and understanding of the situation European states faced. The popular decorated and illustrated maps of the world's oceans showed how the oceans had become another site for the political struggle among the governments of Europe and made those oceans an arena of conflict.

Notes

1. Carla Rahn Phillips and William D. Phillips Jr., *The Worlds of Christopher Columbus* (Cambridge: Cambridge University Press, 1992), 187–88.

2. For a treatment of the subject from a number of different perspectives, see John Hattendorf and Richard W. Unger, eds., *Power and Domination: Europe and Armed Force at Sea during the Middle Ages and the Renaissance* (Woodbridge, England: Boydell and Brewer, 2002).

3. See, for example, Hélène Ahrweiler, *Byzance et la mer: La marine de guerre, la politique, et les institutions maritimes de Byzance aux VIIe–XVe siècles* (Paris: Presses universitaires de France, 1966). See also Ekkehard Eickhoff, *Seekrieg und seepolitik zwischen Islam und Abendland das Mittelmer unter Byzantischer und Arabischer hegemonie (650–1040)* (Berlin: Walter De Gruyter, 1966).

4. There are many treatments of the history of Scandinavia in the age of expansion. See, for example, Gwyn Jones, *A History of the Vikings* (New York: Oxford University Press, 1984).

5. In general, see John H. Pryor, *Geography, Technology, and War: Studies in the Maritime History of the Mediterranean, 649–1571* (Cambridge: Cambridge University Press, 1988).

6. Niels Lund, *Lid, leding og Landeværn Hær og samfund i Danmark i ældre middelalder* (Roskilde, Denmark: Vikingeskibshallen, 1996).

7. Felipe Fernández-Armesto, "Naval Warfare after the Viking Age, c. 1100–1500," in *Medieval Warfare: A History*, ed. Maurice Keen (Oxford: Oxford University Press, 1999), 235.

8. John E. Dotson, "Naval Strategy in the First Genoese-Venetian War, 1257–1270," *American Neptune* 46 (1986): 84–90; and Frederic C. Lane, "The Economic Meaning of the Invention of the Compass," *American Historical Review* 68 (1963): 605–17, reprinted in *Venice and History: The Collected Papers of Frederic C. Lane* (Baltimore: Johns Hopkins University Press, 1966), 331–44.

9. On the use of galleys in a world of full-rigged ships, see John F. Guilmartin, *Gunpowder and Galleys: Changing Technology and Mediterranean Warfare in the Sixteenth Century* (Cambridge: Cambridge University Press, 1974).

10. Michael Oppenheim, *A History of the Administration of the Royal Navy* (London: John Lane, 1896), 6.

11. Fernández-Armesto, "Naval Warfare after the Viking Age," 242–43.

12. Sir George Warner, ed., *The Libelle of Englyshe Polycye: A Poem on the Use of Sea-Power, 1436* (Oxford: Oxford University Press, 1926).

13. James D. Tracy, "Herring Wars: The Habsburg Netherlands and the Struggle

for Control of the North Sea, ca. 1520–1560," *Sixteenth Century Journal* 24 (1993): 254–70.

14. See Jan Glete, *Warfare at Sea, 1500–1650: Maritime Conflicts and the Transformation of Europe* (London: Routledge, 2000).

15. Frederic C. Lane, "Merchant Galleys, 1300–1334: Private and Communal Operation," *Speculum* 38 (1963): 179–205, reprinted in *Venice and History: The Collected Papers of Frederic C. Lane* (Baltimore: Johns Hopkins University Press, 1966), 193–226.

16. See Carlo Cipolla, *European Culture and Overseas Expansion* (Harmondsworth, England: Pelican, 1970), 99–106.

Oceanic Space and the Creation of a Global International System, 1450–1800

ELIZABETH MANCKE

Early modern European expansion (1450–1800) was in fundamental ways an oceanic experience, a mastery of watery space. Profoundly and irreversibly, the major expanding powers—Spain, Portugal, the Netherlands, France, and Britain—politicized and militarized the world's oceans, making them interconnected arenas of conflict over which they attempted to extend their control.[1] In its entirety, this development was new, although we can identify elements of it in other times and places. Prior to European overseas colonization, Austronesians had been the world's great seafaring migrants, settling islands from Rapa Nui (Easter Island) to Madagascar, but they had not maintained the political connections to their hearth societies necessary for oceanic empires.[2] In the fifteenth century, the Chinese had demonstrated the ability to send a naval expedition of thousands of sailors as far as East Africa, but the Chinese emperor decided to dismantle the navy and concentrate on a territorial empire.[3] Muslim traders had carried their wares and religion, but not their political ties, from the Arabian Peninsula to the South China Sea.[4] The early modern empires of Eurasia, whether the Ottoman, Safavid, Mughal, Russian, or Ming, had extended their power by absorbing neighboring territories. None, however, were significant naval powers. In the sixteenth century, the Ottomans developed a navy for the Red Sea and Persian Gulf to counter the Portuguese attempt to control trade through those waters, but the Ottomans never used that navy to support transoceanic expansion.[5]

It is the combination of characteristics (the linkages of political power to transoceanic trade, colonization, and piracy) that makes early modern European empire building a significantly new historical phenomenon.[6] The expanding European powers defined the world's oceans, and not just territo-

rial waters, as political space over which they attempted to exert their jurisdiction, although the nature of that jurisdiction was tenuous, ill defined,
and under frequent negotiation. Before the mid-eighteenth century, early
modern Europeans occupied very little territory in Africa and Asia, and
most land in the Americas was still controlled on a daily basis by indigenous
polities, claims of Europeans notwithstanding.[7] Europeans controlled the
oceans far more successfully, although in the Indian Ocean and South
China Sea, regional powers soon developed strategies for curbing European
pretensions.

There is nothing "natural" or intrinsically obvious about this politicization of the oceans in spite of present-day perceptions. One of the most important changes that the Portuguese introduced into the centuries-old trade
of the Indian Ocean was the idea that suzerainty, if not sovereignty, over the
oceans could be claimed.[8] Connected to this new politicization of the oceans
was the rather remarkable assertion that a monarch's control could reach
across thousands of miles of ocean and around continents, complemented
by its widespread acceptance among Europeans.

This chapter explores how Europeans defined the oceans as a new kind
of political space and argues that this development is a critical link between
early modern state formation and empire building and the emerging definition of a global international system in the early modern era.[9] It makes four
broad points. The first is that the international negotiations over the oceans,
and the extra-European world more generally, created an arena of diplomatic affairs that quickly became more secular and less dynastic than intra-
European affairs, and hence manifested characteristics of the modern state
system earlier than we normally date them. Second, the new importance of
the oceans and their regulation reinforced the coalescence of state power.
Third, the centrality of oceans to these new empires and the small number
of players who regulated their use made global governance a matter of interstate negotiation from which non-Europeans were excluded. Fourth, it was
the profitability of overseas commerce that ultimately made these empires
viable, thus undergirding the ability of mercantile wealth to jockey with
landed wealth in defining the role of the state.[10]

The politicization of the oceans received a foundational, although con-
tested, definition in a series of papal bulls and Luso-Spanish treaties at the
end of the fifteenth and beginning of the sixteenth centuries. The best
known, the 1494 Treaty of Tordesillas, divided the non-Christian world between the Portuguese and the Spanish on a north-south line 370 leagues
west of the Cape Verde Islands. Defining jurisdictional authority over the
territorial waters of seas—whether the North Sea, the Mediterranean, the

Black Sea, the Persian Gulf, or the Red Sea—had an ancient legacy, but the line described in the Treaty of Tordesillas, far from any shore, was new.[11] The treaty, based on four papal bulls issued by Alexander VI in 1493, attempted to mitigate the militarized competition between the Portuguese and the Castilians that had frequently flared after the discovery, conquest, and settlement of the Azores, Madeiras, Canaries, and Cape Verde Islands earlier in the century. It was also intended to preclude conflicts over Portuguese interests in Africa and Castilian interests in the lands newly discovered by Christopher Columbus.[12]

Controversies over the applicability of the Treaty of Tordesillas in specific areas soon developed. Despite a 1495 agreement between the Spanish and Portuguese that they would send out navigators and astronomers to determine the line of demarcation from the Arctic to Antarctic, not until 1512 did either country undertake such an expedition, by which time further Portuguese exploration and claims had complicated the issue.[13] In 1500, Pedro Alvarez Cabral landed in Brazil, which the Portuguese claimed lay on the eastern side of the line of Tordesillas. In the North Atlantic, the Corte-Real brothers claimed that the fishing grounds off Newfoundland lay in Portuguese territory. Meanwhile, in 1498, Vasco da Gama reached India by sailing around Africa, thereby transforming the issue of an eastern line of demarcation from a theoretical to a practical problem. Exploiting their control of the eastern sea route to Asia, the Portuguese claimed the Spice Islands in the South China Sea, aware that they possibly lay in Spanish territory were the line of demarcation to be extended around the world.

In 1519, a disgruntled Portuguese sea captain, Ferdinand Magellan, approached the Spanish crown with a proposal to reach the Spice Islands by sailing west. The success of Magellan's expedition (1519–22), even though he died in the Philippines, precipitated a heated rivalry between the Portuguese and Spanish over their respective claims in Southeast Asia. Spanish plans to settle colonists in the Moluccas were delayed first by Portuguese protests about incursions in their territory and then by Spain's pending war with France and England in Europe. To raise money for the latter, Charles V agreed to accept 350,000 ducats from the Portuguese in exchange for relinquishing the Spanish right to the Moluccas. The 1529 Treaty of Zaragoza confirmed the arrangement and established a pole-to-pole line of demarcation seventeen degrees east of the Moluccas.[14]

This Iberian division of the world contributed to two distinct arenas and dynamics of oceanic conflict in the sixteenth century. The proximity of the Atlantic arena to Europe encouraged the French, English, and, later, the Dutch to contest Iberian claims to hegemony through exploration, piracy, commercial interloping, and diplomatic negotiation. Few non-Iberians, however, sailed beyond the Atlantic basin in the sixteenth century, save for the odd voyage, such as Sir Francis Drake's circumnavigation of the world in 1585 and 1586. The Pacific remained largely unutilized by Europeans until the Spanish settled the Philippines in the 1560s and began regular shipments of bullion from Acapulco to Manila. In the Indian Ocean, where the Portuguese were the only significant European presence during the sixteenth century, Luso-Asian interaction shaped its own distinctive dynamic of politicization.

When the Portuguese rounded the Cape of Good Hope into the Indian Ocean, they entered waters known and traversed by sailors for centuries but largely unmilitarized. The land-based empires bordering on the Indian Ocean or neighboring seas—in particular the emerging Safavid and Mughal empires—did not have navies. This seeming lack of political interest in oceanic control, despite a vibrant maritime economy, can be explained in varying measure by ideology, the geopolitics of Asia, opportunity, and technology. The political power of the land-based empires depended on wealth derived from land and the control of the people who worked it. Commerce, in contrast, functioned at the political margins, and rulers had long accorded merchant communities considerable political autonomy, both in Europe and Asia.[15] As the sultan of Gujarat remarked, "Wars by sea are merchants' affairs, and of no concern to the prestige of kings."[16] In southeastern and western Asia and East Africa, small coastal states (such as Melaka, Hurmuz, and Kilwa) depended on revenues derived from trade, but that commercial basis of fiscal policy did not generally include the politicization and militarization of maritime space.[17] Most Asian rulers shared the opinion of Sultan Ala'uddin of Makassar that God had intended the sea to be used in common and considered it "unheard of that anyone should be forbidden to sail the seas."[18]

Technology influenced the place of the Portuguese in the geopolitics of Asia. In the late fifteenth century, when the Portuguese first sailed into the Indian Ocean, Asian ships did not carry heavy artillery. For sailing in the western Indian Ocean, Asians built ships by lashing together wood with fiber ropes, designed to weather the pounding of the seas but not of cannons. These ships were well suited to trade but not to the artillery-dependent military engagements that the Portuguese introduced into Asian waters.[19] Southeast Asians built large ships (250 to 1,000 tons) with wood-pegged, multisheathed hulls that could withstand cannon fire but were not generally armed for naval engagements.[20]

When the Portuguese used their armed vessels to seize control of islands and ports, they initially met with little Asian resistance. They claimed control over the Indian Ocean's trade routes and focused their resources not on expansive territorial conquests but on the licensing of maritime travel, a regulation of oceanic traffic that had no equivalent in Asian practice.[21] To effect this objective, they captured key ports, such as Goa, Hurmuz, Diu, and Melaka. In some instances, they negotiated trading concessions with local rulers, such as at Surat. The primary organizing principle for harnessing these scattered holdings stretching from East Africa to India and Japan was control of the sea lanes.[22]

Merchant resistance and insufficient resources to coerce thousands of mariners, however, blunted the impact of Portuguese ambitions. Rather than pay for the protection that Portuguese licenses provided, many merchants relocated to Asian-controlled ports. After the Portuguese capture of Melaka in 1511, Gujarati merchants left the city and organized anti-Portuguese actions in other Asian ports. The Keling (Hindu) merchants of Melaka, on the other hand, allied themselves with the Portuguese and provided them assistance in spreading their trade network into ports along the Bay of Bengal. When the Mughal emperor Akbar conquered Gujarat in 1572, he willingly agreed to the Portuguese demand that his ships, many sailing for the annual pilgrimage to Mecca, carry a Portuguese-issued *cartaz* or license.[23]

Asian rulers employed various strategies to curb these newcomers' aggrandizement of power. In the 1520s, the Ming prohibited the Portuguese from trading on the Chinese shore.[24] The Ottomans expanded their naval fleet to keep open the Red Sea route to the Levant after the Portuguese blocked it and to limit Portuguese influence in the Persian Gulf.[25] The Acehnese sultanate, founded in northern Sumatra in the early sixteenth century, organized a trading network between the Indonesian archipelago and South Asia that challenged Portuguese dominance in the intra-Asian trades.[26] The configuration of regional power also constrained the Portuguese. The possession of Hurmuz accorded the Portuguese considerable strategic power in the Persian Gulf trade, but they could not risk offending the Safavids by cutting off that trade or overreaching their sphere of influence. In the long run, peaceful accommodation was more profitable than coercion, and the Portuguese became just another player in the Asian trades.[27]

The Portuguese attempt to claim sovereignty over the Indian Ocean had its greatest European consequence when the Dutch, English, and French arrived, and not because these later European arrivals more successfully subdued their Asian hosts.[28] Like their Portuguese forerunners, they found themselves accommodating Asian practices as well as being drawn into Asian power struggles.[29] In Surat, a major port on the west coast of India, the Mughal emperor granted the English East India Company (EIC) trading rights in an attempt to check the Portuguese, whom he subsequently expelled from the city in 1632. In Persia, the EIC provided Shah Abbas the necessary naval support to oust the Portuguese from Hurmuz in 1622.[30] The Japanese revoked Portuguese trading privileges in Nagasaki in 1634, transferring them to the Dutch East India Company (VOC) instead.[31]

Military decisions and diplomatic negotiations, in these instances, were made between Asian rulers and European officials resident in Asia, whether Portuguese viceroys or officials of the VOC or EIC. This delegation of diplomacy, including the negotiation and ratification of treaties, regionalized international relations between Asians and Europeans by keeping them separate from multilateral European affairs.[32] In contrast to the regionally specific resolution of Euro-Asian conflicts in Asia, many, if not most, intra-European conflicts were negotiated in Europe and influenced multilateral relations, particularly concerning maritime rights and the political and legal definition of oceanic space. During the early modern period, struggles among European rivals in far distant parts of the globe had a much greater impact on the long-term development of international relations than did Euro-Asian, Euro-African, or Euro-American relations.

The signal event that linked developments in the Indian and Atlantic basins was the 1604 capture of a Portuguese ship by the VOC in the waters around the Spice Islands. Chartered in 1602, the VOC was sufficiently capitalized to arm its ships heavily and to challenge the Portuguese militarily. In response to the Dutch threat, the Spanish, who had occupied the Portuguese throne since 1580, claimed that the Dutch were in exclusively Portuguese waters by the terms of the Treaty of Tordesillas. In Europe, this incident gained further import by being wrapped into the Spanish and Dutch negotiations that led to the twelve-year truce (1609–21) in the civil war in the Netherlands. In 1609, the VOC hired the legal theorist, Hugo Grotius, to prepare a legal brief on this piracy charge. In the resulting treatise, *Mare Liberum,* Grotius argued from natural law that the seas were free to the navigation of all people, and no power should restrain that right. The publication of *Mare Liberum* coincided with Anglo-Dutch negotiations over fishing rights in British waters, and the English interpreted the Asian incident as a Dutch pretense for pressing their interests in the North Atlantic waters around Britain. There ensued a century of political and legal writing, as well as diplomatic maneuvering, on the question of whether, and to what extent, any power could claim *dominium,* or property rights, to maritime waters.[33]

ELIZABETH MANCKE

The incident of the Dutch capture of a Portuguese vessel in Asian waters and the publication of *Mare Liberum* conjoined questions of the Indian Ocean as political space with the politicization of maritime space in the Atlantic basin.

Unlike the centuries-old navigation of the Indian Ocean, the more recent and regular crossings of the Atlantic Ocean were a European development. Consequently, neither the Portuguese nor the Spanish faced existing contenders to their claims to control transatlantic navigation. By the same token, there was no existing maritime traffic that they could license and regulate. Rather, they established colonies and sought commerce with local peoples: the Portuguese in Africa and Brazil and the Spanish in the Caribbean basin. Fishermen from both countries frequented the North Atlantic fishing banks. The first serious challenges to the Iberians came from French mariners, who in the first three decades of the sixteenth century had appeared in Newfoundland waters, the Antilles, Africa, and the East Indies. The depredations of corsairs prompted the Castilian Cortés to complain to the French crown in 1523 and 1525. Unmoved by these protests, Francis I of France sponsored Giovanni Verrazano's exploration of the North American coastline in 1524, followed by an attempt at a colony in Brazil in 1530, and Jacques Cartier's first voyage down the St. Lawrence in 1534.[34]

In response to Iberian complaints of French encroachments on their territory, Francis I responded that navigation of the seas was open to all nations, as well as articulated the principle that claims to extra-European territory had to be accompanied by the settlement of subjects. Discovery and papal grants were not sufficient to establish an uncontestable claim.[35] After the late 1550s, these two principles became the ones by which the French and English repeatedly challenged the Iberians' claims, but before then the primacy of European affairs and the marginality of transatlantic ventures made the French and the English, as well as the Iberians, willing to make concessions. The Portuguese sought to protect their mariners from French pirates by agreeing in 1536 that they could use the Azores to prey on Spanish shipping. When that measure failed to deter French corsairs from preying on Portuguese vessels, the Portuguese and Spanish signed a treaty in 1552 to join forces to fight piracy. In a truce signed in 1556, France tentatively agreed with Spain to restrain French navigation to the Indies. Mary Tudor, Queen of England and wife of Philip II of Spain, accepted Iberian claims and prohibited English merchants from trading to Africa. Thus, for the first half of the sixteenth century, it appeared that the Portuguese and Spanish might be able to get other powers to agree to their extra-European claims.

With the accession of Elizabeth I to the throne in 1558, the English consistently challenged Iberian assertions of hegemony in the extra-European world. Responding to Portuguese demands to prohibit her subjects from trading in Guinea, Elizabeth informed Dom Joao II that he should keep Africans from trading with the English if they were, indeed, his subjects. A lack of African obeisance would signal the limits of Portuguese sovereignty. Despite Portuguese naval patrols, trade retaliation, and confiscation of English property in Lisbon, Elizabeth refused to concede that Portugal could legally restrict her subjects' access to Africa, and by extension Asia and the Americas.[36]

Elizabethan defiance of the Portuguese influenced French negotiators of the 1559 Treaty of Cateau-Cambrésis. In the litany of French wartime infractions, the Spanish included commercial interloping in the Caribbean that French diplomats rebutted with claims to freedom of navigation. Spain, unwilling to acknowledge the French position and thereby cede exclusive Iberian sovereignty of Atlantic waters and American land, yet anxious for peace in Europe, agreed that the treaty would apply only in Europe. Europe was defined by "lines of amity," an east-west line along the Tropic of Cancer and a north-south line just east of the Azores. Those lines of amity subsequently became customary text in treaties to distinguish between conflicts in European and extra-European space and to define the times when the terms of treaties would activate in specific regions. This practice reinforced a diplomatic notion that a significant difference existed between affairs in Europe and those in the rest of the world.[37]

By 1560, French and English challenges to Iberian pretensions, particularly their rejection of papal authority to adjudicate claims to the non-Christian world, had secularized negotiations over the extra-European world, both land and water, by elevating the adjudicating authority of interstate negotiations at the expense of the pope. The persistent unwillingness of the Iberians, but especially the Spanish, to accept the French and English positions, subsequently supported by the Dutch, Swedes, and Danes, was to perpetuate and reinforce the need for European interstate negotiations in defining the extra-European world. The three-centuries-long European debate over Iberian claims to the world's oceans Europeanized the discourse over the definition of extra-European space and effectively precluded the inclusion of non-Europeans.[38]

The challenges to Iberian hegemony made the extra-European world into new environments in which early modern Europeans confronted each other, as much as they confronted Africans, Asians, and Americans. The oceans were a primary environment of contest. Significantly, Spain contended that when it acknowledged non-Iberian settlements in the Americas, beginning with concessions to the Dutch in the 1648 Treaty of Munster, it ceded only rights to land.[39] The right of oceanic transit between home societies and colonies was a privilege the Spanish granted, a position evocative of sixteenth-century Portuguese practices in Asia. Spain held that the Atlantic Ocean west of the line established with the Treaty of Tordesillas and the Pacific Ocean, remained its territories, and other Europeans used them at Spanish sufferance.

This point may seem just one of those quaint expressions of national chauvinism that had little larger relevance, but it was not. Rather, this Spanish position influenced economic, political, and military relations in the Atlantic into the mid-eighteenth century. In order to maintain a domestic policy that was consistent with foreign policy, Spain negotiated commercial treaties for the supply of African slaves to Spanish America rather than violate Portuguese space by engaging in the slave trade. The *asiento*, the right to supply slaves to the Spanish colonies, became a fiercely negotiated economic prize after the Portuguese conceded the rights of other Europeans to engage in the African slave trade as part of their diplomacy to restore the Portuguese crown. Spain granted the *asiento* first to the Dutch in 1648, then the French, and after 1713 to the British. Spain's continued claims to the oceans, even when it gave up claims to land, emphasizes the importance of maritime space to the structure of international power and Spain's attempt to use oceanic control to remain the preeminent imperial power, the "lords of all the world."[40]

The freedom of navigation espoused by the French and the English in the sixteenth century largely ended in the seventeenth century, to reemerge in the eighteenth.[41] It is not difficult to see that initially freedom of the seas served their strategic interests vis-à-vis the Iberians. The principle provided diplomatic and political justification for pirates and interloping merchants of both countries to challenge the Iberians.[42] During the wars of the 1580s and 1590s, both England and France issued letters of marque for privateers to prey on Iberian shipping, thereby undermining Spanish war efforts on the continent. After James Stuart succeeded his cousin Elizabeth Tudor on the English throne, the more exclusive Scottish policy on royal claims to territorial waters became English policy. Elizabeth I had asserted *imperium*, or royal jurisdiction, over the waters surrounding England and Ireland, but not *dominium*, or a property right in them. In Scotland, the crown claimed both *imperium* and *dominium*. Based on this claim of *dominium*, James I closed the waters around England, as well as those to the north around Spitzbergen, to Dutch fishermen in 1609. So exclusively were these claims of *dominium* interpreted in Scotland that the Scots argued that James VI did not have the royal right to open Scottish waters to English fishermen just because he was also James I in England. Charles I continued his father's policy of claiming both *imperium* and *dominium* over maritime space and extended his claims westward to the waters off North America.[43]

The Dutch, meanwhile, maintained a policy of freedom of the seas, which they honored in the breach, especially in the waters around the Spice Islands. The states of Holland passed a secret resolve in 1608 to support freedom of the seas, and subsequently pressured the States General to pass a similar resolution, which it did in 1645. As the premier shippers of seventeenth-century Europe, the Dutch were particularly concerned to sort out the rights of neutral shipping (arguing for the most limited rights of search and seizure) and to determine what constituted contraband.[44] The principle of *mare liberum,* or free seas, against claims of *mare clausum,* or closed seas, had received its first global exposition by Hugo Grotius in the early seventeenth century, who based his argument on natural law. The most famous rebuttal to him came from the English theorist John Selden, who argued the legitimacy of *mare clausum,* thereby providing justification for Stuart and, later, Commonwealth policy. His explication of claims over territorial waters set the basis for the subsequent sorting out of territorial limits. The British returned to a policy of freedom of the seas in 1689 with the Glorious Revolution and the crowning of Mary Stuart and her Dutch husband, William of Orange.[45]

Freedom of the seas remained a disputed international principle through the eighteenth century. One of the primary disagreements between Spain and Britain that led to war in 1739 was over navigation in the Atlantic. Beginning in the 1720s, the Spanish *guarda costa* aggressively patrolled Caribbean waters, frequently seizing British trading vessels on the contention that they were sailing on routes unnecessary to reach British colonial holdings. That issue was closely connected to the contract for the *asiento* that the Spanish had granted to the British in 1713, and to the emergence of British merchants as the principle suppliers of manufactured goods to all colonies in the Caribbean, including the Spanish. Trade in manufactured goods, often done under the guise of the slave trade, gave the Spanish further justification for seizing British shipping. The question of freedom of navigation in the Atlantic was largely resolved in 1750, when the Spanish and the Portuguese negotiated a treaty that made "null and void" those parts of the Treaty of Tordesillas pertaining to the "line of demarcation." That treaty complemented another that year signed by Spain and Britain sorting out trading rights in the Caribbean and voiding the British contract for the *asiento.*[46]

ELIZABETH MANCKE

In the mid-eighteenth century, as Spain relinquished its claims to determine navigation in the Atlantic, the international dispute over the control of the oceans shifted to the Pacific, which until then had remained peripheral to European ambitions. After the Treaty of Zaragoza (1529), the Pacific served as a barrier between Portuguese claims in Asia and Spanish claims in the Americas. Then, in 1559, Philip II ordered the viceroy of New Spain to send out people to settle the Philippines. Six years later, an expedition under the command of Miguel López de Legazpi landed in the Philippines and began a settlement that would be the westernmost jurisdiction of the viceroyalty of New Spain. One of the greatest impediments to the colony's success was the lack of an easterly route for sailing from the Philippines to Mexico. Spanish navigators soon determined that by sailing to about thirty degrees north latitude they would pick up trade winds that would carry them across the Pacific and land them in the vicinity of Acapulco. The annual Acapulco-to-Manila run, which took American silver to Asia and brought back fine textiles and spices, was the only routine European crossing of the Pacific for the next 200 years.[47]

The Pacific's vastness, European ignorance of this third of the globe, and Spain's insistence that its American ports were closed to foreign traders limited the impact of European challengers in this ocean basin. In the mid-eighteenth century, however, the British, French, and Russians all breached the constraints that had kept the Pacific a "Spanish lake." The Russians reached North America from the east, a feat that concerned all the expansionist powers of western Europe, not just the Spanish into whose ostensible territory the Russians had penetrated.[48] Meanwhile, the French and British undertook government-sanctioned, if not financed, expeditions of discovery, having recognized that mastery of Pacific navigation, better geographic knowledge, and provisioning stations for Pacific voyages were necessary for any circumglobal ambitions, whether commercial or colonial.

These mid-eighteenth-century challenges to Spain's Pacific claims differed significantly from sixteenth- and seventeenth-century challenges when pirates, interloping merchants, chartered companies, and colonists had undermined Iberian hegemony in the Americas, Africa, and Asia. In the seventeenth century, England, France, and the Netherlands negotiated treaties to restrain piracy in exchange for Spain's and Portugal's acknowledgments of their colonial and commercial claims around the Atlantic and Indian Oceans. Some pirates moved into the Pacific, but limited shipping made plunder on that ocean an unprofitable pursuit. British and French merchants sought trading privileges in Spanish America that would open Pacific ports, but Spain resisted diplomatic pressure for expanded trade.

Commercial expansion into the Pacific also required provisioning stations. The favored locations were the Falklands (or Malvinas) and Juan Fernández, an island off the coast of Chile, but diplomatic concerns and the unprofitability of colonization on these remote island outposts required governmental backing, financially and diplomatically, if not militarily. Finally, Europeans' fragmentary knowledge of the Pacific basin necessitated exploratory expeditions that commercial interests increasingly lobbied governments to finance. These factors all contributed to governmental sponsorship of Pacific exploration and expansion at a level that had not occurred in the Atlantic or Indian Ocean basins.[49]

Diplomatic maneuvering around Spain's insistence on its Pacific claims, those "whimsical notions of exclusive rights in those seas," as Benjamin Keene, Britain's envoy to Madrid, described them, remained necessary until the end of the eighteenth century.[50] In 1749, in response to Spanish protests, the British Admiralty canceled an expedition for assessing the feasibility of settling the Falklands and Juan Fernández. For the British, the completion of diplomatic negotiations over the *asiento* took precedence. To preclude further British or French interest in settling Juan Fernández, the Spanish established a community there in 1750. In 1764, a French expedition under the command of Louis-Antoine de Bougainville planted a settlement on the Falklands, the same year the British reconnoitered those islands for suitable settlement sites. Spain protested the French incursion, and France acceded to the diplomatic demands, in part to thwart British ambitions. In 1767, the Spanish took over the French settlement at Port St. Louis. At the symbolic level, the British renamed the two ships for James Cook's second voyage to the Pacific from *Drake* and *Raleigh* to *Discovery* and *Resolution* to keep from offending the Spanish.[51]

This diplomatic placation of Spain did not keep France and Britain from financing a range of programs that combined scientific endeavors with strategic interests, most with implications for Pacific exploration and expansion. In 1713, Britain offered a reward of twenty thousand pounds to the inventor of an oceangoing device to measure longitude, an incentive the Spanish, Dutch, and French governments soon replicated.[52] The question of the existence or nonexistence of either an "austral" or southern Asia or a northwest passage figured in most eighteenth-century Pacific expeditions. The discovery of either portended enormous strategic and economic benefits that no European power with overseas interests could afford to ignore. The advance of scientific knowledge beyond geography to botany, biology, astronomy, and ethnology became closely associated with Pacific exploration and strategic interests. While James Cook's voyage between 1768 and

1771 on the *Endeavour* set the standard for scientific expeditions, most voyages under official state sponsorship included scientists in a ship's crew.[53]

Commercial penetration of the Pacific in the 1780s and the British decision to establish a convict colony in New South Wales accelerated the strategic jockeying among Spain, France, Britain, and Russia. Reports from diverse expeditions throughout the 1760s and 1770s told of large pods of whales and colonies of seals that could be hunted for the production of oil or furs. Cook's third voyage (1776–81) then brought back news of a potential trade in sea otter pelts in the Pacific Northwest and the fabulous prices they would fetch in China. With the end of the American Revolution in 1783, scores of British and American whalers, sealers, and merchants sailed into Pacific waters. International tensions soon focused on Nootka Sound, a harbor on the coast of Vancouver Island. In response to a growing presence of non-Spanish on the northwest coast of North America, the viceroy of New Spain had sent a naval expedition north to tell foreign traders that they were encroaching on Spanish territory. The Russian presence had been the initial provocation, but in 1789, Estéban José Martínez seized four British merchant ships and the trading posts that British merchants had established at Nootka Sound.[54]

The diplomatic incident that ensued between Britain and Spain encapsulated three centuries of arguments over European claims in the extra-European world. Spain rehearsed its claims based on the papal bulls and Treaty of Tordesillas from the 1490s. Britain responded that claims had to be given substance with occupation. British trading posts on Nootka Sound had effectively established a claim that Spain had violated with its seizure of British property. In the parliamentary debates during the crisis, Henry Dundas defined the heart of the conflict as not "a few miles" on the far western reaches of North America "but a large world." Indeed, the British aspired to establish a transcontinental linkage between its claims in Canada and Rupert's Land and claims on the Pacific coast. Spain and Britain resolved the standoff at Nootka Sound with a secret treaty that allowed for freedom of navigation through the Straits of Magellan and the British right to trade and fish throughout the Pacific basin. This treaty effectively ended Spain's three centuries of oceanic claims.[55]

The early modern conflict over the oceans had been fought between diplomats and political theorists, as much as between navies. The victory of the principle of freedom of the seas was partially illusory. The revocation of the line of demarcation defined in the Treaty of Tordesillas terminated Iberian territorial claims, but it did not end the exclusionary interstate system of oceanic control that had emerged over the previous 300 years. As the British and the French well knew, a few innocuous islands, such as the Falklands, could be gateways to the world, and the right to be gatekeeper was worth a skirmish. An older school of imperial history has emphasized the importance of naval power in the rise of Europeans, particularly the British, to world dominance.[56] Abundant evidence exists for this position, yet the greatest legacy of conflict over the oceans in the early modern era was probably conceptual. Armed conflicts on the oceans were overwhelmingly intra-European, rather than between the West and the rest.[57] While Asian powers successfully checked European pretensions to commercial and military hegemony in Asia for most of three centuries, they largely ignored the intra-European conflicts on the oceans. Those intra-European conflicts, however, ultimately sanctioned European pretensions to global control.

The uninhabitable and global quality of the oceans meant that Europeans, once they created the notion that they could divide the world among themselves, could add substance to it through transoceanic trade, exploration, and colonization in littoral areas without engaging in the messy business of dealing with significant numbers of non-Europeans, the Americas excepted. The oceans could be defined as European political space without challengers, and the European state system could thereby be globalized. Having created the world's first global international system, however exclusive the membership and abstracted from the reality of the world's peoples and territorial powers, Europeans could then set the terms for new members.

Notes

1. Elizabeth Mancke, "Early Modern Expansion and the Politicization of Oceanic Space," *Geographical Review* 89 (1999): 225–36.

2. Ben Finney, *Voyage of Rediscovery: A Cultural Odyssey through Polynesia* (Berkeley: University of California Press, 1994), 14–34.

3. Robert Finlay, "The Treasure-Ships of Zheng He: Chinese Maritime Imperialism in the Age of Discovery," *Terrae Incognitae* 23 (1991): 1–12, reprinted in Felipe Fernández-Armesto, ed., *The Global Opportunity* (Aldershot, England: Variorum, 1995), 93–104.

4. For useful introductions to these issues, see the essays in Ashin Das Gupta and M. N. Pearson, eds., *India and the Indian Ocean, 1500–1800* (Calcutta: Oxford University Press, 1987); and Roderich Ptak and Dietmar Rothermund, eds., *Emporia, Commodities and Entrepreneurs in Asian Maritime Trade, c. 1400–1750* (Stuttgart: Steiner Verlag, 1991). On trade and Islamic polities in Southeast Asia, see Anthony Reid, "Islamization and Christianization in Southeast Asia: The Critical Phase, 1550–

1650," in *Southeast Asia in the Early Modern Era: Trade, Power, and Belief,* ed. Anthony Reid (Ithaca: Cornell University Press, 1993), 151–79.

5. Frederic C. Lane, "Naval Actions and Fleet Organization, 1499–1502," in *Renaissance Venice,* ed. J. R. Hale (London: Faber and Faber, 1973), 146–73; Andrew C. Hess, "The Evolution of the Ottoman Seaborne Empire in the Age of Oceanic Discoveries, 1453–1525," *American Historical Review* 75 (1970): 1892–1919; and S. Ozbaran, "The Ottoman Turks and the Portuguese in the Persian Gulf, 1534–1581," *Journal of Asian History* 6 (1972): 45–87.

6. On the intellectual borrowings of Europeans to explain their expansion, see Anthony Pagden, *Lords of All the World: Ideologies of Empire in Spain, Britain and France, c. 1500–c. 1800* (New Haven: Yale University Press, 1995), 11–28.

7. For a counter position in the Spanish empire, see Peter Bakewell, "Conquest after the Conquest: The Rise of Spanish Domination in America," in *Spain, Europe and the Atlantic World: Essays in Honour of John H. Elliott,* eds. Richard L. Kagan and Geoffrey Parker (Cambridge: Cambridge University Press, 1995), 296–315.

8. M. N. Pearson, "India and the Indian Ocean in the Sixteenth Century," in Gupta and Pearson, *India and the Indian Ocean, 1500–1800,* 71–93; K. N. Chaudhuri, *Trade and Civilisation in the Indian Ocean: An Economic History from the Rise of Islam to 1750* (Cambridge: Cambridge University Press, 1985), 19–33, 63–76; and K. S. Mathew, "Trade in the Indian Ocean and the Portuguese System of Cartazes," in *The First Portuguese Colonial Empire,* ed. Malyn Newitt (Exeter, England: University of Exeter, 1986), 69–84. For the Atlantic, see Geoffrey W. Symcox, "The Battle of the Atlantic, 1500–1700," in *First Images of America: The Impact of the New World on the Old,* ed. Fredi Chiappelli (Berkeley: University of California Press, 1976), 265–77.

9. For other explorations of the globalization of international relations in the early modern era, see the essays by Hedley Bull, Michael Howard, Michael Donelan, and Adam Watson in *The Expansion of International Society,* eds. Hedley Bull and Adam Watson (Oxford: Clarendon Press, 1984).

10. For the limitations of this transition in the Portuguese case, see James C. Boyajian, *Portuguese Trade in Asia under the Habsburgs, 1580–1640* (Baltimore: Johns Hopkins University Press, 1993).

11. Percy Thomas Fenn, *The Origin of the Right of Fishery in Territorial Waters* (Cambridge: Harvard University Press, 1926).

12. Frances Gardiner Davenport, ed., *European Treaties Bearing on the History of the United States and Its Dependencies,* 4 vols. (Washington, D.C.: Carnegie Institution of Washington, 1917–37), 1:56–100.

13. Ibid. 1:101–6.

14. Ibid. 1:146–48, 169–71; Mariano Cuesta Domingo, "The Moluccas Island Voyages," in *Spanish Pacific from Magellan to Malaspina,* ed. Carlos Martínez Shaw (Madrid: Ministerio de asuntos exteriores, 1988), 45–57; and Sanjay Subrahmanyam, *The Portuguese Empire in Asia, 1500–1700: A Political and Economic History* (London: Longman, 1993), 108–19.

15. Philip Curtin, *Cross-Cultural Trade in World History* (Cambridge: Cambridge University Press, 1984), ix-14, 230–54; M. N. Pearson, *Merchants and Rulers in Gujarat: The Response to the Portuguese in the Sixteenth Century* (Berkeley: University of California Press, 1976), chap. 6; and Subrahmanyam, *Portuguese Empire in Asia,* 11–20.

16. This was quoted in C. R. Boxer, *The Portuguese Seaborne Empire, 1415–1825* (London: Hutchinson, 1969), 50.

17. Subrahmanyam, *Portuguese Empire in Asia,* 12–20; and J. Kathirithamby-Wells, "Introduction: An Overview," in *The Southeast Asian Port and Polity: Rise and Demise,* eds. J. Kathirithamby-Wells and John Villiers (Singapore: Singapore University Press, 1990), 1–16.

18. This was quoted in John Villiers, "Makassar: The Rise and Fall of an East Indonesian Maritime Trading State, 1512–1669," in Kathirithamby-Wells and Villiers, *Southeast Asian Port and Polity,* 154.

19. Ahsan Jan Qaisar, *The Indian Response to European Technology and Culture,* A.D. *1498–1707* (Delhi: Oxford University Press, 1982), 20–27.

20. Pierre-Yves Manguin, "The Southeast Asian Ship: An Historical Approach," *Southeast Asian Studies* 11 (1980): 266–76; Pierre-Yves Manguin, "The Vanishing *Jong:* Insular Southeast Asian Fleets in Trade and War (Fifteenth to Seventeenth Centuries)," in Reid, *Southeast Asia in the Early Modern Era,* 197–213; and Geoffrey Parker, *The Military Revolution: Military Innovation and the Rise of the West, 1500–1800* (Cambridge: Cambridge University Press, 1996), 104–6.

21. Pearson, "India and the Indian Ocean," 71–93; and Chaudhuri, *Trade and Civilisation in the Indian Ocean,* 19–33, 63–76.

22. Subrahmanyam, *Portuguese Empire in Asia,* 155.

23. Ibid., 70; and K. S. Mathew, "Akbar and Portuguese Maritime Dominance," in *Akbar and His India,* ed. Irfan Habib (Delhi: Oxford University Press, 1997), 256–65.

24. Boxer, *Portuguese Seaborne Empire,* 49.

25. Hess, "Evolution of the Ottoman Seaborne Empire," 1892–1919; Ozbaran, "Ottoman Turks and the Portuguese," 45–87; and Boxer, *Portuguese Seaborne Empire,* 57.

26. Boxer, *Portuguese Seaborne Empire,* 58; and Subrahmanyam, *Portuguese Empire in Asia,* 133–37.

27. Subrahmanyam, *Portuguese Empire in Asia,* 133–37.

28. For an interpretation that is more sympathetic to European military advantage vis-à-vis Asians, see Parker, *Military Revolution,* 103–45.

29. George D. Winius and Marcus P. M. Vink, *The Merchant-Warrior Pacified: The VOC (Dutch East India Company) and Its Changing Political Economy in India* (Delhi: Oxford University Press, 1991), 74–76; and Subrahmanyam, *Portuguese Empire in Asia,* 144–45.

30. C. R. Boxer, "Anglo-Portuguese Rivalry in the Persian Gulf, 1615–1635," in *Portuguese Conquest and Commerce in Southern Asia, 1500–1750* (London: Variorum Reprints, 1985), 46–129; and Niels Steensgaard, *Carracks, Caravans and Companies:*

ELIZABETH MANCKE

The Structural Crisis in the European-Asian Trade in the Early Seventeenth Century (Odense, Denmark: Studentlitteratur, 1973), 305–43.

31. Om Prakash, "Trade in a Culturally Hostile Environment: Europeans in the Japan Trade, 1550–1700," in *European Commercial Expansion in Early Modern Asia*, ed. Om Prakash (Aldershot, England: Variorum, 1997), 117–28.

32. Holden Furber, *Rival Empires of Trade in the Orient, 1600–1800* (Minneapolis: University of Minnesota Press, 1976), 40–41; Chaudhuri, *Trade and Civilisation in the Indian Ocean*, 75–77, 90–93; and Subrahmanyam, *Portuguese Empire in Asia*, 156–57.

33. C. G. Roelofsen, "Grotius and the International Politics of the Seventeenth Century," in *Hugo Grotius and International Relations*, eds. Hedley Bull, Benedict Kingsbury, and Adam Roberts (Oxford: Clarendon Press, 1992), 104–12; and W. E. Butler, "Grotius and the Law of the Sea," in Bull, Kingsbury, and Roberts, *Hugo Grotius*, 209–20.

34. Davenport, *European Treaties* 1:2–3; Philip Boucher, *Les Nouvelles Frances: France in America, 1500–1815, An Imperial Perspective* (Providence, R.I.: John Carter Brown Library, 1989), 3–12; and William J. Eccles, *France in America* (Markham, Ont.: Fitzhenry and Whiteside, 1990), 1–10.

35. Davenport, *European Treaties* 1:2–3; and Boucher, *Nouvelles Frances*, 5–9. The Spanish had first introduced the idea that extra-European territory had to be occupied by subjects of European rulers in order to be claimed; see Charles Edward Nowell, "The Treaty of Tordesillas and the Diplomatic Background of American History," in *Greater America: Essays in Honor of Herbert Eugene Bolton*, ed. Adele Ogden and Engel Sluiter (Berkeley: University of California Press, 1945), 5.

36. Kenneth R. Andrews, *Trade, Plunder, and Settlement: Maritime Enterprise and the Genesis of the British Empire, 1480–1630* (Cambridge: Cambridge University Press, 1984), 106–12.

37. Davenport, *European Treaties* 1:3, 219–21, 305–14.

38. Glyndwr Williams, "The Pacific: Exploration and Exploitation," in *The Oxford History of the British Empire*, vol. 2, *The Eighteenth Century*, ed. P. J. Marshall (Oxford: Oxford University Press, 1998), 552–75.

39. Davenport, *European Treaties* 1:353–66.

40. Richard Pares, *War and Trade in the West Indies, 1739–1763* (1936; reprint, London: Frank Cass, 1963), 1–64.

41. David Armitage, *The Ideological Origins of the British Empire* (Cambridge: Cambridge University Press, 2000), 100–124.

42. Anne Pérotin-Dumon, "The Pirate and the Emperor: Power and the Law on the Seas, 1450–1850," in *The Political Economy of Merchant Empires*, ed. James D. Tracy (Cambridge: Cambridge University Press, 1991), 196–227.

43. Armitage, *Ideological Origins of the British Empire*, 100–124.

44. C. R. Boxer, *The Dutch Seaborne Empire, 1600–1800* (New York: Alfred A. Knopf, 1965), 90–92.

45. Roelofsen, "Grotius," 103–12; Butler, "Grotius," 209–20; and Armitage, *Ideological Origins of the British Empire*, 124.

46. Pares, *War and Trade;* and Davenport, *European Treaties* 4:78–80.

47. María Lordes Díaz-Trechuelo, "The Philippines Route," in Martínez Shaw, *Spanish Pacific from Magellan to Malaspina,* 59–70; and O.H.K. Spate, *The Spanish Lake* (Minneapolis: University of Minnesota Press, 1979), 100–106.

48. Warren L. Cook, *Flood Tide of Empire: Spain and the Pacific Northwest, 1543–1819* (New Haven: Yale University Press, 1973), 44–55, 134–36.

49. John Dunmore, *French Explorers in the Pacific: The Eighteenth Century* (Oxford: Clarendon Press, 1965), 1:1–56; and Williams, "Pacific" 2:552–75.

50. This was quoted in Glyndwr Williams, "'To Make Discoveries of Countries Hitherto Unknown': The Admiralty and Pacific Explorations in the Eighteenth Century," in *Pacific Empires: Essays in Honour of Glyndwr Williams,* eds. Alan Frost and Jane Samson (Vancouver: University of British Columbia Press, 1999), 18.

51. Alan Frost, "The Spanish Yoke: British Schemes to Revolutionise Spanish America, 1739–1807," in *Pacific Empires,* eds. Frost and Samson, 33–52; Dunmore, *French Explorers in the Pacific* 1:57–64; and Williams, "To Make Discoveries," 24.

52. Dunmore, *French Explorers in the Pacific* 1:36–38.

53. The scientific orientation of British expeditions is well known, while that of the Spanish and French is less recognized. For scholarship on the latter, see Dunmore, *French Explorers in the Pacific* and the essays in Martínez Shaw, *Spanish Pacific from Magellan to Malaspina.*

54. Cook, *Flood Tide of Empire,* 85–199.

55. Davenport, *European Treaties* 4:168–70.

56. This position is associated with the work of Alfred Mahan. See in particular *The Influence of Sea Power upon History, 1660–1783* (Boston: Little, Brown, 1918).

57. Some Asian sailors in the employment of Europeans fought in intra-European naval battles.

ELIZABETH MANCKE

Reimagining the History
of Twentieth-century Navies

JON TETSURO SUMIDA

From the nineteenth century onward, industrial science generated advances in ship propulsion, design, and weaponry that vastly improved the capability of navies. In the twentieth century, fleets that had been transformed by rapid technological change fought two global conflicts. Their operations, which dwarfed previous maritime campaigns, had critical effects on the general course of events. In addition, destructive competition among the navy, other fighting services, and civilian consumption for industrial production during wartime made centralized government direction of the economy essential. During periods of peace, navies were major factors in international relations, while the heavy costs and administrative burdens of building a large and up-to-date force and maintaining it in the face of advances in technology and shifting strategic circumstances begat large financial, political, and managerial difficulties. In short, naval activity in the twentieth century was unprecedented in terms of magnitude, intensity, and significance.

Three conceptual frameworks have dominated scholarly consideration of the history of navies during the period in question. In the first, discussions of naval strategy and national grand strategy revolved around the notion of naval supremacy, also known as command of the sea, exercised by a single power. In the second, the story of the development of naval warfare was told in terms of dramatic changes in warship design—the advent of the all-big-gun battleship, submarine, and aircraft carrier. In the third, the narrative history of navies was concerned with policy, politics, and operations, with relatively little attention paid to economic, financial, or logistical context. This chapter, drawing mainly from the recent historical literature on Britain's Royal Navy, will present alternative approaches to the questions of naval supremacy, development in operational practice, and the form of the master plot. Reimagining the naval history of the twentieth century requires shifting analytical focus from the state to a transnational system, from a single warship type to the fleet as a whole, and from discrete events to institutional process.

The discussion of naval supremacy as something that served the interests of a single state has been concerned primarily with the writings of Alfred Thayer Mahan (1849–1914), an American naval officer and historian; Julian S. Corbett (1854–1922), a British naval historian; and Halford J. Mackinder (1861–1947), a British geographer. Over the course of the twentieth century, the stature of what were thought to be Mahan's ideas diminished, while those of Corbett and Mackinder came to dominate serious consideration of the nature and role of command of the seas. In the late twentieth century, however, reinvestigation of Mahan's views on sea power revealed them to be far different from what they were widely thought to have been and more pertinent to the naval history of the twentieth century than has been supposed.

Mahan opened the debate on the role of naval supremacy in the affairs of nations with the publication in 1890 of *The Influence of Sea Power upon History, 1660–1793*. In this book and the three major accounts of naval warfare in the age of sail that followed, Mahan argued that maritime commerce was essential to the economic prosperity of a great power, that effective attack on or defense of mercantile shipping required command of the sea exercised by a battle fleet, and that in a protracted war, a nation with a navy that was strong enough to control the oceans could defeat an opponent that was superior on land. Many interpreted these propositions as tantamount to the contention that naval supremacy was the prerequisite to ascendancy in the world political order. Because Mahan favored the expansion of the United States Navy, more than a few presumed that his ultimate goal was American international predominance based upon a commanding lead in sea power.[1]

Corbett questioned Mahan's focus on command of the sea by a battle fleet, denigration of commerce raiding, and hostility to amphibious operations whose objectives were military as opposed to those that had naval significance, such as the seizure of territory that would be used to support naval operations. Corbett was concerned with not only the use of a battle fleet to obtain sea command but also the appropriate deployment of all naval forces—including cruisers and the flotilla—in the exercise and exploitation of sea control by a single state through commerce protection and interdiction, and the facilitation of major attacks on land territory from the sea.[2] Mackinder challenged Mahan's positions on the vital significance of trans-

oceanic trade and consequent superiority of sea over land power. He maintained that a single state that controlled the greater part of the Eurasian
landmass would possess the resources to build a navy strong enough to
wrest naval supremacy from even the strongest insular power.[3]

Before 1914, the views of Corbett and Mackinder were little known. What
was believed to be Mahan's conception of sea power, on the other hand, was
famous and widely thought to be valid. During World War I, however,
Britain's battle fleet supremacy did not prevent German submarines from
carrying out attacks on merchant shipping that nearly severed vital maritime lines of supply, while German military prowess came very close to de-
livering victory on the western as well as the eastern front. Proponents of
sea power argued with justice that it was Allied naval supremacy that
starved the Central Powers and enabled the United States to intervene with
substantial military forces. On the other hand, the outcome of the war
might well have been different, and recognition that this was the case
robbed the navalist position of the aura of certitude that it had enjoyed in
many quarters prior to the war's outbreak.[4]

By World War II, even naval war colleges had abandoned the serious
study of Mahan's ideas, which were regarded as either outmoded or platitu-
dinous. During the twentieth century's second global conflict, a German
submarine campaign again came close to success in spite of the Allied
battle fleet supremacy. U.S. submarine attacks on Japan's merchant shipping cut that nation's links to vital raw materials with devastating effect on
its economy, and large-scale amphibious operations in Europe and Asia
were major contributors to victory. These events seemed to validate Corbett's views on the importance of maritime communications and cooperation between land and sea forces. After the war, the United States was confronted by a heavily armed and hostile Soviet Union. As a result, interest
was whetted in both Mackinder's theory of the hegemonic potential of a
great Eurasian state and Corbett's contention that naval supremacy offered
an insular power immunity to invasion and a wide range of offensive options against enemy flanks and detached territory.[5]

By the end of the cold war in the late 1980s, the ideas of Corbett and
Mackinder dominated scholarly discourse on the history of twentieth-century sea power, while those of Mahan were ignored. In the late 1990s, however, careful study of Mahan's many books revealed that major aspects of his
thinking had been misunderstood. The new inquiry demonstrated that the
reduction of Mahan's views on strategy to the simple-minded formula that
battle fleet supremacy was the equivalent of sea command and that attacks
on trade were unrewarding was highly misleading. Mahan actually con-

tended that the best way to interdict merchant shipping was blockade, which required battle fleet command, and that commerce raiding unsupported by a substantial battle fleet could not achieve decisive results against a major naval power, such as Britain had been since the eighteenth century. He did not believe that deployment of the battle fleet or destruction of the enemy battle fleet was always the preferred strategy and on occasion argued otherwise.[6]

Mahan's hostility to amphibious warfare had several aspects. He criticized those who favored support of land campaigns with amphibious operations on the grounds that such action risked the loss of ships and men that could be ill spared so long as command of the sea was less than absolute. He also observed that assaults on land from the sea, though perhaps easy enough to accomplish, burdened a navy with the difficult task of ensuring regular supply to the expeditionary forces. This could cause losses that would ultimately compromise sea control. If maintenance of sea control was not at stake, Mahan was aware of the advantages to be gained from cooperative action by armies and navies. Indeed, his first book, a study of naval action on rivers and coasts during the Civil War, engaged this subject at length and with considerable insight born of his own experience in that conflict.[7]

Above all, Mahan believed in free trade, maintained that neither the elected legislatures of Britain nor the United States were willing to vote the funds required to maintain a navy large enough to command the world's oceans unilaterally, and was convinced that U.S. and British international economic and political interests were in important respects the same. Mahan wanted a stronger U.S. Navy to serve as a partner to Britain's fleet, the two cooperating in the event of war to maintain the security of world maritime trade. Mahan, in other words, wanted a transnational naval consortium to protect an open system of maritime commerce, not a supreme navy whose job was the creation and defense of a far-flung autarkic empire.[8]

Accurate comprehension of Mahan's strategic thinking improves the standing of his work with respect to that of Corbett and Mackinder. Recognition that his views on the role of battle fleets, attacks on commerce, and amphibious operations were complex, nuanced, qualified, and contingent make it possible to see that his positions on these matters were no less sound than those of Corbett and largely validated by twentieth-century experience. Mahan's notion of the exercise of naval supremacy by a transnational consortium seems a more useful perspective than the emphasis on single states adopted by both Corbett and Mackinder. Anglo-American naval collaboration played significant roles in both world wars. Afterward, a coalition of maritime states whose navies protected a global free trade economy proved capable of containing the potential Eurasian hegemony feared by Mackinder.

In the twentieth century, the development of warships and warship armament changed the nature of naval warfare dramatically. The advent of all-big-gun battleships before World War I was associated with a gunnery revolution that more than quintupled the range at which battle fleets were expected to fight. The German deployment of submarines against British merchant shipping with great success during World Wars I and II, and the devastating U.S. submarine attacks on Japan's merchant marine in the latter conflict, indicated that commerce raiding could be a decisive form of naval operations. In World War II, effective carrier-launched air attacks on the Italian and U.S. battle fleets, followed by a series of great carrier fleet encounters in the Pacific, marked the eclipse of the surface capital ship and the traditional line of battle. Thus, the history of twentieth-century naval warfare has been widely understood in terms of innovation in warship design: the radical improvement and decline of the battleship and the rise of the submarine and aircraft carrier.[9]

The foregoing scheme, however, is an unsatisfactory depiction of the development of twentieth-century operational practice because the complexities of naval technology, tactics, and strategy cannot be reduced to a matter of change in three types of warships. Four propositions must be kept in mind when considering alterations in industrial navies and naval combat. First, fleets consist of three major groups of warships—heavy battle units (battleships and later aircraft carriers as well), lighter battle units (cruisers), and small craft (flotilla, which includes submarines)—each of which performs necessary functions, some independently and some in combination with others. Second, fleets were created for specific strategic purposes that differed from power to power and for the same power from time to time. Third, even small changes in technical infrastructure had large effects on naval operational practice. Fourth, the strategic circumstances of the twentieth century were not predestined and constant but contingent and variable, creating major roles for warships that, however critical in the event, were not inevitable.

Before 1914, the naval leadership of Britain, then the world's preeminent naval power, entertained two competing concepts of fleet organization. The standard view was that battleships were to defend home and colonial territorial waters and cruisers were to protect trade. The high costs of this approach, the dangerous need to divide the battle fleet to defend both home and distant seas in the event of strong enemy battle fleet activity in both areas, and the increasing vulnerability of battleships to attacks by flotilla armed with improved torpedoes, prompted a small group of influential officers to argue that the existing system be replaced. They preferred one that would use flotilla to defend home waters, which would free all large surface ships to be deployed in defense of the empire and trade routes. Ideally, battleships were to be superseded by much-improved cruisers, known as battle cruisers, that had the fuel endurance and high speed required to move great distances rapidly. They were supposed to be equipped with advanced gunnery equipment that would enable them to hit their opponents before they could be struck.[10]

The second scheme was well developed by the time of the outbreak of World War I. However, it was not implemented because the naval weakness of Britain's opponents in extra-European waters and the support of powerful naval allies made the dispatch of her heavy surface ships abroad unnecessary. The deployment of all Britain's battleships and battle cruisers together with supporting cruisers and flotilla in what was called a "grand fleet of battle" was thus the result of particular circumstances that arose in 1914 and contingency preparation for which had begun only a few years before. The task, moreover, of controlling such a large and unwieldy formation was far beyond the existing methods of command, control, and communications. In addition, the planned prewar gunnery advances had been disrupted in 1912 by service politics and shifting tactical requirements, and this meant that long-range gunnery was much less efficient than it might otherwise have been. British battle fleet performance in the war's single general engagement was thus unsatisfactory.[11]

German surface cruisers were few and lacked the network of overseas bases required to sustain an effective campaign against British trade. The surface raider threat was for these reasons largely eliminated by British cruisers acting individually or in small squadrons, as in the days of sail. The German resort to unrestricted submarine attacks on shipping in 1917, on the other hand, inflicted heavy losses whose effects were magnified by economic factors that brought Britain to the brink of defeat. The success of submarines unsupported by air reconnaissance depended upon the distribution of large numbers of vulnerable targets across the ocean that could be picked off by underwater raiders moving at random. The simple expedient of grouping merchant shipping in convoys drastically reduced the probability of submarine interceptions, while attached flotilla craft provided adequate defense against single submarines.[12]

During the interwar period, international agreements reduced the size of battleship fleets to well below pre-1914 levels and limited the amount of aircraft carrier tonnage to a fraction of that allowed for battleships. The latter provision was intended to forestall the construction of aircraft carriers as compensation for fewer battleships, and, in effect, it precluded the replacement of the battleship by the aircraft carrier. The combination of a smaller line of battle; advances in command, control, and communications; and the resurrection of the advanced gunnery technology abandoned before the war enabled battleships, aircraft carriers, cruisers, and flotilla to be formed into a maneuverable and hard-hitting combined arms force that was tactically far superior to the poorly integrated and clumsy formation of World War I.[13]

Submarine predation on merchant shipping was limited by treaty, the invention of sonar made submerged submarines detectable and thus much more susceptible to deadly counterattack, convoy had been shown to be an effective defensive tactic, and Germany, Britain's most likely serious enemy in Europe, lacked direct access to the Atlantic. For these reasons, the Admiralty not unreasonably discounted the importance of the submarine threat to Britain's extended lines of maritime supply. The primary peril, British naval leaders believed, would be from fast surface raiders. Trade defense was thus entrusted to cruisers that operated independently or in small groups. Little attention was paid to the development of flotilla forces capable of dealing with a major submarine assault upon transatlantic shipping.[14] In the late 1930s, the priority given to the expansion and modernization of the aging and treaty-restricted battle fleet precluded the buildup of a flotilla force capable of dealing with anticipated serious German air and submarine attacks against British shipping in home waters.[15]

The fall of France at the beginning of World War II, however, not only deprived Britain of a powerful ally but also made French Atlantic ports available to a rapidly expanding German submarine arm that had engaged in unrestricted attacks on commerce in spite of treaty agreements not to do so. German underwater operations, moreover, were enhanced by land-based air reconnaissance that was used to concentrate large groups of submarines against a single convoy. To deal with this more potent form of commerce raiding, Britain, with U.S. industrial assistance, was forced to create a combined-arms force—namely, long-range flotilla, small aircraft carriers, and land-based aircraft—coordinated by improved forms of command, control, communications, and intelligence activity of unprecedented sophistication and effectiveness. The British effort, aided by the similar forces of the United States and Canada, was sufficient to master the German submarine offensive. The Japanese inability to emulate Allied antisubmarine practices enabled U.S. submarines, operating alone for the most part, to ravage weakly protected shipping at relatively small cost.[16]

In European waters, Britain's combined-arms battle fleet was highly successful against German and Italian opponents that always lacked carrier support and frequently cruiser and flotilla backing as well. Striking victories were won when air attacks launched from carriers paved the way for decisive action by battleships. British naval commitments in the European theater precluded the dispatch of a battle fleet that was strong enough to carry out major actions against Japan. The main burden of dealing with the large and efficient Japanese navy was thus left to the United States, Britain's naval consortium partner. Improvised U.S. battle groups built around aircraft carriers were able to fend off Japanese offensives following the heavy loss of battleships at the outbreak of war in the Pacific. In subsequent U.S. naval counteroffensives that shattered the Japanese navy, new fast battleships were joined to carriers, cruisers, and flotilla to form combined-arms strike forces that were integrated and directed by the same kind of command, control, communications, and intelligence resources that had been applied to antisubmarine operations.[17]

The foregoing assessments reveal several serious problems with a view of history centered on the development of three dominant warship forms and progressive changes in their relationships to each other. Before 1914, supposedly the heyday of the battleship, Britain's navy came close to abandoning this type of warship altogether in favor of flotilla defense to prevent invasion and battle cruisers to display power in distant seas. During the period between the wars, the battleship's position was strengthened when a variety of factors increased its effectiveness while limiting that of the aircraft carrier and submarine. In the world wars, the successes of German and U.S. submarines were in large part attributable to nontechnical contingent circumstances, and the accomplishments of the aircraft carrier intertwined with the significant activity of other warship types.

It is analytically and synthetically more satisfying to see the period between the wars in terms of increased cooperation between the warship groups that made up the fleet as a whole. Prior to 1914, the Royal Navy dealt with home defense and trade protection with single groups of warships. During World War I, home defense was placed in the hands of an ill-coordinated combined-arms force made up of different warship groups, while the main burden of trade defense was transferred from cruisers to flotilla. Between the world wars, the tactical integration of the combined-arms battle fleet was greatly improved, while the main responsibility for the protection of merchant shipping returned to cruisers. During World War II, the aircraft carrier replaced the battleship as the principle component of what remained a combined-arms force, while flotilla were enhanced by aircraft carriers and connected to land-based air action. After the war, the operational affiliation of underwater, surface, air, and even space forces was improved by further advances in command, control, communications, and intelligence.[18]

The main story line, or what might be called the master plot, of twentieth-century naval history is devoted to naval policy and operations. The creation and maintenance of large naval forces, however, posed enormous financial, industrial, and operational logistical difficulties that had large effects on naval capability. Moreover, the strategic influence of money, manufacturing, and supply must be connected to the fact that naval supremacy in the twentieth century was not exercised by a single state but, as has been argued earlier, by a transnational consortium. Examination of Britain's efforts to maintain its naval position at five critical junctures—the Anglo-Japanese alliance of 1902, the capital-ship crisis of 1909, the submarine crisis of 1917 and 1918, the Washington Naval Conference of 1921 and 1922, and naval rearmament in the 1930s—indicates how the basic narrative can be remodeled by taking these factors into account.

At the beginning of the twentieth century, Britain's position in the Orient was threatened by the combined fleets of a hostile alliance. In 1901, France and Russia enjoyed a two-to-one advantage in battleships and a 20 percent superiority in cruisers over the British forces in Pacific waters. British fiscal resources were strained by the costs of the war in South Africa and the burden of building and manning warships in unprecedented numbers to maintain control of the Atlantic and Mediterranean. Incapable of either constructing a larger fleet or reducing naval strength in European seas, Britain sought an alliance with Japan. In 1902, the two powers signed a formal agreement that, among other things, guaranteed Britain's Far Eastern naval forces the support of the Japanese fleet in the event of war with France and Russia. This provided strong protection for British colonial territory and commercial interests.[19]

The military-naval alliance between Britain and Japan, however, had been preceded by no less significant fiscal and industrial involvement. In 1896, China paid a large indemnity to Japan through British banks as part of the settlement of the Sino-Japanese War. This financial arrangement provided security for borrowing from London's financial markets and facilitated Japanese purchases of large warships built in British yards. Of the fourteen first-class battleships and cruisers that made up Japan's main naval strength on the outbreak of the Russo-Japanese War in 1904, all six battleships and four of the eight cruisers had been purchased from British shipbuilders in transactions that were assisted by British banks. In return, these acquisitions promoted the strength of Britain's warship-building industry upon which the Royal Navy also depended. Japanese naval power in the early twentieth century, in short, was in large part the creation of British financial and industrial action and reciprocally served important British economic as well as political interests.[20]

Between 1906 and 1909, rapid German construction of surface capital ships appeared to threaten British naval supremacy. Following the accession to power of a Liberal government committed to fiscal retrenchment and social reform in 1905, British construction of battleships and battle cruisers declined. In 1906, 1907, and 1908, nine heavy units were begun, while Germany started no fewer than ten. German building was inflated by the fact that in earlier years it had not laid down its own all-big-gun capital ships, while Britain had started three, but the British margin of superiority in new model capital ships seemed to be too small for comfort. In 1909, rumors that Germany was planning to accelerate her heavy shipbuilding programs compelled the Liberal government to increase capital ship construction to well above what it had planned. In place of four units, the Admiralty was ultimately granted permission to order eight, augmented by two more ships provided by agreements with the dominions of Australia and New Zealand. Thus, while only two heavy ships had been ordered in 1908, no fewer than ten were authorized in 1909.[21]

The British reaction has been attributed to Admiralty fears of German naval expansion. While this was undoubtedly a factor, the great increase in the size of Britain's naval construction program was heavily influenced by other considerations. Admiral Sir John Fisher, the navy's service chief, was the leading proponent of flotilla defense in home waters and the protection of imperial interest and trade routes with battle cruisers. He thus had little reason to respond in kind to the German surface-ship threat in the North Sea. Fisher exploited, if not provoked, the panic over German building in the belief that most if not all the enlarged program would be made up of battle cruisers that would go a long way toward the replacement of a costly force structure of battleships and cruisers with what he believed would be a less expensive one consisting of battle cruisers and flotilla. Fisher was also convinced that the continuation of the reduced building of the previous three years would force contractions in Britain's naval armaments firms that would undermine their abilities to generate essential technical innovations and increase production in the event of an emergency. Fisher failed to get most of his way with regard to the type of capital ship built, but achieved his industrial policy objectives.[22]

In 1915, German submarines began attacks on merchant shipping in retaliation for the British naval blockade. The small numbers of submarines available for operations, antisubmarine countermeasures, and tactical restrictions imposed by the need to meet the objections of neutral countries, including the powerful United States, limited the effectiveness of the German underwater campaign. Beginning in 1917, however, larger numbers of German submarines operating without self-imposed tactical restrictions sank Allied and neutral shipping in much greater numbers than before. Because losses exceeded by a large margin the rate of new construction, insular Britain faced the prospect of soon not having the sea transport required to sustain her war effort. This threat was contained by a combination of more efficient use of shipping, diplomatic pressure on neutrals not to withdraw their vessels from service, increased merchant ship construction by the United States, and the adoption of improved antisubmarine tactics, including the gathering of cargo ships into convoys escorted by warships.[23]

The submarine crisis has generally been understood in military terms, that is, as the product of the operational effectiveness of an innovative weapons system against an unprepared and therefore ineffective defense. Britain's vulnerability to the German submarine offensive, however, was to a great degree created by industrial logistical circumstances. At the start of hostilities, Britain's merchant marine was large enough to suffer heavy losses and still have the capacity to carry what was needed to support the Allied war effort. From 1914 to 1916, an ample margin of safety was eroded by the Royal Navy's voracious appetite for industrial production and ship maintenance assets that brought merchant ship construction to a virtual standstill and left many merchant ships unable to steam for lack of repairs, as well as interfering with army procurement. The efforts of the war cabinet to rein in navy consumption—much of which was not essential—failed, and in the end, the great increases in merchant ship construction that were required to ensure adequate sea transport had to be provided by the United States.[24]

In 1921, the United States invited the world's naval powers to meet in Washington, D.C., to discuss the possibility of general reductions in the size of navies and restrictions on new construction. After considerable deliberation and hard bargaining, agreement was reached in 1922. The Washington Naval Treaty limited the size, number, and armament of battleships, aircraft carriers, and cruisers. In addition, it set ratios of capital ship strength that placed the United States and Britain at parity and Japan at three-fifths that number, and imposed a ten-year ban on new battleship construction with limited exception allowed for the three naval powers just named. Great power consensus at Washington forestalled an expensive three-way build-

ing competition that would have embittered international relations and provoked strong domestic opposition everywhere. Britain gained more from
Washington, however, than just relief from high naval estimates that it
could not afford after a war effort that had nearly exhausted its financial
system.[25]

With the strict Versailles Treaty limitation of German sea power, Britain
faced no serious naval threat in European waters, but had reason to fear
Japanese ambition. Defending her distant colonial and dominion territories
posed a daunting logistical challenge. Existing base facilities in the Orient
were modest, and Admiralty experts estimated that the numbers of tankers
that would be available to Britain for naval use over the next two decades
would limit the size of the battle fleet that could be supplied with fuel to half
that stationed in the North Sea during the late war. Perhaps not coinciden-
tally, the number of battleships allowed Britain under the Washington ac-
cords was nearly exactly this figure, and this was also sufficient to give the
Royal Navy force a 50 percent superiority in capital ships over the treaty-
restricted Japanese fleet. Naval arms limitation thus magnified Britain's
imperial security by preventing the Japanese from building a force that
might have been large enough to outnumber a British Far Eastern contingent whose size had been constrained by logistics.[26]

The state of the Royal Navy on the outbreak of World War II seemed very
much less satisfactory than its condition at the onset of World War I. In
1914, Britain's naval forces were numerically greater than those of her combined enemies and for the most part were made up of new construction
equipped with what was regarded as state-of-the-art weaponry. In 1939, the
Royal Navy outnumbered her immediate adversary but was quantitatively
inferior with respect to the hostile combination that came into being within
two years, while a large proportion of the fleet was made up of warships that
were considerably older than those of other major powers. Insofar as the
critically important naval aviation element was concerned, the fleet was dis-
tinctly weaker than the navies of the United States and Japan. The relative
decline in size and absolute descent in certain areas of quality, however, has
obscured Britain's development of an armaments production scheme that
greatly increased its capacity to expand and sustain its three military services and merchant marine in the event of a long war.

As has been explained previously, Royal Navy consumption of industrial
resources during World War I was so great that it had interfered with important production for the army and compromised adequate production for the
merchant marine, the latter having near war-losing consequences. In the
interwar years, the British government thus created a war-industrial mobili-

zation scheme that minimized destructive interservice competition for limited armaments production and ensured that merchant shipbuilding would not fall below essential requirements. In the 1930s, the deterioration of the international situation prompted general rearmament according to plan, the production effort intensifying after the outbreak of hostilities. Industrial coordination worked well, and it allowed rapid and large increases in the strength of the armed forces and continued high output of new merchant ships. This was enough to enable a besieged Britain to hold on until the United States joined the conflict and brought into play large industrial reinforcements that enabled the Anglo-American naval consortium to win the greatest maritime war in world history.[27]

The serious study of twentieth-century navies is still in its early stages, the considerable work accomplished thus far notwithstanding. Much more detailed investigation of the official papers of the world's navies is needed to increase knowledge about major subjects and promote advances in conceptualization that will in turn foster further intelligent inquiry. Naval personnel recruitment and retention, officer education and promotion, operational training and readiness, steam engineering matériel and practice, electrical and hydraulic technology, industrial intelligence and its effects, weather and tactics, and transnational financial, logistical, and industrial cooperation, for example, have received inadequate attention in spite of what should be their obvious importance. For this reason, the history of twentieth-century navies cannot now be known but must be imagined.[28]

In the past, the instruments of imagination have been three: a theory about the strategic ends of navies, certain notions about the material means of navies, and a master plot that dealt primarily with the application of means to ends. That is to say, naval historians viewed the twentieth century in terms of great power rivalry for sea supremacy as the prerequisite to the international predominance of a single state, a technologically determinist approach to operational practice, and a focus on policy, politics, and operations with little reference to institutional process. Recent scholarship has made it possible to reimagine the period in question by substituting new values in the old formula: naval supremacy was exercised by a transnational consortium in defense of a global system of more or less free trade, the means of naval warfare were conditioned by several major nontechnical as well as technical factors, and the story of navies was just as much about their creation and support as their use as instruments of power. These changes make it possible to think differently about familiar subjects in significant ways, six examples of which follow.

First, naval supremacy in the twentieth century always depended upon international fiscal, industrial, and political cooperation. Second, the displacement of Britain by the United States as the world's strongest naval power was a shift within an ongoing transnational system of naval security, not a substitution of one form of autarkic sea supremacy by another. Third, the world's major naval powers were correct during the interwar period to regard the surface capital ship as the primary component of the battle fleet. Fourth, the most significant changes in naval warfare were about the advent of combined-arms naval forces of various kinds, whose effectiveness depended upon advances in naval command, control, communications, and intelligence. Fifth, for logistical reasons, naval arms control during the interwar period improved Britain's ability—and that of the United States as well—to project naval power for extended periods outside of home waters. Sixth, the advent of protracted wars of industrial attrition made the ability to minimize interservice competition for industrial assets in wartime a naval strategic question of no less importance than the size and quality of the fleet.

Reimagining the history of twentieth-century navies in institutional, informational, and transnational terms has more general implications. Major navies were managed by complex bureaucracies, manned by a highly skilled work force, and equipped with cutting-edge technology that had to be replaced frequently with improved devices. They were thus the precursors and perhaps even progenitors of the large corporate industrial organizations that have come to dominate the economies of the modern world. Naval command, control, communications, and intelligence requirements generated many important advances in technology, including fundamental breakthroughs in computers and related electronics. Navies were for this reason a major contributor to the information revolution of the late twentieth century. Finally, major navies were components of a transnational system of naval security that fostered the growth of international trade. Naval supremacy, therefore, had two faces—as an agent of great power rivalry, to be sure, but contrarily as a force that encouraged international cooperation and the emergence of a global economy.

Notes

1. Jon Tetsuro Sumida, *Inventing Grand Strategy and Teaching Command: The Classic Works of Alfred Thayer Mahan Reconsidered* (Baltimore: Johns Hopkins University Press and Washington, D.C.: Wilson Center Press, 1997).

2. Julian S. Corbett, *Some Principles of Maritime Strategy* (London: Longmans, Green, 1911).

3. Halford J. Mackinder, *Democratic Ideals and Reality* (1919; reprint, New York: W. W. Norton, 1962).

4. Jon Sumida, "Alfred Thayer Mahan, Geopolitician," in *Geopolitics, Geography and Strategy*, eds. Colin S. Gray and Geoffrey Sloan (London: Frank Cass, 1999).

5. Sumida, "Alfred Thayer Mahan"; B. Mitchell Simpson III, ed., *The Development of Naval Thought: Essays by Herbert Rosinski* (Newport, R.I.: Naval War College Press, 1977); and James Goldrick and John B. Hattendorf, eds., *Mahan Is Not Enough: The Proceedings of a Conference on the Works of Sir Julian Corbett and Admiral Sir Herbert Richmond* (Newport, R.I.: Naval War College Press, 1993).

6. Sumida, *Inventing Grand Strategy*.

7. Ibid.

8. Ibid.

9. Bernard Brodie, *Sea Power in the Machine Age* (Princeton: Princeton University Press, 1941); and Robert L. O'Connell, *Sacred Vessels: The Cult of the Battleship and the Rise of the U.S. Navy* (Boulder, Colo.: Westview Press, 1991).

10. Jon Sumida, *In Defence of Naval Supremacy: Finance, Technology, and British Naval Policy, 1889–1914* (Boston: Unwin Hyman, 1989); and Nicholas A. Lambert, *Sir John Fisher's Naval Revolution* (Columbia: University of South Carolina Press, 1999).

11. Sumida, *In Defence of Naval Supremacy*.

12. Arthur Hezlet, *The Submarine and Sea Power* (New York: Stein and Day, 1967), chap. 6.

13. Christopher Hall, *Britain, America and Arms Control, 1921–37* (London: Macmillan, 1987); and Jon Sumida, "'The Best Laid Plans': The Development of British Battle-Fleet Tactics, 1919–1942," *International History Review* 4 (1992).

14. Hezlet, *Submarine and Sea Power*, chap. 7; and Stephen Roskill, *Naval Policy between the Wars*, 2 vols. (London: Collins, 1968–76), 2:452.

15. Joseph Maiolo, *The Royal Navy and Nazi Germany, 1933–39: A Study in Appeasement and the Origins of the Second World War* (New York: St. Martin's Press, 1998).

16. Hezlet, *Submarine and Sea Power*, chaps. 10, 12, and 13; David Kahn, *Seizing the Enigma: The Race to Break the German U-Boat Codes, 1939–1943* (Boston: Houghton Mifflin, 1991); and David Syrett, *The Defeat of the German U-Boats: The Battle of the Atlantic* (Columbia: University of South Carolina Press, 1994).

17. Clark G. Reynolds, *The Fast Carriers: The Forging of an Air Navy* (New York: McGraw-Hill, 1968); Corelli Barnett, *Engage the Enemy More Closely: The Royal Navy in the Second World War* (New York: W. W. Norton, 1991); and John Prados, *Combined Fleet Decoded: The Secret History of American Intelligence and the Japanese Navy in World War II* (New York: Random House, 1995).

18. Captain W.T.T. Pakenham, *Naval Command and Control* (London: Brassey's Defence Publishers, 1989); and Gordon R. Nagler, ed., *Naval Tactical Command and Control* (Washington, D.C.: AFCEA International, n.d.).

19. Paul M. Kennedy, *The Rise and Fall of British Naval Mastery* (New York: Charles Scribner's Sons, 1977), 212–14.

20. Toshio Suzuki, *Japanese-Government Loan Issues on the London Capital Market, 1870–1913* (London: Athlone, 1994); Ian Nish, "Japan and Sea Power," in *Naval Power in the Twentieth Century*, ed. N.A.M. Rodger (Annapolis, Md.: Naval Institute Press, 1996); David C. Evans and Mark R. Peattie, *Kaigun: Strategy, Tactics, and Technology in the Imperial Japanese Navy, 1887–1914* (Annapolis, Md.: Naval Institute Press, 1997), chap. 3; and Hugh B. Peebles, *Warshipbuilding on the Clyde: Naval Orders and the Prosperity of the Clyde Shipbuilding Industry, 1919–1939* (Edinburgh: John Donald, 1987).

21. Sumida, *In Defence of Naval Supremacy*; and Lambert, *Sir John Fisher's Naval Revolution*.

22. Lambert, *Sir John Fisher's Naval Revolution*.

23. Hezlet, *Submarine and Sea Power*, chaps. 4 and 6.

24. Jon Sumida, "Forging the Trident: British Naval Industrial Logistics, 1914–1918," in *Logistics in Western Warfare from the Middle Ages to the Present*, ed. John A. Lynn (Boulder, Colo.: Westview Press, 1993), 217–49.

25. Roger Dingman, *Power in the Pacific: The Origins of Naval Arms Limitation, 1914–1922* (Chicago: University of Chicago Press, 1976).

26. Jon Sumida, "British Naval Operational Logistics, 1914–1918," *Journal of Military History* 57 (1993).

27. W. K. Hancock and M. M. Gowing, *British War Economy* (London: HMSO, 1949); H. Duncan Hall, *North American Supply* (London: HMSO, 1955); and G.A.H. Gordon, *British Seapower and Procurement between the Wars: A Reappraisal of Rearmament* (Annapolis, Md.: Naval Institute Press, 1988).

28. Jon Sumida and David Rosenberg, "Machines, Men, Manufacturing, Management and Money: The Study of Navies as Complex Organizations and the Transformation of Twentieth-Century Naval History," in *Doing Naval History: Essays toward Improvement*, ed. John B. Hattendorf (Newport, R.I.: Naval War College Press, 1995).

Odysseus's Oar

Archetypes of Voyaging

ROBERT D. FOULKE

One of the oldest emblems in sea literature is Odysseus's oar, symbolizing the unnaturalness of treading the "sea-road," as the Homeric formula is often translated, and introducing the motif of leaving the sea forever. During Odysseus's visit to the underworld, the prophet Tiresias tells Odysseus what he must do to complete his penance for offending Poseidon. You will recall that he had not only tricked and blinded the cyclops Polyphemus but also taunted this stricken son of Poseidon as he sailed away. The vengeance of the god of the sea brings suffering to Odysseus throughout his long voyage home, destroys all his ships and men, and, after his last shipwreck, leaves him a lone swimmer facing a brutal surf pounding into a towering cliff. As if this were not enough penance, he must turn his back on the sea and make a journey inland after he has reclaimed his kingship in Ithaca. Tiresias makes this clear to him:

> go forth once more, you must . . .
> carry your well-planed oar until you come
> to a race of people who know nothing of the sea,
> whose food is never seasoned with salt, strangers all
> to ships with their crimson prows and long slim oars,
> wings that make ships fly. And here is your sign—
> unmistakable, clear, so clear you cannot miss it:
> When another traveler falls in with you and calls
> that weight across your shoulder a fan to winnow grain,
> then plant your bladed, balanced oar in the earth
> and sacrifice fine beasts to the lord god of the sea,
> Poseidon.[1]

The theme of escaping bondage to the sea and living out of sight of it persists throughout sea literature from Homer to Conrad, and it is often associated with Odysseus's emblematic oar. In *The Mirror of the Sea*, Joseph Conrad consciously draws a parallel between Dominic Cervoni and Odysseus. Cervoni, who has had to deliberately wreck his ship to avoid capture by the Spanish coastal guard, comes ashore with an oar:

> I gazed after the strangely desolate figure of that seaman carrying an oar on his shoulder up a barren, rock-strewn ravine under the dreary leaden sky of the *Tremolino's* last day . . . walking deliberately, with his back to the sea. . . . And Dominic Cervoni takes his place in my memory by the side of the legendary wanderer on the sea of marvels and terrors, by the side of the fatal and impious adventurer, to whom the evoked shade of the soothsayer predicted a journey inland with an oar on his shoulder, till he met men who had never set eyes on ships and oars. It seems to me I can see them side by side in the twilight of an arid land, the unfortunate possessors of the secret lore of the sea, bearing the emblem of their hard calling on their shoulders, surrounded by silent and curious men: even as I, too, having turned my back on the sea, am bearing those few pages in the twilight, with the hope of finding in an inland valley the silent welcome of some patient listener.[2]

Like the character who waylays an unsuspecting wedding guest in Samuel Taylor Coleridge's poem "Rime of the Ancient Mariner," both Odysseus and Conrad have tales to tell, ones that will barely be understood on land, and the lure of the sea is so strong that one must carry the oar far enough inland to be out of its sight and sound.

Writing about seafaring is loaded with dichotomies between the sea and the land, and among them, in voyage narratives, the strongest polarity is the impulse to sail outward set against the desire to return home. Such ambivalence is as unstable as the sea itself, and its currents can flow either way. Odysseus's voyage follows the ancient Greek pattern of the *nostos*, or "return." Yet most of his adventures and disasters come from the opposite impulse, an insatiable curiosity and brashness that leads him into trouble time after time. One of the most telling moments in *The Odyssey* occurs in the Aeolus episode, when curious and avaricious crewmen unseal the bag of winds and release gales that drive the homecoming fleet back to sea just as they have made a landfall on Ithaca—years before the return that no one but Odysseus will see. In his poem "Ulysses," Alfred, Lord Tennyson, reverses the *nostos* and strengthens the impulse to be outward bound as he focuses on an older hero, safely home but bored. His restive Ulysses, stuck with an aging Penelope and an unimaginative son, Telemachus, cannot wait to clear out of the Ithaca he sought through ten years of the long and difficult voyage home:

> There lies the port; the vessel puffs her sail;
> There gloom the dark, broad seas. My mariners,
> Souls that have toiled, and wrought, and thought with me;—
> That ever with a frolic welcome took
> The thunder and the sunshine, and opposed
> Free hearts, free foreheads—you and I are old;
> Old age hath yet his honor and his toil.
> Death closes all; but something ere the end,
> Some work of noble note, may yet be done,
> Not unbecoming men that strove with gods.
> The lights begin to twinkle from the rocks;
> The long day wanes; the slow moon climbs; the deep
> Moans round with many voices. Come, my friends,
> 'Tis not too late to seek a newer world.
> Push off, and sitting well in order smite
> The sounding furrows; for my purpose holds
> To sail beyond the sunset, and the baths
> Of all the western stars, until I die.[3]

This Victorian Ulysses strikes out on a new voyage of discovery, while one of his twentieth-century successors, the hero of *The Odyssey; a Modern Sequel* by Nikos Kazantzakis, also leaves Ithaca to create new havoc in an aftermath of the Trojan War and embark on a symbolic dark journey through ancient Egypt and primordial Africa toward death. These reworked heroes, one romantic and the other thoroughly ironic, reflect both the tenor of their ages and the radically different possibilities inherent in voyaging. Tennyson and Kazantzakis did not misread *The Odyssey* but simply pulled out of it the burning curiosity that leads to Odysseus's adventures and usually gets him into desperate trouble.

The polarity between the urge to explore unknown seas and the longing to return home emerges most directly and poignantly in an anonymous Anglo-Saxon lyric entitled "The Seafarer":

> Little the landlubber, safe on shore,
> Knows what I've suffered in icy seas
> Wretched and worn by the winter storms,

Hung with icicles, stung by hail,
Lonely and friendless and far from home.
In my ears no sound but the roar of the sea,
The icy combers, the cry of the swan;
In place of the mead-hall and laughter of men
My only singing the sea-mew's call,
The scream of the gannet, the shriek of the gull;
Through the wail of the wild gale beating the bluffs
The piercing cry of the ice-coated petrel,
The storm-drenched eagle's echoing scream.
In all my wretchedness, weary and lone,
I had no comfort of comrade or kin. . . .
Yet still, even now, my spirit within me
Drives me seaward to sail the deep,
To ride the long swell of the salt sea-wave.
Never a day but my heart's desire
Would launch me forth on the long sea-path,
Fain of fair harbors and foreign shores.
Yet lives no man so lordly of mood,
So eager in giving, so ardent in youth,
So bold in his deeds, or so dear to his lord,
Who is free from dread in his far sea-travel,
Or fear of God's purpose and plan for his fate.[4]

Here we have it all in simple contiguity—cold misery and loneliness in an environment devoid of human comfort set against renewed wanderlust and the urge to sail, tempered by justifiable fear. In "Ballads and Songs of the American Sailor" (an unpublished manuscript), Stuart Frank notes the prevalence of the theme of farming in sailors' longing for life ashore. One song from the ship *Florida* of New Bedford in the 1840s echoes the ambivalence of the Anglo-Saxon seafarer more than a millennium later:

Yes I was once a sailor lad
I plowed the restless sea
I saw the sky look fair and glad
And I felt proud and free.
    I breathed the air of many a clime
Saw beauties fair and gay
My hopes were fixed on future time
The present slipped away
    Experience sad hope's brilliant view

ROBERT D. FOULKE

Like mist dissolved away
I found small harvest did accrue
To plowmen of the sea
    I found my team would range and rove
'Twas but the fickle wind
That plowing o'er the rolling sea
No furrow left behind
    Days have passed by I'm snug on shore
Safe from the sea's alarms
I have a never failing store
A fifteen acre farm
    Oh, sweet it is to till the soil
'Neath our New England sky
And sweet when I have eased my toil
To muse on days gone by.[5]

Such polarities between life at sea and life ashore proliferate throughout sea literature in the nineteenth century, and the image of the disappearing furrow often gets expanded into a broader vision of trackless ocean that retains no imprint of human activity or civilization. Richard Henry Dana makes this observation:

> Much has been said of the sunrise at sea; but it will not compare with the sunrise on shore. It lacks the accompaniments of the songs of birds, the awakening hum of humanity, and the glancing of the first beams upon trees, hills, spires, and housetops, to give it life and spirit. There is no scenery. But although the actual rise of the sun at sea is not so beautiful, yet nothing will compare for melancholy and dreariness with the early breaking of day upon "Old Ocean's gray and melancholy waste." There is something in the first gray streaks stretching along the eastern horizon and throwing an indistinct light upon the face of the deep, which combines with the boundlessness and unknown depth of the sea around, and gives one a feeling of loneliness, of dread, and of melancholy foreboding, which nothing else in nature can. This gradually passes away as the day grows brighter, and when the sun comes up, the ordinary monotonous sea day begins.[6]

Herman Melville deepens the polarity of sea and shore values through paradox in his miniature elegy for Bulkington, a seaman who has shipped on board the ill-fated *Pequod* after returning from a four-year voyage. Here the land becomes the menace and the raging sea the refuge:

ODYSSEUS'S OAR: ARCHETYPES OF VOYAGING

Let me say that it fared with him as with the storm-tossed ship, that miserably drives along the leeward land. The port would fain give succor; the port is pitiful; in the port is safety, comfort, hearthstone, supper, warm blankets, friends, all that's kind to our mortalities. But in that gale, the port, the land, is that ship's direst jeopardy; she must fly all hospitality; one touch of land though it but graze the keel, would make her shudder through and through. With all her might she crowds all sail off shore; in so doing, fights 'gainst the very winds that fain would blow her homeward; seeks all the lashed sea's landlessness again; for refuge's sake forlornly rushing into peril; her only friend her bitterest foe![7]

Of course, Melville has other themes at work in this passage, both autobiographical and metaphysical, but in doing so, he taps into the fear of a lee shore based on centuries of shipwrecks. The sea both attracts and repels, calling us to high adventure and threatening to destroy us through its indifferent power. In *The Mirror of the Sea*, Conrad untangles the intertwined bundle of human attitudes generated by the sea:

For all that has been said of the love that certain natures (on shore) have professed to feel for it, for all the celebrations it had been the object of in prose and song, the sea has never been friendly to man. At most it has been the accomplice of human restlessness, and playing the part of dangerous abettor of world-wide ambitions. Faithful to no race after the manner of the kindly earth, receiving no impress from valour and toil and self-sacrifice, recognizing no finality of dominion, the sea has never adopted the cause of its masters like those lands where the victorious nations of mankind have taken root, rocking their cradles and setting up their gravestones. He—man or people—who, putting his trust in the friendship of the sea, neglects the strength and cunning of his right hand, is a fool! As if it were too great, too mighty for common virtues, the ocean has no compassion, no faith, no law, no memory. Its fickleness is to be held true to men's purposes only by an undaunted resolution and by a sleepless, armed, jealous vigilance, in which, perhaps, there has always been more hate than love. *Odi et amo* may well be the confession of those who consciously or blindly have surrendered their existence to the fascination of the sea.[8]

Such complex attitudes toward the sea and seafaring persist to this day for those who put to sea under sail—awe and fear, ennui and anxiety, zest and weariness, and even elation and despair. I experienced some of these

ROBERT D. FOULKE

contradictory feelings during my first ocean race around the island of Oshima off the east coast of Japan in 1953, when I was stationed there in the navy during the Korean War. A fellow naval officer owned a very able twenty-nine-foot double-ended Aitken yawl, so we set out with justified confidence even though gale warnings had been posted before the race. As we beat out of Sagami Wan into the open Pacific at night, the wind piped up to force seven, perhaps even force eight at times, and we were forced to take down our heavily reefed mainsail entirely, riding the seas under jib and jigger alone. Unfortunately, the hibachi pot in the cabin that heated our coffee also produced fumes, and I became violently seasick during a brief watch below. For the rest of the night, on deck, we tacked back and forth against huge seas and a strong adverse current, in pitch blackness except for a single lighthouse on the island that we never succeeded in weathering until the gale abated at dawn. Of course, most of our Japanese competitors, with more experience and better detailed charts, had abandoned the race and scooted into the harbor on the island. When we crossed the finish line late the next day after twenty-four hours of misery, seasickness, lack of food, and a healthy dose of awe and anxiety, I still remember feeling elated. Ah, youth! Most of those who have been to sea in sailing vessels have similar tales to tell—of more rigorous encounters with the sea in its angry mood, of unexpected visions of beauty, of inexplicable conflict among crew members during long voyages, and of the deep companionship that shipmates can never duplicate on land.

Some years later I recall reading the final peroration in Conrad's story "Youth" with a sense of recognition. Here is Conrad's narrator, Marlow, talking to older, shore-bound men who had once been seamen:

> "Ah! The good old time—the good old time. Youth and the sea. Glamour and the sea! The good, strong sea, the salt, bitter sea, that could whisper to you and roar at you and knock your breath out of you . . . and, tell me, wasn't that the best time, that time when we were young at sea; young and had nothing, on the sea that gives nothing, except hard knocks—and sometimes a chance to feel your strength—that only—what you regret?"
>
> And we all nodded at him: the man of finance, the man of accounts, the man of law, we all nodded at him over the polished table that like a still sheet of brown water reflected our faces, lined, wrinkled; our faces marked by toil, by deceptions, by success, by love; our weary eyes looking still, looking always, looking anxiously for something out of life, that while it is expected is already gone—has passed unseen, in a

sigh, in a flash—together with the youth, with the strength, with the romance of illusions.[9]

That final phrase, "the romance of illusions," brings us back to the ambivalence that seafaring always seems to generate.

Much of the consistency in attitudes toward the sea throughout the centuries stems from the nature of the ocean environment and its effects on those who put to sea on extended voyages. I must pause for one caveat here. It would seem that the description that follows is anachronistic in the twenty-first century, an era in which the sea commerce of the world is carried out in supertankers and container ships and its pleasure cruises, in larger and larger floating palaces with atriums piercing ten decks, resemble luxury hotels ashore. Yet as I was writing this paragraph, rescue efforts were underway for the crew of a container ship sunk some 400 miles northwest of Bermuda, and the past few years have brought the usual range of sea maladies to cruise ships—engine failures, strandings, fires, and even a Greek cruise ship's spectacular plunge to the bottom off the coast of South Africa. The endless and often inane public fascination with the *Titanic* story derives from its emblematic quality as a parable of hubris that an indifferent ocean can shatter in a moment. Twice I have sped across the North Atlantic at a cruising speed of twenty-eight knots on board the *Queen Elizabeth II*. On a morning visit to the bridge to watch the ship dodge around fishing boats on George's Bank (it takes seven miles to stop her at that speed), I learned that we had been using radar to identify icebergs the night before, at the same speed. Technology, however, will never tame the sea entirely, and for many vessels—fishing boats, sail-training ships, cruising yachts—the sea environment has changed very little. Although the fishing fleet is shrinking in some parts of the world's oceans, there are more people out there in tall ships and small sailboats than at the turn of the previous century, so contemporary seafaring experience is likely to produce more voyage narratives like Peter Matthiessen's *Far Tortuga*, Robert Stone's *Outerbridge Reach*, and Sebastian Junger's *Perfect Storm*, as well as a host of accounts of single-handed circumnavigations and around-the-world yacht races.

The environment of long sea passages promotes reflection in thoughtful seafarers. Once committed to the open sea, human beings are enclosed irrevocably by the minute world of the vessel in a vast surround. That world reverses many physical and social realities. Ashore, healthy human beings desire bodily movement and gain a sense of freedom and power through it, notably in activities like walking, running, dancing, or skiing. At sea, motion is imposed upon one, with temporary but debilitating effects. Again,

ROBERT D. FOULKE

many individuals ashore can join and leave groups at will, but at sea, all are compressed within a single, unchanging society, and one traditionally and sensibly marked by a rigid hierarchy at that. It is often possible to choose a solitary life ashore, or at least to regulate contact with others, but at sea, the absolute isolation of the vessel makes adapting to the fixed society on board unavoidable. In this fragmentary but self-contained world, seafarers have time on their hands, and they spend much of it standing watch—literally watching the interaction of ship, weather, and sea while waiting for something, or nothing, to happen. Their world demands keen senses because they live on an unstable element that keeps their home in constant motion, sometimes soothing them with a false sense of security, sometimes threatening to destroy them.

Although the vision of those at sea is bounded by a horizon and contains a seascape of monotonous regularity, what is seen can change rapidly and unpredictably. Unlike the land, the sea never retains the impress of human civilization, as Dana and many others have observed, so seafarers find their sense of space suggesting infinity and solitude, on the one hand, and prisonlike confinement, on the other. That environment contains in its restless motion lurking possibilities of total disorientation: in a knockdown, walls become floors, and doors become hatches. In Conrad's magnificent novella *Typhoon*, a somewhat stupid but orderly Captain MacWhirr first realizes that he may lose his ship not by watching the furious seas that engulf her but by going below and finding his cabin in total disarray.

The seafarer's sense of time is equally complex. It is both linear and cyclical. It is linear in the sense that voyages have beginnings and endings, departures and landfalls, and starting and stopping points in the unfolding of chronological time. Yet time is also cyclical, just as the rhythm of waves is cyclical because the pattern of a ship's daily routine, watch on and watch off, highlights endless recurrence. Space and time have always merged more obviously at sea than they do in much of human experience. Until late in the eighteenth century, European ocean navigators calculated their latitude by taking the altitude of the sun or a star and their longitude by deduced reckoning, measuring the number of miles they had sailed a particular course by combining time and speed. The invention of reliable chronometers made more precise celestial navigation possible by interlocking measurements of time and space in a more sophisticated way. Before the era of electronic Loran and global satellite positioning systems, in order to find longitude, you had to have a precise reading of the time at another place, Greenwich, England. Then to really get a fix on where you were on the planet, you added to that time measurement a spatial one by taking the

altitude of a celestial body. It is no wonder that mariners tended to be reflec-
tive when they had to deal with abstract time and celestial space just to find
out where they were in the watery world. They still live suspended between
sky and sea in a world where time and space merge, where the real and the
virtual may not be distinguishable. Solo voyagers have been subject to hallu-
cinations since Joshua Slocum first set out, and control of the world-encom-
passing dimensions of navigation can lead to delusions. Like Donald Crow-
hurst in the first nonstop, solo ocean race around the world, Owen Browne,
the protagonist of Robert Stone's *Outerbridge Reach*, fabricates false positions. When Browne can no longer "pursue the fiction of lines" and is weary
"of pretending to locate himself in space and time," he jumps overboard.[10]

It is not surprising that such conditions of seafaring, taken together, have
generated a rich and lasting literature. Because voyages in real experience
have built-in momentum and directionality, driven by the urge for exploration and discovery or simply by the desire to reach a known port safely, their
narration requires very little artifice in plot. They tap into an innate teleol-
ogy and an undercurrent of human purposes and goals. We embark on voyages not only to get somewhere but also to accomplish something, and, in
Western culture, often to discover more about the ways human beings can
expect to fare in the world. In this sense, voyages are a natural vehicle for the
human imagination exploring the unknown, whether it be discovering
strange new lands, finding out the truth about ourselves, or searching for
those more perfect worlds we call utopias. These purposes and intentions,
as well as tension between the lure of new experience and the desire to get
home, mark every stage of Odysseus's return from the Trojan War. As he
recapitulates the whole of his extraordinary voyage to Penelope, he tells the
first returning seaman's yarn in the Western world. Because *The Odyssey*
spawned a host of literary patterns, it became an archetype of voyage narratives in Western literature, and its basic structure of the *nostos*, the long and
difficult voyage home, recurs down through the centuries in narratives as
different as Conrad's *Nigger of the "Narcissus*," Eugene O'Neill's *Bound East
for Cardiff* and *The Long Voyage Home*, and John Barth's *Sabbatical*.

In addition to exploration, discovery, and return, voyage narratives as-
similate and develop many other literary patterns. One is the hunt for a
big fish, perhaps best exemplified in twentieth-century literature by Ernest
Hemingway's classic *The Old Man and the Sea*. When the pursued object is
overtly symbolic, like the Golden Fleece in the voyage of the Argonauts, the
hunt borrows the conventions of romance and is transformed into a quest.
If those engaged in a quest endow a part of the natural world with super-
natural powers and implications, the quest turns metaphysical and often

becomes tragic. The most striking example in American literature is, of course, *Moby Dick,* with an obsessed Captain Ahab pursuing evil made incarnate in the form of a white whale.

Another frequent and natural pattern for voyage narratives is the anatomy of society, in which the small world of the ship serves as a microcosm of civilization as a whole. The usual action is a sudden decrease in entropy, a revolution or mutiny in shipboard terms; *Mutiny on the Bounty* and *The Caine Mutiny* represent a whole class of narratives. Because the ship is self-contained, isolated, and organized as a rigid hierarchy, it is also a natural setting for exploring ethical dilemmas such as the conflict between virtue and authority in Melville's *Billy Budd* or the degeneration of a whole society in Katherine Anne Porter's *Ship of Fools,* which develops the medieval motif of the world as a ship. Similarly, the voyage can be used as a vehicle for getting to utopia—literally no place on Earth—as in Jules Verne's *Twenty Thousand Leagues under the Sea,* or to dystopias, as in three of the four voyages in *Gulliver's Travels.*

Initiation is a third important literary pattern developed within voyage narratives. In its simplest form, an initiation at sea puts a young person (usually a boy until recent decades) into an unfamiliar situation, tests his or her worth in a crisis, and rewards those who pass muster with full acceptance as adults. This is the design of Outward Bound schools, and it is reflected in much sea literature, such as Rudyard Kipling's *Captains Courageous.* More complex versions of the pattern are innumerable, including Apollonius of Rhodes's *Argonautica,* Tobias Smollett's *Roderick Random,* Frederick Marryat's *Mr. Midshipman Easy,* many of James Fenimore Cooper's sea novels, Dana's *Two Years before the Mast,* Melville's *Redburn* and *White-jacket,* Conrad's "Youth," Jack London's *Sea Wolf,* Stephen Crane's "Open Boat," and scores of less well known but memorable sea stories. The multitude of examples is not surprising, since life at sea removes the initiate from the familiarity and comfort of shoreside places and provides a full range of potential tests—storm, fire, stranding, collision, falling from aloft or overboard, disease, starvation, and sinking—all threatening injury or death.

When the test becomes more menacing and the probability of failure greater, the stakes change from growing up to risking moral destruction. This is the usual case in Conrad: In *Heart of Darkness,* Marlow nearly loses his own identity in the voyage up the Congo River to Kurtz's Inner Station; Lord Jim in the novel of the same name discovers a fatal "soft spot" in his character when he jumps from the bridge of a steamship that he thinks is sinking; and in "The End of the Tether," Captain Whalley violates all responsibility when he continues to navigate his ship while going blind. Sometimes the protagonist is an overaged innocent, like Conrad's Captain MacWhirr in *Typhoon* or Melville's Captain Delano in "Benito Cereno," who can either ignore or survive exposure to the "destructive element." The usual archetype for such a dark initiation is descent, both obvious and natural as a ship sinks to the bottom of the sea. In this way, sinking is a psychic repetition of myths of visiting the underworld—Odysseus in Hades or Jonah in the belly of a whale. Such myths are usually displaced (i.e., made more naturalistic) in modern literature. The central scene in the storm section of Conrad's *Nigger of the "Narcissus"* is a descent into the deckhouse of a nearly capsized ship to rescue its source of dissension, James Wait; the climactic scene in Melville's *White-jacket* is a spectacular fall from high in the rigging deep into the sea.

Another archetype, immobilization, represents the more subtle threat of prolonged calm or stranding on the rocks and beaches of coastlines. Samuel Coleridge's "Rime of the Ancient Mariner" and Conrad's *Shadow-Line* depend upon the powerlessness of human effort in calm and use many images of stagnation and stillness. Similarly, stranding gives the ship back to the land that produced her in an unnatural way; waves that a hull had parted now rip it to pieces, and those who swarm over the ship are no longer builders but wreckers bent upon booty. There is a whole subgenre of sea writing about shipwrecks and disasters in coastal regions, perhaps because at those dramatic moments the power and danger of the sea impinge upon the imagination of landsmen. Gerard Manly Hopkins catches the irony of a storm stranding, the fact that the disaster takes place within sight of safety before witnesses powerless to help, in the magnificent stanzas of "The Wreck of the 'Deutschland.'"

These patterns and their modulations occur in all varieties of voyage narrative, whether they purport to be reportorial or fictitious. There is an unusually close relationship between historical accounts of voyages and literary fictions based on them—so close that it is often difficult to determine the purpose of a narrative by looking at its structure. Historical and literary voyage narratives are often nearly identical in structure and substance: there is usually no clear demarcation between fact and fiction, or experience and imagination. Among narrative forms, voyages cling to the inescapable realities of life at sea on the one hand, and, on the other hand, simultaneously project human desires and fantasies. They record strenuous human enterprise, serve as emblems of the course of life, and, in ambitious narratives like *The Odyssey* or *Moby Dick*, leap back and forth between a precise rendering of events in the sea world and moral or metaphysical interpretations of that world. Herein lies a related and complicated subject of an essay for another day.

One classic voyage narrative that lies midway between literature and history is Richard Henry Dana's *Two Years before the Mast,* which sometimes reads like pure reportage, sometimes like fiction, but most frequently shares the conventions of both. Dana also develops the sea meditation, a mode of reverie that is found throughout voyage narratives and essays on seafaring, from *The Odyssey* to *The Mirror of the Sea* and beyond. The sea meditation springs from one segment in the broad essay genre; it stands with feet planted firmly in everyday reality on board a ship and has a head stuffed with metaphor and fancy. Ashore the tradition flourished for centuries in writers as varied as Montaigne, Pascal, Ruskin, Carlyle, Emerson, and Thoreau; such writers share the impulse to connect quotidian detail with larger intuitions, by either burrowing within an observation or leaping from it in flashes of illumination. At sea, the meditation or reverie is nourished by the immensity of the ocean, isolation, and ample time for reflection. With strong roots in Dana, Melville, and Conrad, the meditation has been explored by twentieth-century writers such as Alan Villiers, H. M. Tomlinson, John Muir, Jan de Hartog, Hilaire Belloc, Joshua Slocum, and Peter Matthiessen. Often it is intermixed with narration, momentarily suppressing the energy of unfolding events. Thus, in *Two Years before the Mast,* we hear Dana meditating on the breathing of whales, the vacuum caused by a death at sea, the beauty of ships, the boredom of gales, and dozens of other subjects.

Although sea meditations are often contained within large and powerful narrative structures—voiced by Ishmael in *Moby Dick* and Marlow in *Lord Jim,* where they are intertwined with the advance of the story—sometimes they become the container themselves. One notable example is *The Mirror of the Sea,* growing from an impulse that Conrad describes in letters as "the *wonderfulness* of things, events, people—when looked back upon" and "an imaginative rendering of a reminiscent mood."[11] The impulse is emblematic, and it suppresses narrative energy throughout, with the exception of two autobiographical sections on rescuing the crew of a sinking ship ("Initiation") and a smuggling expedition along the Spanish coast ("The Tremolino"). Both are encased in meditation, and throughout *The Mirror,* incidents become exemplar their complications are pared away, and their growing room is confined by the point they are meant to illustrate. In many ways, the structure of the whole resembles that of a classical elegy on departed ships—beginning with connections between death and time, moving to shared experiences of prowess demonstrated and difficulty overcome, then to expressing grief at lives of ships cut short, resting momentarily in two versions of completed voyages, reaching a climax with poignant reflections on the meaning of shipwrecks for the speaker, and closing with the celebration of a continuing maritime tradition. This was Conrad's elegy for the end of the commercial sailing-ship era, three-quarters of a century before tall ships began roaming the seas again under the new auspices of sail training. He would be astounded, I think, by the collection of sailing ships we saw in Tall Ships 2000.

Voyage narratives of previous centuries also employed a number of nautical character types to embellish their action. From the Restoration onward, sailor types abound in anecdotes, caricatures, ballads, sketches, plays, and novels. Familiar types include the jolly tar, the picaresque rogue in naval togs, the hawse-hole captain, the bully mate, the brawny bos'n, the stowaway, the jinx, the landlubber greenhorn, the wise old seaman mentor, the ancient mariner who must tell his tale ashore, the malingerer, the handsome sailor, the coal heaver, the oiler, and others. The list is lengthy because work roles onboard ship are very tightly defined, necessarily, and any elaboration or deviation is instantly noticeable. Some have become stereotypes, the butt of ridicule, like the jolly tar whose drunken revels resound throughout the world's ports, or the harsh but good-hearted hawse-hole captain who brings his sea ways and lingo ashore, to the amusement of all. In Restoration and eighteenth-century drama, we meet Captain Manly in Wycherly's *Plain Dealer*, Ben Legend in Congreve's *Love for Love*, and a whole cast of nautical characters in Shadwell's novel *Fair Quaker of Deal*—Commodore Flip, Captains Worth and Mizen, Midshipman Derrick, Jack Hatchway, and Dick Binnacle. As the novel grew in importance throughout the eighteenth century, its nautical characters included Daniel Defoe's buccaneer, Captain Singleton, and a host of figures from Tobias Smollett's *Roderick Random* and *Peregrine Pickle*—Captain Oakum, Lieutenant Tom Bowling, Jack Rattlin, Commodore Hawser Trunion, Lieutenant Hatchway, and Boatswain Pipes. In the early nineteenth century, Frederick Marryat continued the tradition of the naval novel in Smollett's wake, again using young midshipman protagonists like Peter Simple and Jack Easy to survey whole shiploads of seagoing types. The nautical names of these characters reveal their springs of motivation, almost like the humors of Renaissance drama, and determine their responses to a series of encounters, both afloat and ashore. Although exaggeration often clothes these sea types in literary settings, they do grow from real persons and frequently repeated human situations at sea.

Most of the playwrights and novelists who used sailors had some experience at sea, but when Sir Walter Scott wrote *The Pirate* (1822), his unfamil-

FIGURE 18. *Defeat the Kaiser and His U-Boats*, 1917–18, signed Steele, silkscreen print. Peabody Essex Museum collections, M21237. 21½ x 14 in.

iarity with seamen and ships spurred James Fenimore Cooper to write *The Pilot* (1824) as an antidote. Thus began the tradition of American sea fiction, and Cooper's twelve sea novels produced a string of memorable characters, including captains like Tuck and Daggett and seamen like Long Tom Coffin and Boltrope. More important was a sea change in the conception of character itself. The gallery of sea eccentrics who display their oddities in shore society gave way to extended portraits of multifaceted seamen, enmeshed in a compressed and isolated shipboard society, who face not only the ills of that society but larger issues raised by precarious human interaction with the sea. Cooper only began to realize the full potential of complex characters acting within an immense, totally fluid environment of sea and sky, but others followed, including Dana's persona in *Two Years before the Mast*, Melville's Ahab, Ishmael, and "Starry" Vere, Conrad's Lord Jim and Marlow, Hemingway's Santiago, William Golding's Edmund Talbot, William Mc-Phee's Captain Washburn, and Matthiessen's Raib Avers.

In this evolution of sea fiction and nonfiction, largely begun in America but transported back to Britain as well, type characters did not disappear but were transformed. Some have important narrative functions to perform: the stowaway and the jinx serve as the intruder and the scapegoat in shipboard society, and the bully mate becomes the enforcer of rigid rules that encroach upon the crew's slender margin of freedom. Yet others, like the greenhorn or neophyte, become the central figures who grow to manhood at sea; they usually cross class barriers as soon as they set foot in the forecastle and need the help of the older seamen who become their mentors. This is the familiar narrative pattern of the sea Bildungsroman, seen in its simplest form in novels like Melville's *Redburn* and Kipling's *Captains Courageous*. Some highly specialized types that belong to a specific era of seafaring upset the equilibrium of shipboard society and provide the central impetus of the narrative. For example, the malingerer—the seaman who shirked and dodged all the hard work on sailing ships because he was paid by the day no matter what he did—often became the focus of hatred tinged with envy, the disturbing role both Donkin and Wait play in Conrad's *Nigger of the "Narcissus."* The handsome sailor, on the other hand, is the very stuff of the young hero, combining physical beauty and seamanlike competence with the simple goodness of the untutored "natural man" who is undefiled by the ways of the world. He appears again and again in sea narratives and in sea experience. Dana describes one he met in Monterey:

> He had been at sea from a boy, having served a regular apprenticeship of seven years, as all English sailors are obliged to do, and was then

about four or five and twenty. He was tall; but you only perceived it when he was standing by the side of others, for the great breadth of his shoulders and chest made him appear but little above the middle height. His chest was as deep as it was wide; his arm like that of Hercules; and his hand "the fist of a tar—every hair a rope yarn." With all this he had one of the pleasantest smiles I ever saw. . . . He had a good deal of information, and his captain said he was a perfect seaman, and worth his weight in gold on board a vessel, in fair weather and in foul. His strength must have been immense, and he had the sight of a vulture. It is strange that one should be so minute in the description of an unknown, outcast sailor, whom one may never see again, and whom no one may care to hear about; but so it is. Some people we see under no remarkable circumstances, but whom, for some reason or other, we never forget. He called himself Bill Jackson; and I know no one of all my accidental acquaintances to whom I would more gladly give a shake of the hand than to him. Whoever falls in with him will find a handsome, hearty fellow, and a good shipmate.[12]

Melville had also met such men and remembered them well enough to build the character of Billy Budd. In *Rites of Passage*, Golding inverts the type with Billy Rogers, also a foretopman, and gives him the clever malice of a Claggart. Clearly, in these last two instances and many others, the focus has shifted from the surface appearance of sailors to their innate characteristics.

The sea has been a "place" of extraordinary importance in the evolution of Western culture. It is the environment that has encompassed human beings during major movements of expanded awareness—the Greek colonization westward through the Mediterranean during the Archaic era; the Portuguese explorations of the South Atlantic, at first tentative then bold; the early Spanish voyages to the Indies and later ones to the Americas; Renaissance circumnavigations of the world; explorations of the Pacific during the eighteenth century; polar expeditions to the Arctic and Antarctic during the nineteenth and early twentieth centuries; and undersea exploration to profound depths of the ocean in recent decades. From *The Odyssey* to the present, the sea has served as a place for literary portraits of adventure, disaster, quests, hunts, and tests of human endurance. Throughout all centuries, unlike the land, the sea has been a constant for those who sailed on it, variable in mood but immutable in essence—a place with a character much like that attributed to Poseidon, by turns placid and turbulent, serene and menacing. For seafarers, these are the defining dimensions of the place they live in, largely unchanged since the first separation of earth and water.

ROBERT D. FOULKE

Notes

1. Homer, *The Odyssey*, trans. Robert Fagles (New York: Penguin Books, 1996), 11:138–49.

2. Joseph Conrad, *The Mirror of the Sea* (London: J. M. Dent, 1946), 182–83.

3. Alfred Lord Tennyson, "Ulysses," in *An Anatomy of Literature*, eds. Robert Foulke and Paul Smith (New York: Harcourt Brace Jovanovich, 1972), 320.

4. Anonymous, "The Seafarer," in *Moods of the Sea: Masterworks of Sea Poetry*, eds. George C. Solley and Eric Steinbaugh (Annapolis: Naval Institute Press, 1981), 27–28.

5. Stuart Frank, "Ballads and Songs of the American Sailor," unpublished manuscript.

6. Richard Henry Dana, *Two Years before the Mast* (Hammondsworth, England: Penguin, 1981), 14.

7. Herman Melville, *Moby-Dick: An Authoritative Text*, ed. Harrison Hayford and Hershel Parker (New York: W. W. Norton, 1967), chap. 23, p. 97.

8. Conrad, *Mirror of the Sea*, 135.

9. Joseph Conrad, *Youth, Heart of Darkness, and The End of the Tether* (London: J. M. Dent, 1946), 42.

10. Robert Stone, *Outerbridge Reach* (New York: Ticknor and Fields, 1992), 382.

11. William Blackburn, ed., *Joseph Conrad: Letters to William Blackwood and David S. Meldrum* (Durham, N.C.: Duke University Press, 1958), 138; and G. Jean-Aubry, *Joseph Conrad: Life and Letters* (Garden City, N.Y.: Doubleday, Page, 1927), 2:34.

12. Dana, *Two Years before the Mast*, 134–35.

ABOUT THE CONTRIBUTORS

John Armstrong is a professor of business history at Thames Valley University, London. His most recent book on maritime history (with Andreas Kunz) is *Coastal Shipping and the European Economy, 1750–1980* (2002).

Lionel Casson is professor of classics emeritus at New York University. He is the author of the standard reference work *Ships and Seamanship in the Ancient World*, 3rd ed. (1995).

Felipe Fernández-Armesto is a professorial Fellow of Queen Mary, University of London, where he teaches history and geography, and director of the global history program at the Institute of Historical Research, University of London. His recent books include *Millennium* (1999), and *The Americas: a Hemispheric History* (2003).

Daniel Finamore is the Russell W. Knight Curator of Maritime Art and History at the Peabody Essex Museum. He is the author of *Rendezvous with the Sea: The Glory of the French Maritime Tradition* (2002).

Brendan Foley has participated in investigations of ancient deep-sea shipwrecks using Remotely Operated Vehicles, Autonomous Underwater Vehicles and the U.S. Navy's submarine NR-1. His academic interests include developing methodology for archaeology in deep water and historical research on social and technological change in the U.S. Navy.

Robert Foulke has taught at Minnesota, Trinity College, and Skidmore College. His publications include *An Anatomy of Literature* (1972) and articles on voyage narratives in *The Journal of British Studies, Modern Fiction Studies, The Literature and Lore of the Sea*, and *The American Neptune*.

John B. Hattendorf is chairman of the Naval War College's Maritime History Department in its Center for Naval Warfare Studies. He is the author of more than eighty articles as well as being the author, coauthor, editor, or coeditor of more than thirty books on British and American maritime history.

Olaf U. Janzen is professor of history at the Sir Wilfred Grenfell College campus, Corner Brook of Memorial University of Newfoundland. He is a Fellow of the Royal Historical Society, edits the yearbook of the Association for the History of the Northern Seas, and is reviews editor of the International Journal of Maritime History.

Elizabeth Mancke is an associate professor of history at the University of Akron. She has published a number of essays on the intersection of empire building, state formation, and the development of a global system of international relations in the early modern era.

Justin E. Manley is lead ocean engineer at Mitretek Systems, a nonprofit engineering and research organization working in the public sector, where he supports the National Oceanic and Atmospheric Administration (NOAA) and its Office of Ocean Exploration.

Carla Rahn Phillips is professor of history at the University of Minnesota. Her publications include *Ciudad Real, 1500–1750: Growth, Crisis and Readjustment in the Spanish Economy* (1979); *Six Galleons for the King of Spain: Imperial Defense in the Early Seventeenth Century* (1986); and (coauthored with William D. Phillips Jr.) *The Worlds of Christopher Columbus* (1992).

William D. Phillips Jr. is the president of the Society for Spanish and Portuguese Historical Studies. He works in the history of slavery, and is presently working on the interactions of medieval Europe and the rest of the world.

Jon Tetsuro Sumida is an author and editor of many articles. He is a leading authority on twentieth-century naval history, particularly with regard to the influence of finance, administration, and technology on policy, and strategic theory.

ABOUT THE CONTRIBUTORS

Richard W. Unger is professor of early European history at the University of British Columbia. He is the author of *A History of Dutch Brewing, 900–1900: Economy, Technology and the State* (2001) and coeditor of *Armed Force at Sea in the Middle Ages and the Renaissance: Power and Theories of Domination* (2003).

INDEX

Illustrations are indicated by italic type.

NEW PERSPECTIVES ON MARITIME HISTORY AND NAUTICAL ARCHAEOLOGY
James C. Bradford and Gene A. Smith, Series Editors

This series is devoted to providing lively and important books that cover the spectrum of maritime history and nautical archaeology broadly defined. It includes works that focus on the role of canals, rivers, lakes, and oceans in history; on the economic, military, and political use of those waters; and upon the people, communities, and industries that support maritime endeavors. Limited neither by geography nor time, volumes in the series contribute to the overall understanding of maritime history and can be read with profit by both general readers and specialists.

Maritime Heritage of the Cayman Islands,
by Roger C. Smith (1999) first paperback edition, 2000

The Three German Navies after World War II: Dissolution, Transition, and New Beginnings, 1945–1960, by Douglas C. Peifer (2002)

The Rescue of the Gale Runner: Death, Heroism, and the U.S. Coast Guard, by Dennis L. Noble (2002)

Brown Water Warfare: The U.S. Navy in Riverine Warfare and the Emergence of a Tactical Doctrine, 1775–1970, by R. Blake Dunnavent (2003)

Medieval Naval Warfare and the Battle for Sicily: The Catalan-Aragonese Fleet in the War of the Sicilian Vespers, by Lawrence V. Mott (2003)

An Admiral for America: Sir Peter Warren, Vice Admiral of the Red, 1703–1752, by Julian Gwyn (2004)

Maritime History as World History, edited by Daniel Finamore (2004)